A Russian Diary

ALSO BY ANNA POLITKOVSKAYA

A Dirty War: a Russian Reporter in Chechnya

Putin's Russia

Anna Politkovskaya

A Russian Diary

TRANSLATED
FROM THE RUSSIAN
BY

Arch Tait

WITH A FOREWORD BY

Jon Snow

Harvill *Secker*
LONDON

Published by Harvill Secker 2007

2 4 6 8 10 9 7 5 3

Copyright © The Estate of Anna Politkovskaya 2007
English translation copyright © Arch Tait 2007
Foreword © Jon Snow 2007

First published in Great Britain in 2007 by
Harvill Secker
Random House, 20 Vauxhall Bridge Road,
London SW1V 2SA

www.randomhouse.co.uk

Addresses for companies within The Random House Group Limited can be found at:
www.randomhouse.co.uk/offices.htm

The Random House Group Limited Reg. No. 954009

A CIP catalogue record for this book
is available from the British Library

ISBN 9781846551024 (hardback)
ISBN 9781846550461 (trade paperback)

The Random House Group Limited makes every effort to ensure that the papers used in its books
are made from trees that have been legally sourced from well-managed and credibly certified
forests. Our paper procurement policy can be found at: www.randomhouse.co.uk/paper.htm

Typeset in Adobe Garamond by Palimpsest Book Production Limited,
Grangemouth, Stirlingshire

Printed and bound in Great Britain by
Clays Ltd, St Ives plc

Contents

Foreword

Reading Anna Politkovskaya's *A Russian Diary* in the knowledge of her terrible end – at the hand of an assassin in the stairwell of her Moscow apartment block – it seems to foretell that she could not possibly be allowed to live. What she reveals here, and demonstrated in her earlier writings, are such wounding and devastating truths about the regime of President Vladimir Putin that someone, sooner rather than later, was bound to kill her. In some ways it is miraculous that she lived as long as she did.

More miraculous is that amid the post-Soviet upheavals a journalist arose who almost single-handedly brought to the world's attention the scandalous tragedy of Chechnya and so many more of modern Russia's misdeeds. The behaviour she exposed, and continues to expose in this record, represents a vast body of systemic political and human rights abuse. For this is the diary she kept during the period from the corrupted parliamentary elections of December 2003 to the end of 2005 and the aftermath of the Beslan school siege.

As I read *A Russian Diary* I wondered what on earth we have embassies in Russia for. How did it happen that our leaders so steadfastly ignored what they knew Putin was up to? Was it the hunger for gas? For the riches of the outrageous post-Communist sell-off of Russian state assets and manufacturing resources, through which our financial institutions participated in the rise of the thieving oligarchs? Or was it the blind desire to keep Russia 'on side', whatever the cost to her own impoverished people?

It was those people that Anna Politkovskaya travelled huge distances to talk to, and to represent. The risks she took were terrifying but the intense reality she portrays is breathtaking. After the 2004 bombing of the Moscow Metro in which thirty-nine people were killed, she visits some of the victims' homes. She discovers that 'cause of death' on a number of the death certificates is simply crossed out – even in death, she writes, 'the Russian state can't refrain from dishonesty. Not a word about terrorism.'

Anna's journalism meant that she very quickly became a rallying point for those the state made suffer. One night, after 11.00 p.m., she takes an anguished call from Ingushetia. '"Something terrible is going on here! It's a war", women were screaming into the telephone, "Help us! Do something! We are lying on the floor with the children!"'

Anna's formative years as a journalist were lived under the yoke of Communism. She came of radical campaigning age as, in 1991, the USSR transmogrified into the Russian Federation, led by President Boris Yeltsin. As the new countries of the former Soviet Union began to stand on their own feet a number of internal wars broke out. One of the most serious was the First Chechen War (1994–6) when predominantly Islamic Chechen rebels sought to found a breakaway, independent state. Anna was one of those whose reporting created the circumstances which made possible the eventual peace settlement and Russian troop withdrawal. Indeed, she identifies stopping that war as the media's greatest achievement during the relatively free Yeltsin years.

Vladimir Putin's arrival in the Kremlin and his initiation of the Second Chechen War in 1999 raised both the military and the journalistic stakes. Drawing on his secret service background, Putin took measures to ensure that the media would not be able to embarrass him with reports of Russia's brutal activities in Chechnya. Anna was to visit Chechnya on more than fifty occasions. The newspaper for which she worked, *Novaya gazeta*, remained one of the very few publications which would not bow to Kremlin pressure to reduce or tone down their coverage.

By 2002, Putin was taking full advantage of the Bush–Blair 'war on terror' as cover for Moscow's wholesale crackdown in Chechnya. Anna became increasingly isolated. She reported the extra-judicial killings, kidnappings, rapes, torture and disappearances that characterised the Russian forces' methods as they struggled to contain the Chechen War, and she often reported these alone. Increasingly Anna felt, and wrote publicly, that Putin's policies actively nurtured the very terrorists they were supposedly designed to defeat. Threaded through these accounts is her deep conviction that Putin's path to the presidency was shaped around, and dependent upon, his pursuit of the Chechen conflict. She even links some of the specific torture practices that she uncovers in Chechnya to those extolled by the KGB and its successor the FSB in their training manuals.

Her account of Putin's re-election in 2003 is astonishing both for her own bravery and for the facts she discloses. The disappearance of Ivan Rybkin, one of the candidates challenging Putin, could read like fiction were it not so serious. Having disappeared from Moscow, where he says he was drugged, Rybkin surfaces in London. As Anna observes, 'a defecting presidential candidate is a first in our history'. But she is in no doubt that it is the political culture engendered by Putin's camp that has led to this state of affairs.

Shortly after the election, a young activist lawyer, Stanislav Markelov, is beaten up on the Moscow Metro by five youths. Anna describes them shouting at him, '"You've made a few speeches too many! . . . You had this coming"'. It was to prove a nasty foretaste of things to come. Needless to say, as Anna reports, the police refused to open a criminal case, and we still do not know who attacked Markelov nor who ordered them to.

In September 2004 Anna fell victim to poison introduced into a cup of tea aboard the plane she was taking to Rostov. She was making her way to the school siege at Beslan. Thereafter, the combination of her isolation and the increasing pressure upon her from the 'authorities' served to push Anna beyond reporting into campaigning and fighting for the rights of those she perceived to be victims of the Kremlin's policies.

During the Moscow theatre siege in October 2002, Anna had taken an active role as an intermediary between the authorities and the kidnappers. Her intention was to do the same at Beslan. It is at this point that some journalists might judge that she had crossed the Rubicon from objective reporter to partisan. But Russia was in a state of post-Communist evolution, if not revolution. Anna regarded respect for human rights as the Rubicon. Once, as she saw it, the Putin regime committed itself to a wholesale disregard for human rights in Chechnya, she felt she had no alternative but to oppose it.

Anna will, however, be judged on the full body of her work. That includes this remarkable book. In this, as in all her writing, her tireless commitment to getting at the truth shines through, but so do the eventually fatal risks she took in order to report.

For many of us who continue to aspire to the highest standards of journalism, Anna Politkovskaya will remain a beacon burning bright, a yardstick by which integrity, courage and commitment will be measured. Those who met her over the years can testify that she never allowed her feet to leave the ground, never basked in fame or celebrity. She remained modest and unassuming to the end.

Who killed Anna and who lay beyond her killer remain unknown. Her murder robbed too many of us of absolutely vital sources of information and contact. Yet it may, ultimately, be seen to have at least helped prepare the way for the unmasking of the dark forces at the heart of Russia's current being.

I must confess that I finished reading *A Russian Diary* feeling that it should be taken up and dropped from the air in vast quantities throughout the length and breadth of Mother Russia, for all her people to read.

Jon Snow
February 2007

Translator's Note

Some of Anna's diary entries include comments which she added at a later date, and these are separated by a centred asterisk. Comments in round brackets are her own. Her murder just as the translation was being completed meant that final editing had to go ahead without her help. Information added by the translator is enclosed in square brackets. An asterisk in the text indicates an entry in the glossary.

PART ONE

The Death of Russian Parliamentary Democracy
December 2003–March 2004

How Did Putin Get Re-Elected?

According to the census of October 2002, there are 145.2 million people living in Russia, making us the seventh most populous country in the world. Just under 116 million people, 79.8 per cent of the population, describe themselves as ethnically Russian. We have an electorate of 109 million voters.

7 December 2003

The day of the parliamentary elections to the Duma, the day Putin began his campaign for re-election as President. In the morning he manifested himself to the peoples of Russia at a polling station. He was cheerful, elated even, and a little nervous. This was unusual: as a rule he is sullen. With a broad smile, he informed those assembled that his beloved Labrador, Connie, had had puppies during the night. 'Vladimir Vladimirovich was so very worried,' Mme Putina intoned from behind her husband. 'We are in a hurry to get home,' she added, anxious to return to the bitch whose impeccable political timing had presented this gift to the United Russia party.

That same morning in Yessentuki, a small resort in the North Caucasus, the first 13 victims of a terrorist attack on a local train were being buried. It had been the morning train, known as the student train, and young people were on their way to college.

When, after voting, Putin went over to the journalists, it seemed he would surely express his condolences to the families of the dead. Perhaps even apologise for the fact that the Government had once again failed to protect its citizens. Instead he told them how pleased he was about his Labrador's new puppies.

My friends phoned me. 'He's really put his foot in it this time. Russian people are never going to vote for United Russia now.'

Around midnight, however, when the results started coming in, initially from the Far East, then from Siberia, the Urals and so on westwards, many people were in a state of shock. All my pro-democracy friends and acquaintances were again calling each other and saying, 'It can't be true. We voted for Yavlinsky*, even though . . .' Some had voted for Khakamada*.

By morning there was no more incredulity. Russia, rejecting the lies and arrogance of the democrats, had mutely surrendered herself to Putin*. A majority had voted for the phantom United Russia party, whose sole political programme was to support Putin. United Russia had rallied Russia's bureaucrats to its banner – all the former Soviet Communist Party and Young Communist League functionaries now employed by myriad government agencies – and they had jointly allocated huge sums of money to promote its electoral deceptions.

Reports we received from the regions show how this was done. Outside one of the polling stations in Saratov, a lady was dispensing free vodka at a table with a banner reading 'Vote for Tretiak', the United Russia candidate. Tretiak won. The Duma* Deputies from the entire province were swept away by United Russia candidates, except for a few who switched to the party shortly before the elections. The Saratov election campaign was marked by violence, with candidates not approved of by United Russia being beaten up by 'unidentified assailants' and choosing to pull out of the race. One, who continued to campaign against a prominent United Russia candidate, twice had plastic bags containing body parts thrown through his window: somebody's ears and a human heart. The province's electoral commission had a hotline to take reports of irregularities during the campaign and the voting, but 80 per cent of the calls were simply attempts to blackmail the local utility companies. People threatened not to vote unless their leaking pipes were mended or their radiators repaired. This worked very well. The inhabitants of the Zavod and Lenin Districts had their heating and mains water supply restored. A number of villages in the Atkar District finally had their electricity and telephones reconnected after several years of waiting. The people were seduced. More than 60 per cent of the electorate in the city voted, and in the province the turnout was 53 per cent. More than enough for the elections to be valid.

One of the democrats' observers at a polling station in Arkadak noticed people voting twice, once in the booth and a second time by filling out a ballot slip under the direction of the chairman of the local electoral commission. She ran to phone the hotline, but was pulled away from the telephone by her hair.

Vyacheslav Volodin, one of the main United Russia functionaries who was standing in Balakov, won by a landslide, with 82.9 per cent of the vote; an unprecedented victory for a politician devoid of charisma who is renowned only for his incoherent speeches on television in support of Putin. He had announced no specific policies to promote the interests of local people. Overall in Saratov Province, United Russia gained 48.2 per cent of the vote without feeling the need to publish or defend a manifesto. The Communists got 15.7 per cent, the Liberal Democrats* (Vladimir Zhirinovsky's* party) 8.9 per cent, the nationalistic Rodina (Motherland) Party* 5.7 per cent. The only embarrassment was that more than 10 per cent of the votes cast were for 'None of the above'. One-tenth of the voters had come to the polling station, drunk the vodka and told the lot of them to go to hell.

According to the National Electoral Commission's figures, over 10 per cent more votes were cast in Chechnya*, a territory totally under military control, than there are registered voters.

St Petersburg held on to its reputation as Russia's most progressive and democratically inclined city. Even there, though, United Russia gained 31 per cent of the vote, Rodina about 14 per cent. The democratic Union of Right Forces* and Yabloko* (Apple) Party got only 9 per cent each, the Communists 8.5 and the Liberal Democrats 8 per cent. Irina Khakamada, Alexander Golov, Igor Artemiev and Grigorii Tomchin, democrats and liberals well known throughout Russia, went down to ignominious defeat.

Why? The state authorities are rubbing their hands with glee, tut-tutting and saying that 'the democrats have only themselves to blame' for having lost their link with the people. The authorities suppose that, on the contrary, they now have the people on their side.

Here are some excerpts from essays written by St Petersburg school students on the topics of 'How my family views the elections' and 'Will the election of a new Duma help the President in his work?':

My family has given up voting. They don't believe in elections any more. The elections will not help the President. All the politicians promise to make life better, but unfortunately ... I would like more truthfulness ...

The elections are rubbish. It doesn't matter who gets elected to the Duma because nothing will change, because we don't elect people who are going to improve things in the country, but people who thieve. These elections will help no one – neither the President nor ordinary mortals.

Our Government is just ridiculous. I wish people weren't so crazy about money, that there was at least some sign of moral principle in our Government, and that they would cheat the people as little as possible. The Government is the servant of the people. We elect it, not the other way round. To tell the truth, I don't know why we have been asked to write this essay. It has only interrupted our lessons. The Government isn't going to read this anyway.

How my family views the elections is they aren't interested in them. All the laws the Duma adopted were senseless and did nothing useful for the people. If all this is not for the people, who is it for?

Will the elections help? It is an interesting question. We will have to wait and see. Most likely they won't help in the slightest. I am not a politician, I don't have the education you need for that, but the main thing is that we need to fight corruption. For as long as we have gangsters in the state institutions of our country, life will not get better. Do you know what is going on now in the Army? It is just endless bullying. If in the past people used to say that the Army made boys into men, now it makes them into cripples. My father says he refuses to let his son go into an Army like that. 'For my son to be a cripple after the Army, or even worse – to be dead in a ditch somewhere in Chechnya, fighting for who knows what, so that somebody can gain power over this republic?' For as long as the present Government is in power I can see no way out of the present situation. I do not thank it for my unhappy childhood.

These read like the thoughts of old people, not the future citizens of New Russia. Here is the real cost of political cynicism – rejection by the younger generation.

8 December

By morning it is finally clear that while the left wing has more or less survived, the liberal and democratic 'right wing' has been routed. The Yabloko party and Grigorii Yavlinsky himself have not made it into the Duma, neither has the Union of Right Forces with Boris Nemtsov and Irina Khakamada, nor any of the independent candidates. There is now almost nobody in the Russian Parliament capable of lobbying for democratic ideals and providing constructive, intelligent opposition to the Kremlin.

The triumph of the United Russia party is not the worst of it, however. By the end of the day, with more or less all the votes counted, it is evident that for the first time since the collapse of the USSR, Russia has particularly favoured the extreme nationalists, who promised the voters they would hang all the 'enemies of Russia'.

This is dreadful, of course, but perhaps only to be expected in a country where 40 per cent of the population live below even our dire official poverty line. It was clear that the democrats had no interest in establishing contact with this section of the population. They preferred to concentrate on addressing themselves to the rich and to members of the emerging middle class, defending private property and the interests of the new property owners. The poor are not property owners, so the democrats ignored them. The nationalists did not.

Not surprisingly, this segment of the electorate duly turned away from the democrats, while the new property owners jumped ship from Yabloko and the Union of Right Forces to United Russia just as soon as they noticed that Yavlinsky, Nemtsov and Khakamada seemed to be losing their clout with the Kremlin. The rich decamped to where there was a concentration of the officials without whom Russian business, which is mostly corrupt and supports and feeds official corruption, cannot thrive.

Just before these elections, the senior officials of United Russia were saying openly, 'We have so much money! Business has donated so much we don't know what to do with it all!' They weren't boasting. These were bribes that meant, 'Don't forget us after the elections, will you?' In a corrupt country, business is even more unscrupulous than in countries where corruption has at least been reduced to a tolerable level and where it is not regarded as socially acceptable.

What further need had they of Yavlinsky or the Union of Right Forces? For our new rich, freedom has nothing to do with political parties. Freedom is the freedom to go on great holidays. The richer they are, the more often they can fly away, and not to Antalya in Turkey, but to Tahiti or Acapulco. For the majority of them, freedom equals access to luxury. They find it more convenient now to lobby for their interests through the pro-Kremlin parties and movements, most of which are primitively corrupt. For those parties every problem has its price; you pay the money and you get the legislation you need, or the question put by a Duma Deputy to the Procurator-General's Office. People have even started talking about 'Deputies' denunciations'. Nowadays these are a cost-effective means of putting your competitors out of business.

Corruption also explains the growth of the chauvinistic 'Liberal Democratic Party', led by Zhirinovsky. This is a populist 'opposition', which is not really an opposition at all because, despite their propensity for hysterical outbursts on all sorts of issues, they always support the Kremlin line. They receive substantial donations from our completely cynical and apolitical medium-sized businesses by lobbying for private interests in the Kremlin and adjacent territories such as the Procurator-General's Office, the Interior Ministry, the Federal Security Bureau, the Ministry of Justice and the courts. They use the technique of Deputies' denunciations.

That is how Zhirinovsky got into the Duma both last time and this. Now he has an enviable 38 seats.

The Rodina party is another chauvinistic organisation, led by Dmitry Rogozin* and created by the Kremlin's spin doctors specifically for this election. The aim was to draw moderately nationalist voters away from the more extreme National Bolsheviks. Rodina has done well too, with 37 seats.

*

Ideologically, the new Duma was orientated towards Russian traditionalism rather than towards the West. All the pro-Putin candidates had pushed this line relentlessly. United Russia encouraged the view that the Russian people had been humiliated by the West, with openly anti-Western and anti-capitalist propaganda. In the pre-electoral brainwashing there was no mention of 'hard work', 'competition' or 'initiative' unless in a pejorative context. On the other hand, there was a great deal of talk of 'indigenous Russian traditions'.

The electorate was offered a variety of patriotism to suit every taste. Rodina offered rather heroic patriotism; United Russia, moderate patriotism; and the Liberal Democrat Party, outright chauvinism. All the pro-Putin candidates made a great show of praying and crossing themselves whenever they spotted a television camera, kissing the Cross and the hands of Orthodox priests.

It was laughable, but the people blithely fell for it. The pro-Putin parties now had an absolute majority in the Duma. United Russia, the party created by the Kremlin, took 212 seats. Another 65 'independents' were to all intents and purposes also pro-Kremlin. The result was the advent of a one-and-a-half party system, a large party of government plus several small 'barnacle' parties of similar persuasion.

The democrats talked so much about the importance of establishing a genuine multi-party system in Russia. It was something in which Yeltsin* took a personal interest, but now all that was lost. The new configuration in the Duma excluded the possibility of significant disagreement.

Shortly after the elections, Putin went so far as to inform us that Parliament was a place not for debate, but for legislative tidying up. He was pleased that the new Duma would not be given to debating.

The Communists won 41 seats as a party, plus a further 12 through individual Communists standing independently. It pains me to say that today it is the Communist Deputies who are the most moderate and sensible voices in the Fourth Duma. They were overthrown only 12 years ago, yet by late 2003 they had been transfigured into the great white hope of Russia's democrats.

In the months that followed, the arithmetic in the Duma changed somewhat, with Deputies migrating from one party to another. Absolutely everything the Presidential Administration wanted passed got approved by a majority vote. Although in December 2003 United Russia had not obtained a sufficient majority large enough to change the Constitution (for which 301 votes are required), this was not to prove a problem. In practical terms, the Kremlin 'engineered' a constitutional majority.

I choose the word advisedly. The elections were carefully designed and executed. They were conducted with numerous violations of electoral law and, to that extent, they were rigged. There was no possibility of legally challenging any aspect of them because the bureaucrats had already taken control of the judiciary. There was not a single ruling against the results by any legal institution, from the Supreme Court down, no matter how indisputable the evidence. This judicial sanctioning of the Big Lie was justified as being 'in order to avoid destabilising the situation in the country'.

The state's administrative resources swung into action in these elections in just the same way as in the Soviet period. This was also true in no small measure of the elections in 1996 and 2000 in order to get Yeltsin elected, even though he was ill and decrepit. This time, however, there was no holding back the Presidential Administration. Officialdom merged with the United Russia party as enthusiastically as it used to with the Communist Party of the Soviet Union (the CPSU). Putin revived the Soviet system as neither Gorbachev* nor Yeltsin had done. His unique achievement was the establishment of United Russia, to the cheers of officials who were only too glad to become members of the new CPSU. They had plainly been missing Big Brother, who always did their thinking for them.

The Russian electorate, however, was also missing Big Brother, having heard no words of comfort from the democrats. There were no protests. United Russia's election slogans were stolen from the Communists and were all about rich bloodsuckers stealing our national wealth and leaving us in rags. The slogans proved so popular precisely because it was now not the Communists proclaiming them.

It has also to be said that in 2003 a majority of our citizens heartily supported the imprisonment, through the efforts of members of United Russia, of the oligarch Mikhail Khodorkovsky*, head of the Yukos oil company. Accordingly, although manipulating the state's administrative resources for political ends is no doubt an abuse, the politicians had public support. It was just a matter of the Administration leaving nothing to chance.

8 December

Early in the morning, political analysts assembled on the *Free Speech* programme to discuss the results as they came in. They were jittery. Igor Bunin talked of a crisis of Russian liberalism, about how the Yukos affair had suddenly aroused a wave of anti-oligarchic feeling in the middle of the campaign. They talked about the hatred that had accumulated in the hearts of many people, 'especially decent people who could not bring themselves to support Zhirinovsky', and the fact that the eclectic United Russia party had managed to unite everybody, from the most liberal to the most reactionary. He predicted that the President would now stand in for the liberals in the ruling elite.

On the same programme, Vyacheslav Nikonov, the grandson of Molotov, suggested that young people had not turned out to vote and this was the main reason for the democrats' defeat. 'Ivan the Terrible and Stalin are more to the taste of the Russian people.'

The evening's television continued. The programme was funereal, with an added sense of impending stormy weather. Those in the studio seemed more inclined to take shelter than to fight. Georgii Satarov, a former adviser to President Yeltsin, insisted that the outcome had been decided by the 'nostalgia vote' of those who pined for the USSR. The democrats came in for a lot of flak. The writer Vasilii Aksyonov complained that the liberals had failed to exploit the unsavouriness of the Yukos affair. He was quite right. The democrats failed to take a stand one way or the other over the issue of Khodorkovsky's treatment.

*

Free Speech was shortly to be taken off the air by its parent company, NTV, to which Putin commented, 'Who needs a talk show for political losers?' He was referring, no doubt, to Yavlinsky, Nemtsov and the other defeated liberals and democrats.

Vyacheslav Nikonov was to transform himself a few months later into a raging apologist for Putin. There were to be many such conversions among political analysts.

So, where would we go from here? Our freedoms were bestowed upon us from above, and the democrats kept running to the Kremlin for guarantees that they would not be revoked, in effect accepting the state's right to regulate liberalism. They kept compromising, and now had nowhere left to run to.

On 25 November, 13 days before the elections, a number of us journalists had talked for five hours or so to Grigorii Yavlinsky of the Yabloko party. He seemed very calm and confident, to the point of arrogance, that he would make it into the Duma. We suspected some bargain had been struck with the Presidential Administration; provision of administrative resources to support Yabloko in return for 'burying' a number of issues during the campaign. For me and many others who used to vote for Yabloko, this made our flesh creep.

Yavlinsky had no time for the idea of an alliance between Yabloko and the democratic Union of Right Forces party.

'I consider that the Union of Right Forces played an enormous part in unleashing the Chechen war. It was the only party which could in any way be described as democratic and in favour of civil society, yet they chose to say that the Russian Army was being reborn in Chechnya, and that anybody who thought otherwise was a traitor who was stabbing the Russian troops in the back.'

'So who else could Yabloko now unite with against the war in Chechnya?'

'Now? I don't know. If the Union of Right Forces were to admit that they had been wrong, we could discuss the possibility of an alliance with them. But while Nemtsov is pretending to be a dove of peace and Chubais* is talking about the liberal ideal, you'll have to forgive me, I'm not prepared to discuss that possibility. Whom else we could unite with I don't know.'

'But it was not the Union of Right Forces who began the Second Chechen War.'

'No, it was Putin, but they supported him as a candidate for the presidency and, incidentally, legitimised him as a war leader in the eyes of the intelligentsia and the entire middle class.'

'You are at daggers drawn with the Union of Right Forces. You don't want an alliance with them, but you have embarked on a number of compromises with the President and his Administration in order to obtain some degree of administrative support for your campaign. As I understand it, and there have been many rumours to this effect, the war in Chechnya is precisely the compromise in question. You have agreed not to make too much noise about the Chechen issue, and in return you have been guaranteed the necessary percentage of votes to get you into the Duma.'

'Don't rely on rumours. That is a completely wrong approach. There are rumours about your own newspaper too. No other paper is allowed to write about Chechnya, but you are not shut down for doing so. The rumour is that they give you that leeway so they can go to Strasbourg and wave your newspaper about to show what a free press we have. See what is being written about Chechnya in *Novaya gazeta*! I don't suppose for a moment that is really the way things are . . .'

'All the same, please give a straight answer.'

'I never struck any such deal or agreed any such compromise. It is out of the question.'

'But you did have talks with the Administration?'

'No, never. They talked about giving us money back in September 1999.'

'Where was that money coming from?'

'We didn't get down to that kind of detail, because I said it was unacceptable. I said I was not against Putin – I had only just set eyes on the man – but to say I would endorse everything he was going to do six months in advance was impossible. I was told, "Then in that case we cannot reach agreement with you, either." Later, after the elections, when the leaders of the parties were invited to the Kremlin and seated in accordance with their percentage of the vote, one of the most highly placed officials in the land said, "And you could have been sitting here . . ." I replied, "Well, that's just the way it is." This time they didn't even offer.'

'When did you last speak to Putin?'

'On 11 July, about the Khodorkovsky affair and the searches at Yukos.'

'At your request?'

'Yes. They assembled the entire State Council and the leaders of the political parties at the Kremlin to discuss economic programmes, etc. The meeting ended at half-past ten at night and I told Putin I needed to talk to him urgently. At half-past eleven I met him at his home. We discussed various problems, but the main one was Khodorkovsky.'

'Did you realise that Khodorkovsky would be imprisoned?'

'There was no knowing that in advance, but it was clear that the affair was being taken very seriously. I realised something bad would happen to Khodorkovsky when the *Financial Times* in London published an enormous article with photographs of Khodorkovsky, Mikhail Fridman* and Roman Abramovich, under a very large headline, which they don't usually do. The story was to the effect that those oligarchs were transferring their wealth to the West and preparing to sell everything here. There were quotes from Fridman saying it was impossible to create modern businesses in Russia, that although they themselves were really pretty good managers, there was no way, in the midst of all the corruption, you could establish proper companies in our country.'

'Have you already reconciled yourself to the fact that Putin will win a second term?'

'Even if I don't reconcile myself to that, he will get it.'

'How do you realistically assess your chances?'

'How should I know? Our own research tells us we have eight or nine per cent, but we are talking about elections where votes get added here, added there, and they call it "managed democracy". People just give up.'

'I have the impression that you are giving up too. After all, people in Georgia* rejected the results of rigged elections and used extra-parliamentary methods to alter the situation. Perhaps you should do the same? Perhaps we all should? Are you prepared to resort to extra-parliamentary methods?'

'No, I'm not going down that path, because I know that in Russia it would end with the spilling of blood, and not mine, either.'

'What about the Communists? Do you think they might take to the streets?'

'Everybody is gradually being fed the information that they are going to get twelve to thirteen per cent. It has already become the conventional wisdom. I don't rule that out, because politically Putin has very successfully stolen their clothes. United Russia is hardly going to take to the streets because it's been awarded thirty-five per cent and not thirty-eight, and there are no other mass parties. They simply don't exist. Forming a political opposition in Russia became a practical impossibility after 1996. Firstly, we lack an independent judiciary. An opposition has to be able to appeal to an independent legal system. Secondly, we lack independent national mass media. I mean television, of course, and primarily Channel One and Channel Two. Thirdly, there are no independent sources of finance for anything substantial. In the absence of these three fundamentals it is impossible to create a viable political opposition in Russia.

'There is no democracy now in Russia, because democracy without an opposition is impossible. All the prerequisites for a political opposition were destroyed when Yeltsin beat the Communists in 1996, and to a large extent we allowed them to be destroyed. There isn't even the theoretical possibility of a 100,000-strong demonstration anywhere in Russia today.

'It is a peculiarity of the present regime that it doesn't just brutishly crush opposition, as was done in the era of totalitarianism. Then the system simply destroyed democratic institutions. Now all manner of civil and public institutions are being adapted by the state authorities to their own purposes. If anyone tries to resist, they are simply replaced. If they don't want to be replaced, well then, they'd better look out. Ninety-five per cent of all problems are resolved using these techniques of adaptation or substitution. If we don't like the Union of Journalists, we will create Mediasoyuz. If we don't like NTV with this owner, we will re-invent NTV with a different owner.

'If they began taking an unwelcome interest in your newspaper, I know perfectly well what would happen. They would start buying up your people, they would create an internal rebellion. It wouldn't happen quickly, you have a good team, but gradually, using money and other methods, inviting people to come closer to power, turning the screws, cosying up, everything would start to fall apart. That's how they dealt with NTV. Gleb Pavlovsky stated openly that they had murdered public politics. It was no more than the truth. The authorities also deliberately create pairings, so that everybody has someone to shadow. Rodina can take on the Communists; the Union of Right Forces can take on Yabloko; the People's Party can take on United Russia.'

'But if they are up to all this trickery, what are they afraid of?'

'Change. The state authorities act in their corporate interests. They don't want to lose power. That would put them in a very dangerous situation, and they know it.'

Yavlinsky was not to make it into the Duma.

Were we seeing a crisis of Russian parliamentary democracy in the Putin era? No, we were witnessing its death. In the first place, as Lilia Shevtsova, our best political analyst, accurately put it, the legislative and executive branches of government had merged and this had meant the rebirth of the Soviet system. As a result, the Duma was purely decorative, a forum for rubber-stamping Putin's decisions.

In the second place – and this is why this was the end and not merely a crisis – the Russian people gave its consent. Nobody stood up. There were no demonstrations, mass protests, acts of civil disobedience. The electorate took it lying down and agreed to live, not only without Yavlinsky, but without democracy. It agreed to be treated like an idiot. According to an offical opinion poll, 12 per cent of Russians thought

United Russia representatives gave the best account of themselves in the pre-election television debates. This despite the fact that the representatives of United Russia flatly refused to take part in any television debates. They had nothing to say other than that their actions spoke for them. As Aksyonov remarked, 'The bulk of the electorate said, "Let's just leave things the way they are."'

In other words, let's go back to the USSR – slightly retouched, slicked up, modernised, but the good old Soviet Union, now with bureaucratic capitalism where the state official is the main oligarch, vastly richer than any property owner or capitalist.

The corollary was that, if we were going back to the USSR, then Putin was definitely going to win in March 2004. It was a foregone conclusion. The Presidential Administration concurred, and lost all sense of shame. In the months that followed, right up until 14 March 2004 when Putin was indeed elected, the checks and balances within the state vanished, and the only restraint was the President's conscience. Alas, the nature of the man and the nature of his former profession meant that was not enough.

9 December

At 10.53 a.m. today a suicide bomber blew herself up outside the Nationale Hotel in Moscow, across the square from the Duma and 145 metres from the Kremlin. 'Where is this Duma?' she asked a passer-by, before exploding. For a long time the head of a Chinese tourist who had been next to her lay on the asphalt without its body. People were screaming and crying for help, but although there is no shortage of police in that area, they didn't approach the site of the explosion for 20 minutes, evidently fearing another explosion. Half an hour after the incident the ambulances arrived and the police closed the street.

10 December

There is little comment on the terrorist incident, or on why such acts take place.

Russia's upper chamber, the Soviet of the Federation, has announced the date of Putin's re-election. Putin immediately goes into top gear, using all sorts of anniversaries and special days to present himself to the country and the world as Russia's leading expert on whatever is being celebrated. On Cattle-Breeders' Day he is our most illustrious cattle-breeder; on Builders' Day he is our foremost brickie. It is bizarre, of course, but Stalin played the same game.

Today, as luck would have it, is International Human Rights Day, so Putin summoned our foremost champions of human rights (as selected by him) to the Kremlin for a meeting of the Presidential Commission on Human Rights. It began at 6.00 p.m. and was chaired by Ella Pamfilova*, a democrat from the Yeltsin era.

The paediatrician, Dr Leonid Roshal, spoke for one minute about how much he loves the President; Lyudmila Alexeyeva of the Moscow Helsinki Group spoke for five minutes about improper use of state resources during elections (which Putin didn't deny); Ida Kuklina of the League of Committees of Soldiers' Mothers spoke for three minutes about the exploitation of soldiers as slave labour and other Army horrors; Valerii Abramkin of the Centre for Reform of the Criminal Justice System spoke for five minutes about the things that go on in places of detention (the President seemed to appreciate his speech more than the other speeches); Ella Pamfilova spoke at great length about the dismal relations between human-rights campaigners and the law-enforcement agencies; Svetlana Gannushkina of the Memorial Human Rights Centre had three minutes to explain the implications of the new law on citizenship; Tamara Morshchakova, Adviser to the Constitutional Court, had seven minutes to present proposals for making the state authorities publicly accountable; Alexey Simonov spoke for three minutes on freedom of speech and the predicament of journalists; and Sergey Borisov and Alexander Auzan of the Consumers' Association talked of the need to protect small businesses.

Ranged against them were the Head and Deputy Head of the Presidential Administration; the Procurator-General of Russia, Vladimir Ustinov; the Minister of the Interior, Boris Gryzlov; the Minister of Justice; the Minister for the Press; the Chairmen of the Constitutional, Supreme and Business Arbitration Courts. Nikolai Patrushev, Director of the FSB*, was also present at the beginning, but left shortly afterwards.

All the campaigners in turn set about Procurator-General Ustinov. In between their attacks, Putin would also give him a dressing down and accuse him of unjustifiable rulings. Tamara Morshchakova kept up a legal commentary on what was being said, urging for example that a social worker should be present during the questioning and court appearances of minors. This is standard practice in many countries, but to the Kremlin it sounded radically new. Ustinov parried by claiming this would be contrary to Russian law, and Morshchakova brought him up short by pointing out that the laws he was referring to simply did not exist. This meant either that the Procurator-General did not know the law, which is clearly unthinkable, or that he was deliberately misleading his hearers. With Putin present this was hardly thinkable either, which led back to the first possibility, which is incompatible with holding the office of Procurator-General.

'It is only when they have direct personal experience of something that you can get anywhere,' Svetlana Gannushkina told me. 'While the President was talking on the telephone to Bush, I went over to Viktor Ivanov, the Deputy Head of the Presidential Administration and chairman of a working group on migration legislation. I unexpectedly found that we had equally negative feelings about residential registration. Ivanov's wife had recently spent five hours queuing to get temporary registration of friends who had come to stay with them in Moscow. It had made her furious.'

This prompted Ivanov to recognise the folly of reviving residential registration and he vowed to fight it. An FSB general, he offered to set up a joint working group with Gannushkina to reform it. 'Give me a call,' he said. 'Draw up a list of members for the group. We'll work on it together.'

Another example of the triumph of personal involvement over bureaucratic inertia came when Valerii Abramkin, a champion of prisoners' rights, told the President a dreadful story about two juvenile girls who had been wrongfully convicted. Their juvenile status was overlooked both by the court and the prison authorities and was picked up only after the girls had been transported under guard into exile, at which point they were released. Unexpectedly, Putin reacted very strongly to this. Something human flashed in his eyes. It turned out that his family had come across a similar incident involving two young girls who had suffered from disregard for the law, and to whom his wife was now giving support. It really seems that some personal experience is a prerequisite to the Administration focusing on the victims of injustice.

'You have the impression that on certain issues the President's information is very low-grade and sketchy. He doesn't do anything about it,' was Svetlana Gannushkina's reaction.

For the most part, Putin listened to what was being said and, when he did speak, presented himself as being on their side. He mimicked being a human-rights campaigner. Evidently, now that the democrats have been silenced, he will represent Yabloko and the Union of Right Forces for us. The prediction of the political analysts on the night of the parliamentary elections has come to pass.

This was probably Putin's main purpose in meeting the human-rights campaigners: to show them that their concerns were his. He is an excellent imitator. When need be, he is one of you; when that is not necessary, he is your enemy. He is adept at wearing other people's clothes, and many are taken in by this performance. The assembly of human-rights campaigners also melted in the face of Putin's impersonating of them and, despite a fundamentally different take on reality, they poured out their hearts to him.

At one moment someone actually did blurt out that they had the feeling Putin understood them much better than the security officials. Putin was unabashed and fired right back, 'That is because at heart I am a democrat.'

Needless to say, after this everyone's joy just grew and grew. Dr Roshal asked to speak 'just for a moment'. 'Vladimir Vladimirovich,' he said, 'I like you so much.' He has said this before. Vladimir Vladimirovich looked down at the table.

The doctor went on, '. . . and I do not like Khodorkovsky.' Vladimir Vladimirovich suddenly stiffened. Heaven only knew where this paediatrician was heading. And sure enough, his boat was heading straight for the reef. 'Although I like you and do not like Khodorkovsky, I am not prepared to see Khodorkovsky under arrest. After all, he is not a murderer. Where do we think he might run away to?'

The President's facial muscles worked, and those present bit their tongues. After that nobody mentioned Khodorkovsky again, as if Putin were a dying father and Khodorkovsky his prodigal son. The human-rights campaigners did not press home the attack, as might have been expected, but tucked their tails between their legs. The sky darkened, and only one person was to be found who, after the slip-up over Yukos, dared to broach another topic that the President's entourage always ask one not to mention, for fear of him losing control of himself. Svetlana Gannushkina raised the question of Chechnya.

Concluding her short speech on the problems of migration, which had been cleared by the Administration, Gannushkina went on to say that she could not expect the President to talk about Chechnya, and accordingly wished simply to present him with a book that had just been published by the Memorial Human Rights Centre, *People Live Here: Chechnya, A Chronicle of Violence*.

This was unexpected. The minders had no time to intervene. Putin took the book and, also unexpectedly, showed interest in it. He leafed through it for the remainder of the meeting, until 10.30 p.m. In the end he himself started talking about Chechnya.

'In the first place,' Gannushkina recalls, 'he is certain that it is all right to trample human rights underfoot in the course of the campaign against terrorism. There are grounds that justify not observing the law, circumstances in which the law can be flouted. In the second place, browsing through the book, Putin commented, "This is badly written. If you wrote so that people could understand, they would follow you and you could exert real influence on the Government. But the way this is presented is hopeless."'

Of course, what he had in mind was not Chechnya, but the defeat of Yabloko and the Union of Right Forces in the election. 'Putin is right,' Gannushkina believes. She has long been a member of Yabloko, and worked in the Duma assisting the Yabloko Deputies. 'We are incapable of explaining to people that we are neither on one side nor the other, but defending rights.'

After that the conversation turned of its own accord to Iraq. The campaigners said there was no comparison: the Chechens were Russian citizens, unlike the Iraqis. Putin parried this by saying that Russia gave a better impression of itself than the USA, because we have pressed charges against military personnel who have committed crimes in Chechnya far more frequently than the United States has against its war criminals in Iraq.

The Procurator-General chimed in: 'More than six hundred cases.' The human-rights campaigners didn't let that pass: how many of those had led to sentences being passed? The question hung in the air, unanswered.

Lyudmila Alexeyeva, leader of the Moscow Helsinki Group and an unofficial doyenne of Russian human-rights campaigners, someone whom the state authorities have raised to iconic status as personifying the human-rights community as far as the Kremlin is concerned, proposed convening a round table with the same participants to discuss the problems of Chechnya with the President. 'We'll need to think about that,' Putin muttered as he was saying his farewells, which meant, 'There's no way that is going to happen.'

*

There were indeed no discussions on Chechnya between Putin and the human-rights campaigners, but after their December meeting some of them, along with some of the democrats, decided to switch allegiance from the defeated Yavlinsky and Nemtsov to the newly democratic Putin, whom they evidently supposed would serve just as well.

The same fate befell a number of well-known journalists. Reputations were compromised before our very eyes. We watched as Vladimir Soloviov, a popular television and radio presenter, one of the boldest, best-informed and most democratic of reporters, who not long ago had exposed Government wickedness, for example, over the chemical attack in the *Nord-Ost* disaster [when 912 members of the audience of a musical were taken hostage by Chechens], suddenly and publicly proclaimed his passionate support for Putin and the Russian state.

This happened to him because he was brought in closer to the Kremlin and sweetened up. He transmogrified. It is a recurrent Russian problem: proximity to the Kremlin makes people slow to say no, and altogether less discriminating. The Kremlin knows this full well. How many of them there have been already, stifled by the Kremlin. First they are gently clasped to the authorities' breast. In Russia the best way to subjugate even the most recalcitrant is not money, but bringing us in from the cold, at arm's length at first. The rebellious soon begin to subside. We have seen it with Soloviov, with Dr Roshal, and now even the admirers of Sakharov* and Yelena Bonner* are beginning to talk about Putin's charisma, saying he gives them grounds for hope.

Of course, this is not the first time in recent history that we have seen this coming together of the regime and defenders of human rights, the regime and the democrats. It certainly is the first time, though, that it has been so devastating for former dissidents. What hope is there for the Russian people if one part of the opposition has been bombed out of existence, and another, almost all that remains, is being set aside for later use?

11 December

This morning there was more of the same, a reputation destroyed by the Kremlin's embrace. Andrey Makarevich was an underground rock musician in the Soviet period, a dissident, a fighter against the KGB*, who used to sing with passion, 'Don't bow your head before the changeful world. Some day that world will bow its head to us!' It was the anthem of the first years of democracy under Yeltsin. Today, on live television on the state-run Channel One, he is being presented with a medal 'For Services to the Fatherland'.

Makarevich came out in support of United Russia and took part in their pre-election get-togethers. He really did bow his head to Putin and his United Russia party. He told the people what a good guy Vladimir Vladimirovich was and, lo and behold, we now see him in receipt of official favours; a former dissident who wasn't embarrassed to join the Kremlin party.

Putin gave a reception for the leaders of the Duma parties as this is the last day of the Third Duma. He spoke of positive developments in relations between the branches of state power. Yavlinsky smiled wryly.

Soon, across the road from the Kremlin, the final session of the departing Parliament was held in the Duma building. Almost everybody was there. United Russia were in holiday mood and made no attempt to disguise the fact. Why would they? Every day newly elected Deputies from other parties are defecting to them, moving closer to Putin. United Russia is inflating like a hot-air balloon.

Yavlinsky stood apart from everyone else, as always, alone. He was morose and taciturn. What was there to applaud? The destruction of Russian parliamentary democracy has been accomplished on the tenth anniversary of the First Duma under Yeltsin's presidency. Tomorrow, 12 December, is also the tenth anniversary of Russia's new, 'Yeltsin' Constitution.

Nemtsov is trying to give as many interviews as possible while people are still interested in him. He explains. 'The Union of Right Forces and Yabloko are doing the impossible, something that before 7 December seemed a fantasy: we are trying to unite.' People do not entirely believe him. All the pro-democracy voters were praying they would merge before 7 December in order to have an impact in the elections, but they just were not interested.

Gennadii Seleznyov, the Speaker, makes a farewell speech to which nobody listens. He knows his days as Speaker are over, because in future the Speaker will not be elected by Parliament, but appointed by the Kremlin. Everybody also knows who it is going to be: Boris Gryzlov, Putin's friend and one of his most loyal henchmen, the Leader of United Russia and Minister of the Interior. It is unquestionably a historic moment. As we bid farewell to the Third Duma, we are bidding farewell to a political epoch. Putin has crushed our argumentative Parliament.

The exigencies of politics have not caused the Kremlin to neglect money matters. The attack on Yukos continues, with our business world trying to get its teeth into parts of it while everything is still up for grabs. The Arbitration Court of Yakutia has found in favour of Surgutneftegaz, a company that lost out to Sakhaneftegaz, subsequently part of Yukos, in an auction of oil and gas rights held in March 2002. The verdict strips Yukos of the Talakan field with its oil reserves of 120 million tonnes and 60 billion cubic metres of gas, and awards its rival a licence to exploit the central concession of the field in perpetuity.

Tsentrobank reports another record in replenishing the gold and foreign-currency reserves. To 5 December these are $70.6 billion. But is this a triumph? One of the main reasons why companies are dumping their foreign-currency profits on the market is the predicament of Yukos, with claims by the state that it concealed its earnings for tax-evasion purposes. The others are not tempting providence and are converting their profits into roubles. The hullabaloo over Yukos is doing the state no harm at all, which is why it can pay off its foreign debt. The Russian people rejoices, without having a clue as to what is going on.

Today is also the ninth anniversary of the start of Russia's latest wars against the Chechens. On 11 December 1994 the first tanks entered Grozny, and we saw the first soldiers and officers burned alive in them. There was no mention of this today on any of the television channels. The anniversary has been removed from Russia's calendar.

The unanimity of the television stations cannot be coincidental and must reflect instructions from the Presidential Administration, which means we can be sure that Putin's presidential campaign will exclude all mention of Chechnya. That's the way he operates: since he doesn't know what to do about Chechnya, Chechnya will not be on the agenda.

In the evening there was a televised debate between Valeriya Novodvorskaya, a democrat to the marrow of her bones, and Vladimir Zhirinovsky. She talked about the monstrous irresponsibility of the war in Chechnya, the blood and the genocide. Zhirinovsky's response was to shriek hysterically, 'Get out of this country! We will never give in to them!' In the vote at the end of the programme, viewers cast 40,000 votes in favour of Zhirinovsky to 16,000 for Novodvorskaya.

12 December

Constitution Day. A holiday. Moscow is flooded with militiamen and agents in plain clothes. There are dogs everywhere, searching for explosives. The President held a grand reception in the Kremlin for the political and oligarchic elite and made a speech about human rights, predicated on the notion that they had triumphed in Russia. Yeltsin was there, looking fitter and younger, but with mental problems written all over his face. He was there because the Constitution was adopted during his presidency. He is not usually invited to Putin's Kremlin.

A survey revealed that only 2 per cent of Russians have much idea of what the Constitution actually says. Forty-five per cent thought its main guarantee was of the 'right to work', and only 6 per cent mentioned free speech as something fundamental to their way of life.

18 December

A television phone-in. A big occasion as Putin meets the people. It was announced that more than a million questions had been submitted. The President's virtual dialogue with the country was hosted by his favourite television presenters, Sergey Brilev from the Rossiya channel and Yekaterina Andreyeva from Channel One.

Andreyeva to Putin: This is the third time you have appeared on this direct line. Me too. Are you nervous?

Putin: No. Don't offer what you can't deliver and don't lie, then you have nothing to fear.

Brilev, choking with joy: Very much like our work . . .

Putin: Everything that Russia has achieved has been achieved by hard work. There have been many difficulties and setbacks, but Russia has shown herself to be a country that stands firmly on her own feet and is developing rapidly. I have brought some statistics along. In 2002 our rate of growth was 4.3 per cent. Five per cent was projected for this year, but we shall achieve 6.6, or even 6.9. Payments on our foreign debt have been reduced. We have paid off 17 billion dollars and the country didn't even notice it. The gold and foreign-currency reserves in 2000 were $11 billion. In 2003 they rose to $20 billion, and today they are $70 billion. These are not empty statistics. A number of factors are involved here. If we continue with our present economic policy, there will be no more currency defaults. On the other hand, in early 2003 there were 37 million people whose income was beneath the subsistence level. In the third quarter of 2003 that number had fallen to 31 million, but this is still humiliating. The average subsistence level is 2,121 roubles [£40] a month, which is very low, and 31 million people live below that level.

A question from Komsomolsk-on-Amur, Khabarov Region: Ours is the third-largest city in the Far East of Russia, an enormous industrial centre, a city of young people, but a very long way from Moscow. My name is Kirill Borodulin. I work in the Amur shipyard. At present we are only working on export orders. When are we going to see orders from the Russian defence industry? We want to be needed by Russia.

(The questions do not give the impression of being spontaneous, and the answers appear to have been prepared. Putin reads out statistics from his notes even though the question was asked 'live on air'. He will evidently only be answering questions he wants to answer.)

Putin: The fact that you are working for export is entirely positive. There is a battle being waged for the arms market, and Russia is not doing at all badly. We have an armaments procurement programme up to the year 2010 and it is being fully financed. Of course, there are problems; one would always like to allocate more to our Armed Forces. The priorities for procurement are decided by the Ministry of Defence, which has placed new aircraft only eighth on its list of priorities, even though today's wars are fought using aircraft. You can be entirely sure that your services will be required.

Katya Ustimenko, student: I have voted for the first time. What can we expect from the new Duma?

Putin: No civilised state can live without a legislative institution. A great deal depends on the Duma. We expect efficient, systematic work.

Alexander Nikolaevich: I live in Tula, in the house where my father lived before me. The foundations are breaking up. We are in an excavation zone. Why does the state talk so much, but still doesn't resolve the problem of crumbling accommodation?

Putin: I have been to Tula. I was surprised at the state of the residential accommodation. There are ways and means. What are they? Only a few years ago the state allocated practically no funds. For the first time we made funds available in 2003: 1.3 billion roubles [£24.5 million] from the federal budget. The same amount again was to be added from local government budgets. The way out is to develop mortgage lending. If mortgages had been introduced, you would have been able to make use of one. What is your monthly salary? You are working in an efficient region.

Alexander Nikolaevich: 12,000 roubles [£226].

Putin: You would qualify for a mortgage. We need to make some legislative changes.

Yury Sidorov, Kuzbass: Working as a miner is dangerous. Why has the miners' pension been reduced to the statutory rate? What sort of pension is that?

Putin: The average salary of miners is 12,000 roubles a month, against a national average salary of 5,700 [£108]. The logic of the pensions reform is for pensions to directly reflect the contributions made from salary. Your pension will differ from the average to your advantage; it will be higher. This change has been introduced. The national pension fund is opening a network of consultation centres around the country and in the workplace. You need to go and talk to them.

Valentina Alexeyevna from Krasnodar: You have not so far announced whether you are intending to stand in the presidential election. What are your plans?

Putin: Yes, I shall be standing. I shall make an official announcement in the near future.

Alexey Viktorovich, naval repair yard, Murmansk Province: We have had no salary or holiday pay since August. When is this going to be sorted out?

Putin: We have sorted matters out as far as the budget is concerned. Delays must not exceed two days for salaries. As far as industry is concerned, there are a number of variations here. There are state enterprises, some of which are being reclassified as budget-financed enterprises. A number are in a parlous financial state. In other cases it is the owners and management who are responsible.

Question from Brilev: How do you feel about having your portrait in government offices?

Putin: The President is a symbol of the state, so there is nothing terrible about that. Everything is good in moderation. When that is forgotten, it gives rise to concern.

Sergeant Sergey Sergeyevich, Russian military base in Kant, Kirghizia*: The Americans have managed to capture Saddam Hussein, but there is going to be a second Vietnam in Iraq. Everybody will run away. The chaos there will affect everyone.

Putin: Sergey Sergeyevich, it is not in our national interest to see the USA defeated in its struggle against international terrorism. As far as Iraq is concerned, that is a separate issue. There were no international terrorists there under Saddam Hussein. Without the sanction of the United Nations Security Council the invasion cannot be regarded as legal, to put it mildly. In all ages, however, great empires have had delusions regarding their invulnerability, a sense of their grandeur and infallibility. This has invariably caused them a great deal of trouble. I hope this will not happen to our American partners.

Vitalii Potapov, electrician, Borovichi, Novgorod Province: Before the Duma elections your dog had puppies. How are they getting on?

Putin: They are doing well. They are very lively, but haven't opened their eyes yet. As to their future, we have had many requests from people wanting to adopt them. I and my children and my wife have to think about that. We have to make sure the puppies go to good homes. We need to know who we are giving them to.

Balkarov, a Kabardinian, Nalchik: I work in the Russian theatre. The

Abkhazians [from a disputed part of Georgia] are related to the Kabardinians [who are citizens of Russia]. Perhaps we should bring Abkhazia into the Russian Federation* and avert a new war?

Putin: This is a very acute question, for Russia as a whole, and especially for the south of our country. Maintaining the territorial integrity of the state was recently one of our own main problems and priorities. By and large that task has been accomplished. Following these principles, we cannot refuse to apply them to our neighbours. We are a member of the United Nations and we will fulfil our international obligations. There are peculiarities to do with the fact that the family of hill-dwelling peoples are a special community, with links of kinship between them, which go back many centuries. We are far from indifferent to the fate of these peoples. After the collapse of the USSR many conflicts broke out, in South Ossetia, Karabakh, Abkhazia. It would be a mistake to suppose they can all be resolved by Russia. I say, agree matters between yourselves and we will act as an honest guarantor. We will keep a close eye on the Abkhaz problem, but we respect the territorial integrity of Georgia.

Akhmad Sazaev, Balkarian writer: Inflaming ethnic strife is forbidden by law, but during the election campaign certain parties campaigned under the slogan, 'Russia for the Russians'. Why were these parties allowed to broadcast such sentiments on television?

Putin: Anyone who says 'Russia for the Russians' is either an idiot or a troublemaker. Russia is a multinational country. What do they want, partition? The dismemberment of Russia? Most likely these are mischief-makers looking for easy gains, who want to show how radical they are. As regards the election campaign, I didn't see this on television. If it did happen, I shall talk to the Procurator-General. Action should be taken.

Natalia Kotenkova, Krasnoyarsk: Is it not time to end privatisation and begin renationalisation?

Putin: This is not a new question and I have my own views on the matter. When the country began privatisation, it was assumed that the new property owners would be more efficient. That was quite right. Developed economies, however, have a well-established system of administration. By receiving taxation revenue from private enterprises, the state resolves social problems for its citizens. We ran into a snag. The administrative apparatus was not in place and the necessary resources did not flow into the Treasury. I am quite certain that what is needed is to strengthen the state's institutions and legislation and improve our system of administration. Not to stop privatisation.

Dmitry Yegorov, 25: I listen to heavy rock. What kind of music do you like?

Putin: Light classical music and Russian big-band music with vocals.

Alexey, Sverdlovsk Province: Were you very strict in bringing up your daughters?

Putin: No, unfortunately. Or fortunately. My girls have grown up independent, with a sense of their own worth. I think that is a good result.

Irina Mozhaiskaya, teacher: In the past three years there have been 12 terrorist outrages in Staropoliye. Forty-five people were killed in Yessentuki. How can this be stopped?

Putin: What is the root of the problem? It is a problem stemming not only from Chechnya. There are people in the world who consider they have the right to influence the outlook of people who adhere to Islam. They consider that they have a right to take control of territories densely populated by Muslims. This is extremely relevant to our country. 'International terrorists' is our name for these people. They have exploited the problems of the disintegration of the USSR, which are related to what has happened in Chechnya, but they have other goals. They want, not independence for Chechnya, but secession of all territories with a high Islamic population. If the Balkanisation of Russia were to begin, that would be terrible. We must fight that. The threat comes from abroad. The Islamic extremist groups in Dagestan* consist 50 per cent of foreigners. The only way is not to give in to their pressure, not to panic. We must act firmly and systematically, and the law-enforcement agencies need to improve the way they work.

Anatoly Nikitin, Murmansk Province: The Internal Affairs Offices and traffic militia seem to think they are in business to make a profit. Are you fully informed about what goes on in these agencies?

Putin: In the current year there have been more than 19,000 irregularities within the Interior Ministry's area of responsibility, and of these more than 2,600 were outright violations of the law. Many officials have faced criminal charges. The security services will be further strengthened. To give you a straight answer, yes, I am aware of the real situation in the agencies of law and order.

Sergey Tatarenko: Is the state planning to stop the migration of Chinese into the Far East?

Putin: Not to stop it, but to regulate it. We need to know where, how many and what kind of migrants we require, and devise a way of attracting the manpower we need. The level of corruption in this sphere is very high.

Lidiya Ivanovna, Khimki, Moscow Province: Will a mechanism be created to fight corruption in the procurators' offices and the courts? And in the executive institutions of the state?

Putin: Apart from becoming tougher over this, we need to introduce fundamental changes. We need to start a real administrative reform. The fewer opportunities officials have to interfere in the taking of decisions, the better. The court system should be independent, but transparent – accountable to society. The judges already have a system of self-regulation. I hope it will start working.

Ivetta, student, Pedagogical University, Nizhny Novgorod: They say you are a political pupil of Anatoly Sobchak, one of the founders of the democratic movement. What is your attitude towards the defeat of the forces on the political right?

Putin: Sobchak was my teacher at University. The defeat of the forces of the right gives me no pleasure. All the country's political voices should be represented in our Parliament. Their absence is a major loss, but it is a result of their policies. They made mistakes both in the tactics and in the strategy of their political campaign. They had access to administrative resources – Chubais is in charge of Russia's entire electricity system. They had everything, apart from an understanding of what people expect from a political party. There was also a lack of political will on the part of the miscellaneous forces on the right to agree on a joint course of action. I hope their defeat will not result in their disappearing from the political map. We shall help them too. We shall have discussions with the Union of Right Forces and Yabloko and try to make use of their human resources.

Vladimir Bykovsky, Chuvashia: Do you allow yourself emotions?

Putin: Unfortunately, I do.

Dobroslava Diachkova, pensioner, Vyborg: I work in a Hope Centre for the elderly and disabled, and talk a lot to those who are resting there. Many have relatives and friends in the Baltic States. Why does Russia not undertake more positive action to defend the Russian population in the Baltic States?

Putin: In recent years our Ministry of Foreign Affairs has been increasingly devoting attention to this. Many things there give us cause for concern. It cannot be said that these people are in full possession of their rights and freedoms. We are trying to help them both diplomatically and in court cases at various levels, but certain West European standards that are seen as appropriate in a number of other hotspots should also apply to the Baltic States. If in Macedonia the Organisation for Security and Cooperation in Europe and the European Community believe there should be representation for the Albanian population in the south of Macedonia, why is this principle not applicable in Riga, where 25 per cent of the population is Russian? Why are there different standards? In order not to do more harm than good for our compatriots, we shall approach this matter cautiously.

Anna Novikova, university teacher: People who distribute drugs should be given a life sentence!

Putin: I proposed changes to make penalties more severe. The Third Duma passed them, the Soviet of the Federation supported them, and a week ago I signed these amendments into law. There is a considerable increase in severity – up to 20 years' imprisonment for certain categories. I think it is a significant improvement.

Putin then read out a question he himself had chosen from those sent in by e-mail: What is your attitude towards increasing the term for presidents?

Putin: I am against it.

Immediately after this communion with the people, Putin told the press: 'Our state system is not yet fully established. In Russia everything is still evolving. Direct communication with citizens is extremely useful.'

That is how Putin concluded the event, and it may explain why he appeared on the phone-in in the first place: 'Strengthening demoracy has a practical importance in Russia. A situation has developed that will allow us to create a unique multi-party system, with a powerful right centre, social democracy on the left, allies to either side and also with representatives of marginal groups and parties. This is now an achievable goal.'

A strange statement that does not reflect reality.

If we consider the phone-in from a pre-election viewpoint, the main planks of Putin's platform as of 18 December would seem to be: the fight against poverty, defence of the Constitution, the creation of a multi-party system, the struggle against corruption, the struggle against terrorism, and the development of mortgage lending.

How much of this is our virtual President likely to implement?

20 December

Today is Secret Policeman's Day. The Cheka-OGPU-NKVD-KGB-FSB have been at it for 86 years. On the television news this is the lead item. How awful. The tone of the report is very dispassionate, as if millions of lives had not been sacrificed to this blood-soaked service. What else can we expect in a country whose leader openly admits that, even while in the post of President, he remains 'in the active reserve of The Firm'?

The final official summary of the parliamentary election results: United Russia, 37.55 per cent (120 seats); the Communist Party, 12.6 per cent (40 seats); the Liberal Democratic Party, 11.45 per cent (36 seats). Rodina obtained 29 seats. In three constituencies, in Sverdlovsk and Ulianovsk Provinces and also in St Petersburg, by-elections will be held on 14 March because the successful candidate last time was 'None of the above'. From tomorrow the parties can propose their presidential candidates.

Deputies are scuttling over to join United Russia. Particularly painful is the defection of Pavel Krashenninikov, elected as an independent candidate, but previously known to the electorate as a liberal and a member of the Union of Right Forces. The Duma is becoming a one-party show.

21 December

Yavlinsky has declined to stand as a presidential candidate for Yabloko. He also declared that they would 'create a major democratic party', but made the announcement with the haughty expression that puts everybody off voting for him. Proof, if proof were needed, that we need new faces and new leaders. Today's are incapable of forming a democratic opposition.

Khakamada also announced that the Union of Right Forces would not be putting forward a candidate. Her explanation was convincing: 'From the way people voted, it is clear that they don't want us leading the country.' The Communists also say they want no part in the election.

A boycott of the presidential election by the opposition on the right and left: is this the only way left for them to play a part in the country's politics after the December elections?

22 December

Today Putin submitted applications to the Central Electoral Commission from a group of electors who wish to start collecting signatures in support of his candidacy. The Kremlin's public opinion survey indicates that 72 per cent of the electorate would vote for Putin if the election were held today.

Who is standing against him? As of now, the only alternative to Putin is Gherman Sterligov, an undertaker who makes coffins. He has no party behind him, only lots of money and 'The Russian Ideal'. He is a rank outsider. The other potential runner is Vladimir Zhirinovsky. He has stated that the Liberal Democratic Party will field a candidate. He too is an outsider, but has done his bit to become an insider with the Kremlin. Putin looks ridiculous in such company. Presumably in the next few weeks the Administration will cobble together a group of rather more respectable candidates for Putin to defeat.

Nobody quite believes yet that Khodorkovsky is going to be found guilty. Most people think this is all just a Kremlin ploy, which will be dropped after Putin has been re-elected. On 30 December the period for which Khodorkovsky can be detained will expire, but hearings have been arranged well in advance at the Basmanny Court in Moscow to extend his imprisonment.

This evening it became clear that the Procurator-General's Office is asking that Khodorkovsky should be held until 25 March. That is, he will see Putin's re-election from prison. Khodorkovsky was brought to the court only at 4.00 p.m. or so. Some time after 6.00 p.m., when all the judges, employees, witnesses, plaintiffs and defendants in other cases had left, the doors of the Basmanny Court were closed and the hearing of his case began.

What are they so scared of? Is Khodorkovsky really the most dangerous man in Russia? Not even terrorists get this treatment, and Khodorkovsky is only charged with seven counts of financial irregularities. He was taken back to the Matrosskaya Tishina prison at about 10.00 p.m. The application of the Procurator-General's Office was granted.

Some results of last Sunday's local elections of governors: in Tver Province 9 per cent of the electorate voted for 'None of the above'. In Kirov Province it was 10 per cent.

Those who vote 'against' are the real democrats in Russia today. They have done their duty as citizens by turning out to vote, and are mostly thoughtful people with an aversion to all those now in power.

23 December

Ritual murders are taking place in Moscow. A second severed head has been found in the past 24 hours, this time in the district of Golianovo in the east of Moscow. It was in a rubbish container on Altaiskaya Street. Yesterday evening, a head in a plastic bag was found lying on a table in the courtyard outside Apartment Block 3 on Krasnoyarskaya Street. Both men had been dead for 24 hours before the discovery. The circumstances in the two cases are almost identical: the victims are from the Caucasus, aged 30–40, and have dark hair. Their identities are unknown. The heads were found a kilometre apart.

Such are the results of racist propaganda in the run-up to the parliamentary elections. Our people are very susceptible to fascist propaganda, and react promptly. In Moscow, Dmitry Rogozin's Rodina party won 15 per cent of the vote earlier this month.

The Union of Right Forces and Yabloko have unveiled their new joint project: the United Democratic Council, an inter-party body to which each party will nominate six members. At the announcement, not even party workers seemed to have much faith that the union would last. The general public seem totally uninterested in what has become of Yavlinsky, Nemtsov and the Yabloko party luminaries.

Putin has held a meeting with the business elite, or rather there has been a meeting of the Board of the Chamber of Commerce and Industry, which the President attended.

Putin favours the Chamber over the RUIE, the Russian Union of Industrialists and Entrepreneurs, which is considered the oligarchs' trade union. It was from the RUIE that Anatoly Chubais spoke out in defence of Khodorkovsky shortly after his arrest. He didn't pull his punches, talking of an 'escalation of the actions of the authorities and the law-enforcement agencies in respect of Russian business'. He warned that the business community's confidence in the Government had been undermined: 'Russian business no longer trusts the current system of law enforcement or those running it.' This was a direct accusation by the oligarchs' trade union that the forces under Putin's command were destabilising society. Chubais called for Putin to adopt a 'clear and unambiguous position'. These were unprecedently harsh words from business to the Government.

Putin's response was to tell them publicly to 'cut out the hysterics', and to advise the Government 'not to get drawn into this discussion'. He ignored the substance of the oligarchs' complaint and expressed his complete confidence in the law-enforcement agencies. When in January Boris Gryzlov was appointed Speaker of the Duma, Putin promoted Rashid Nurgaliev to be Minister of the Interior, one of the most odious militia bosses. This may also have been a response to whisperings at that time about Putin's supposed weakness as a leader, an attempt to demonstrate the robustness of the regime.

Putin's meeting with the Chamber of Commerce and Industry was much calmer, though. He sees the Chamber as being in a different category from the RUIE. The President of the CCI, that wily old Soviet fox Yevgeny Primakov, read his speech and quoted Putin on five occasions, prefacing his words with, 'as Vladimir Vladimirovich has correctly remarked . . .' Primakov assured Putin that 'an oligarch and a major entrepreneur are quite different things . . . The word oligarch sounds pejorative. After all, what is an oligarch? Someone who gets rich through devious manipulation of, among other things, his tax bill, who may trip up his business comrades or make crude attempts to interfere in politics, corrupting officials, parties, Deputies . . .', and so on. Primakov's entire speech was in the register of Soviet servility, and Putin clearly loved it.

Then it was time for questions. Naturally, they asked whether there was to be a review of the results of privatisation. Even if they are not the oligarchs' trade union, the Yukos affair was on everybody's mind.

Putin suddenly bawled like a market trader, or a prison guard, 'There will be no review of privatisation! The laws were complicated, muddled, but it was perfectly possible to observe them! There was nothing impossible about it, and those who wanted to, did! If five or ten people failed to observe them, that does not mean everybody failed to! Those who observed them are sleeping soundly now, even if they didn't get quite so rich! Those who broke the law should not be treated the same as those who observed it.'

'To be sleeping soundly now' is also a Russian euphemism for being in the grave.

After Putin's outburst, the proceedings continued smoothly. The businessmen made their reports to Putin and gave 'socialist undertakings' to meet various targets, just as in the days of the USSR. Primakov carried on doing what nobody had sunk to since the advent of Gorbachev, namely licking the boots of the country's leader and vowing that no words could be more profound than his.

(In December 2003 this grated on the ear and many were dismayed by Primakov's behaviour. It subsequently became clear that he was just the first to see the way the wind was once more blowing. Soon everybody who made speeches in Putin's presence was quoting him copiously – just as was the practice in the Brezhnev era – and not asking him awkward questions.)

Valeriya Novodvorskaya, the leader of the Democratic Union Party, received the Starovoytova Award in St Petersburg for 'her contribution to the defence of human rights and strengthening democracy in Russia'. The award is named after Galina Starovoytova, leader of the Democratic Russia Party, who was murdered by Special Operations hitmen from the Army's Central Intelligence Directorate (GRU) in the entrance to her own home. At the ceremony, Novodvorskaya said, 'We are not in opposition to, but in confrontation with, the present regime. We shall not take part in the forthcoming elections. We shall boycott them, although this will not change anything.'

The opposition in Russia is first and foremost words, but Novodvorskaya uses them with exceptional accuracy and is the first to take on the state.

The Moscow Municipal Court has increased the compensation awarded to one of the *Nord-Ost* widows, Alla Alyakina, whose husband, a businessman, died in the theatre siege on 26 October 2002, by two copecks [a fraction of a penny].

24 December

The first meeting of the United Democratic Council of Yabloko and the Union of Right Forces, at which the main issue is the prospects for joint political survival. An item about fielding a presidential candidate representing a united democratic front was removed from the agenda. From a conversation with Grigorii Yavlinsky:

'Why is Yabloko refusing to participate in the presidential election?'

'Because our elections are no longer even relatively democratic.'

'Then why did you take part in the parliamentary elections?'

'It was precisely the questionable results of the parliamentary elections which made it clear that things could not go on like that. During the last elections unsanctioned political involvement of business was crushed. No businessman now dares to contribute money to a political cause without permission from the Kremlin.'

'How do you see the future for Yabloko?'

'The same as for the rest of Russia. They will probably set up a decorative pseudo-democratic parallel party, or fight us to extinction. I don't suppose for a moment that we shall be left in peace to prepare for the next elections.'

'A one-party Duma? But the Communist Party is still in there.'

'Formally, yes. But if you took five people from the remaining parties, put them in different rooms and asked them crucial questions like, "What should be done in Chechnya? How should the Army be reformed? What should be done about education and health? What should our relations be with Europe and America?" they would all give the same answers. We have a pseudo-multi-party parliament, pseudo-free and fair elections, a pseudo-impartial judiciary and pseudo-independent mass media. The whole set-up is a Potemkin façade, a sham.'

'Do you see this lasting for a long time?'

'Things are changing rapidly, and anybody who thinks any of this will last for a long time is mistaken. Although to you and me, perhaps, it will seem quite long enough.'

I take an interest in what Yavlinsky has to say almost from force of habit. Other journalists are completely uninterested.

In Moscow, the victorious United Russia party holds its conference. Boris Gryzlov, the newly appointed Speaker of the Duma, declares, 'More than thirty-seven per cent of Russia's citizens, more than twenty-two million people, voted for us. We have obtained a majority in the Duma, which lays a great responsibility on us, and I do not believe in walking away from responsibility. I submitted an application to Putin and he made the arrangements for my transfer to the Duma. Permit me to express my especial gratitude to President Vladimir Vladimirovich Putin. It is by following his course that victory has been assured. Our candidate in the forthcoming elections is already known: the President – Vladimir Vladimirovich Putin. Our duty is to ensure that he wins decisively.'

After the conference came the first meeting of the parliamentary United Russia party. Gryzlov told us about his vision of the Duma's political role. Political debate, it seems, is mere chatter and should be excluded. For Gryzlov, a Duma without debate will be a step forward.

The Central Electoral Commission has registered a lobby group of electors proposing Putin's candidacy. As of today they can conduct their campaign officially, as if they haven't been doing just that until now.

26 December

The fifteenth conference of the misleadingly named Liberal Democratic Party begins in Moscow under the slogan 'Russians are tired of waiting!' Zhirinovsky will not stand for President. 'We will put forward a complete unknown, but I personally will lead the party during the election of the President,' he announced. The conference nominated Oleg Malyshkin, a wrestling coach who is Zhirinovsky's bodyguard and a complete imbecile. In his first television interview as a presidential candidate he had some difficulty remembering what his favourite book was.

Putin does not simply lack a field of competitors against whom to run. The whole background against which the election is being organised is an intellectual desert. The affair has no logic, no reason, no sparkle of genuine, serious thinking. The candidates have no manifestos, and one cannot imagine them being able to conduct a political debate.

What can we do? Election campaigns and hustings have been devised by democratic societies partly in order to allow the population some input into the deciding of their future, to give candidates advice and instructions.

We have been told just to pipe down. Candidate No. I knows best what everybody needs and accordingly requires no advice from anyone. There is nobody to moderate his arrogance. Russia has been humiliated.

27 December

Sterligov, the coffin-maker, has been disqualified from standing by the Central Electoral Commission. Viktor Anpilov, a clown from the Workers' Russia Party, promptly put himself forward. A horseradish is no sweeter than a radish.

28 December

At last they have found a worthy opponent for Putin: Sergey Mironov*, the Speaker of the Soviet of the Federation, has been proposed by the Party of Life (another of the dwarf parties set up by the Presidential Administration's Deputy Head, Vladislav Surkov*). He immediately announced, 'I support Putin.'

The conference of the Russian Communist Party is taking place. The Communists have proposed Nikolai Kharitonov, an odd, garrulous man who used to be a KGB officer. How wonderful!

Ivan Rybkin has announced he will stand. He is the creature of Putin's main opponent, Boris Berezovsky*, now in exile abroad. Rybkin used to be the Speaker of the Duma and Chairman of the National Security Council. Who is he today? Time will tell.

Meanwhile, Moscow is at a standstill. The rich haven't a care in the world; they are all abroad on holiday. Moscow is very rich. All the restaurants, even the most expensive, are crammed or closed for corporate parties. The tables are laden with delicacies beyond the imaginings of the rest of Russia. Thousands of dollars are spent in an evening. Is this the last fling of the twenty-first century's New Economic Policy?

29 December

The first sitting of the new Duma. Putin announced that the Parliament 'must remember that power derives from the people. Our main priorities are first and foremost to concentrate on issues affecting the quality of life of our citizens . . . It has taken considerable time and effort to move the Duma away from political confrontation to constructive work . . . It is essential to break through on every front . . . We have every right to call this a time that is seeing the strengthening of parliamentary democracy in Russia . . . All debate is useless . . .'

Vladislav Surkov, from the Presidential Administration, was also present. He is the spin doctor to whom United Russia owes its constitutional majority, a designer of political parties, slippery and dangerous.

Vladimir Ryzhkov*, an independent candidate from the Altai region, announced that he intends to challenge the composition of the Duma in the courts. 'The electorate did not give United Russia the mandate for a constitutional majority.' Really? Well, what are you going to do about it? We're living in times when the state authorities are entirely without shame.

Sergey Shoygu, Minister for Emergency Situations and a leading functionary of United Russia and by no means the stupidest of them, suddenly proposed that 'United Russia should become the party providing public accountability in the fulfilling of the President's decisions.'

Irina Khakamada may after all stand for President. All the democrats and liberals are condemning her in advance, saying the Administration has offered her a deal in order to have at least one intelligent opponent for Putin to defeat. Viktor Gerashchenko, formerly the head of Tsentrobank and now a Deputy of the Rodina party, has also decided to stand.

30 December

Irina Khakamada has confirmed she will stand as a candidate. She thought it over for 24 hours after a lobby group proposed it to her. Was it sent by the Kremlin?

She has until 28 January to collect two million signatures. Viktor Gerashchenko will not need to collect signatures, because Rodina is a party with seats in the Duma. Rodina was dreamed up by Vladislav Surkov and is financed by various oligarchs. Sergey Glaziev, also from Rodina, will stand as an independent.

Putin needed competitors, and he has received them as a New Year's gift. The new candidates have all promptly declared that the main thing is not to win, but to take part.

31 December

It is a sad farewell to 2003. The Duma elections were a great victory for Putin's absolutism, but how long can you go on building empires? An empire leads to repression and ultimately to stagnation, and that is where we are heading. Our people have been exhausted by having political and economic experiments conducted on them. They want very much to live better lives, but do not want to have to fight for that. They expect everything to come down to them from above, and if what comes from above is repression, they resign themselves to it. The joke most popular on the Internet: 'It is evening in Russia. Dwarfs are casting enormous shadows.'

The viewers of NTV's *Free Speech* programme have voted for the Russian of the Year. Among the nominations were Vladislav Surkov (for bringing about the crushing victory of United Russia); Academician Vitalii Ginzburg (Nobel Prize 2003, for work in quantum physics); the Novosibirsk film director, Andrey Zvyagintsev (whose first film, *The Return*, won the Lion d'or at the Venice Film Festival); Georgii Yartsev (who coached the Russian football team to victory against Wales); and Mikhail Khodorkovsky (for creating the most honest and transparent company in Russia, becoming the country's richest man and ending up in jail).

The viewers chose Ginzburg. Surkov came last.

At the end of the programme, the presenter Savik Shuster revealed the rating of the nominees in a poll commissioned earlier from the Romir public-opinion survey service. There too Ginzburg came first and Surkov last. This shows a divergence between the Putin Administration's model of reality and what actually exists.

The virtual world of the official television stations is quite different. *Vremya*, the country's main news programme, also ran a popularity poll for 2003. In first place was Putin, in second Shoygu and in third Gryzlov. So there!

Now, as it is almost time for the Kremlin chimes to ring out at midnight, a final thought for the year. Why are so many people emigrating? In the past year, the number of our citizens applying to live in the West has increased by 56 per cent. According to the Office of the

UN High Commissioner for Refugees, Russia is ahead of every other country in the world in terms of the number of its citizens seeking to emigrate.

4 January 2004

The conference of the Party of Life confirms Sergey Mironov as its presidential candidate. He repeats that he hopes Putin will win.

Mironov is one of a number of props for the candidacy of Putin. Leaving nothing to chance is one of the main features of this campaign. Why are they so worried?

In the Chechen village of Berkat-Yurt, Russian soldiers have abducted Khasan Chalaev, who works for the Chechen militia. His whereabouts are unknown.

5 January

Putin holds a Cabinet meeting. 'We need to explain the Government's priorities to the Duma Deputies,' he insists repeatedly. He is not in a good mood. The Rose Revolution* has triumphed in Georgia and Saakashvili* is celebrating victory. Provisional results suggest he gained about 85 per cent of the vote. This is a wake-up call to the heads of the other countries of the Commonwealth of Independent States*. All those sitting round the table with Putin are well aware of this. There is a limit to how long you can trample people underfoot. When they really want change, there is nothing you can do to stop it. Is this what they are afraid of?

6 January

The final day for presidential candidates to lodge their documents. Kharitonov, Malyshkin, Gerashchenko and Mironov have been proposed by parties in the Duma. There are now six independent candidates (Putin, Khakamada, Glaziev, Rybkin, Aksentiev and Bryndalov). Khakamada has problems with her right-wing political colleagues. Neither the Union of Right Forces nor Yabloko is in any hurry to support her or help with the collection of signatures. This makes her something of an outcast, which in itself might make Russians vote for her. We like pariahs, but we also like winners. People admire Putin for the way he manages to cheat everybody else. Those in the middle lose out.

This is the night before the Russian Orthodox Christmas, when people traditionally give presents and do good deeds (although not in public). Putin flew by helicopter to Suzdal. He has an election to win, so his personal life is public property. In Suzdal he walked round the ancient churches, listened to the singing of the novices in one of the convents, and posed for the television cameras and, no doubt, the press pack at the beginning of the Christmas service. The television shot was arranged to show Putin alone with the simple village congregation of little children and local women in their headscarves. Not a bodyguard in sight. He crossed himself. Thank God, there is progress in the world; he crosses himself very competently nowadays.

Another Russian tradition is that those at the top and bottom of our society might as well be living on different planets. Exhibiting Putin among ordinary people at Christmas time does not mean life will change for them. I set off to see the most underprivileged of all in a place where none of the elite set foot: Psycho-Neurological Orphanage No. 25 on the outskirts of Moscow.

Moscow's outskirts are not like the city centre, which nowadays is improbably opulent. The outskirts are quiet and hungry. Here there are no benefactors with toys and gifts, books and Pampers. Not even at Christmas.

'Let's go to see the children,' says the wise Lidia Slevak, director of this orphanage for the very smallest children, in a tone that suggests this will answer all my questions.

Little Danila is sticking out like a candle from the adult arms of a carer. He seems to be with you, in that he has almost put his arms around you, but also not with you, lonely, distant. The world has passed him by, he is on his own. He holds his thin little back very straight, like a yogi. His shock of fair curly hair is like the candle's flame. The slightest breeze wafting in through the door from the corridor makes his silken locks flicker. He is a Christmas miracle, an angel.

The only question is: to whom does this angel belong? Nobody is allowed to adopt him because of our idiotic laws. Danila's official status is a problem to which there is no solution. His natural mother did not officially renounce her maternal rights before running away. The militia are supposed to track her down, but they have more important things to worry about. This means that he cannot be adopted, even though he is such a little wonder. The sooner he is adopted, the better his chances in life will be, the sooner he will recover and will forget all that has happened to him. But the state too has more important things to worry about.

The surroundings here are warm and clean, as in a good nursery. A sign above the door tells us that the group to which Danila and 11 other little boys and girls belong is called the Baby Starlings. Their patient carers are kind, very tired, overworked women. Everything here is good, except that the children don't cry. They are silent or they howl. There is no laughter to be heard. When he is not grinding his teeth, 15-month-old Danila is silent, peering attentively at the strangers who have arrived. He does not look at you as you would expect of a 15-month-old baby; he peers straight into your eyes, like an FSB interrogator. He has catastrophically limited experience of human tenderness.

It is the night before Christmas in the orphanage on Yeletskaya Street and a Christmas present has just been delivered. His name is Dmitry Dmitrievich and he has severe liver and kidney insufficiency. He was born in December 2002 and in May 2003 his mother 'forgot' him in the entrance to a block of flats. Amazingly enough, the militia managed to track her down and she wrote out the necessary declaration: 'I apply to renounce my parental rights.'

Dmitry Dmitrievich has been brought to the orphanage from hospital. He has spent half his life in intensive care and now has no hair on the back of his head. It has rubbed off because he has always been lying on his back. The new boy in the group sits in a special baby-walker and studies this unfamiliar place. There are rattles and toys in front of him, but Dmitry Dmitrievich seems more interested in people. He examines the consultant. He wants to take a good look at her, but does not yet know how to work his little legs, which, since he's been bedridden for so long, are not helping him to turn the baby-walker to face Lidiya Konstantinovna. She doesn't intervene. She wants him to learn how to get what he wants.

'Come on, Dmitry Dmitrievich,' she says. 'Take a grip on life! Fight back!'

Unaided, Dmitry Dmitrievich does fight back, and a few minutes later he has won and is facing Lidiya Konstantinovna.

'What kind of work do you feel you are doing here? The work of Mother Teresa, or of someone who has to clean up after our society. Or do you just feel very sorry for these children?'

'The children do not need pity,' Lidiya says. 'That is the most important lesson I have learned. They need help. We are helping them to survive. Because of the work we do, they can hope to find foster parents. I and my staff never refer to this as an orphanage in front of them. We call it a nursery so that later, in a quite different life if they are adopted, the children will not have even a subconscious memory of having once been in an orphanage.'

'You are working so that the children entrusted to your care should be adopted?'

'Yes, of course. That is the most important thing I can do for them.'

'What do you think about adoption by foreigners? Our patriotic politicians demand that we should put a stop to it.'

'I think adoption by foreigners is a very good thing. There are some horror stories about Russian foster families too, only they don't get mentioned. Right now there is talk of withdrawing one of our children from his Russian foster parents. He will be coming back to us. Another problem is that Russian foster parents will not take children from the same family. Foreigners are happy to do that, which means that brothers and sisters are not separated. That is very important. We had a family of six children adopted in America. Natasha, the youngest of the six, was brought in to us wrapped in a piece of wallpaper. Her four-year-old brother wrapped her up in that to keep her from freezing because there was nothing else in the house to use. So what is bad about the fact that all six of them are now in the United States? I feel very happy when I look at the photograph I was sent from there. Nobody would believe the state they were in here. Only we remember that. In the past year, fifteen of the twenty-six children who have been adopted from our orphanage have been taken by foster parents from abroad, mainly from the USA and Spain. There were three pairs of brothers and sisters. Russian people just wouldn't take them.'

'They didn't want to or they couldn't afford to?'

'They didn't want to. And, as a rule, rich people in Russia don't adopt children at all.'

What kind of people will they grow up to be, the way our country has turned out now?

The wave of charitable giving in Russia came to a stop in 2002 when the Putin Administration revoked tax privileges for charities. Until 2002, children in our orphanages were showered with gifts and New Year presents. Now the rich no longer give them presents. Pensioners bring them their old, tattered shawls.

The World Bank has a special programme called A Chance to Work, which gives disadvantaged children work experience and a chance to learn valuable job skills. If anyone did that in our society they would most likely be viewed with suspicion. 'What's in it for them?' the neighbours would wonder.

It is the orphans themselves who show compassion. Nadya left the orphanage when she was too old to remain, and was allocated a room by the local authority as the law requires. She promptly moved in four other orphans. Completely unfamiliar with the ways of the world, they had exchanged their own rooms for mobile phones and had found themselves on the street.

Now Nadya is feeding them, but she is penniless. None of them can find work. Hers is true charity. She can see no point in trying to approach the banks and other wealthy institutions. They wouldn't let her past security.

Meanwhile, our nouveau riche are skiing this Christmas in Courchevel. More than 2,000 Russians, each earning over half a million roubles [£10,000] a month, congregate there for the 'Saison russe' in the Swiss Alps. The menu offers eight kinds of oysters, the wine list includes bottles at £1,500, and in the retinue of every nouveau riche you can be sure of finding the government officials, our true oligarchs, who deliver these vast incomes to the favoured 2,000. Not a word is heard in the televised Christmas reports from Courchevel about hard work having led to the amassing of these fortunes. The talk is of success, of the moment when everything just fell into place, of the firebird of happiness caught by its tail feathers, of being trusted by the state authorities. The 'charity' of officialdom, otherwise known as corruption, is the quickest route to Courchevel. It is a modern version of the tale of Ivan the Fool, who just couldn't be poor, no matter how badly his brothers cheated him: just pay the Kremlin and riches and power will come your way.

8 January

Zhirinovsky's bodyguard has been registered by the Central Electoral Commission as the first candidate in 2004 for the presidency of Russia. Hip-hip-hooray! Zhirinovsky has power of attorney over Malyshkin.

In Krasnoyarsk Region the peasants are being paid in sick calves. The potentate ruling over this region is the oligarch closest to Putin, indeed his representative there, Vladimir Potanin. No wages have been paid in cash at the dairy farm in Ustyug for more than three years; the peasants are given calves instead. All the machinery has been sold off to settle debts. The vet was sacked long ago, so there is nobody to look after the ailing calves.

9 January

This really is a first for us. The pupils of the International Orphanage in Ivanovo are on hunger strike. The orphanage was founded in 1933 to provide for children from many different countries whose parents were in the prisons of 'states with reactionary or fascist regimes'.

The children are demanding that the International Orphanage should be left alone, not broken up and privatised and the building sold. (They were successful.)

10 January

In the Chechen village of Avtury unidentified soldiers have abducted the human-rights campaigner Aslan Davletukaev from his home. The kidnappers drove up in three armoured personnel carriers and two armoured UAZ jeeps.

13 January

Today is Russian Press Day. In anticipation, the Romir public-opinion survey asked people, 'Which social institutions do you most trust?' Nine per cent trust the media; 1 per cent trust political parties; 50 per cent trust Putin; 28 per cent trust nobody; and 14 per cent trust the Russian Orthodox Church. The Government and the Army scored 9 per cent each. Local government and the trade unions scored 3 per cent, and the law-enforcement agencies managed 5 per cent. People were, of course, at liberty to trust more than one institution. Some did.

Victims of the terrorist acts of recent years have sent an open letter to all the presidential candidates. It reads:

> The presidential election is a time for reviewing the past and for the outgoing authorities to account for what they have been up to while in office. There must be few people in Russia who have suffered more in this period than we. We lost those dear to us when apartment blocks were blown up in 1999 and when the theatre on Dubrovka was seized by terrorists in 2002. We call upon you to include investigation of these terrorist acts in your manifestos.

. . . We would like to know what each of you will do if elected. Will you set up genuine, independent and impartial inquiries, or will the conspiracy of silence surrounding the deaths of our loved ones continue? We have tried in vain to obtain credible explanations from the state authorities. The present President of the Russian Federation was under an obligation to reply, not only by virtue of his position, but simply as a matter of conscience. The deaths of our loved ones were, after all, directly related to his political career and to decisions taken by him. The blowing up of apartment blocks persuaded the Russian people to support his hard line on Chechnya during the last presidential election, and he personally gave the order to use gas in Dubrovka.

The signatories then submit a list of questions to the candidates, which they have previously addressed to Putin without any response.

Regarding the blowing up of the apartment blocks:

1. Why did the authorities obstruct the investigation of events in Ryazan when FSB agents were caught red-handed preparing to blow up an apartment block?
2. How did the Speaker of the State Duma come to issue a statement about the blowing up of the apartment block in Volgodonsk three days before it occurred?
3. Why was there no investigation of the discovery of the high explosive, hexogen, in sacks labelled 'Sugar' at the Army base in Ryazan in the autumn of 1999?
4. Why, under pressure from the FSB, was the investigation closed into the transfer of hexogen from Army storage facilities to fictitious firms through the Roskonversvzryvtsentr Research Institute?
5. Why was the lawyer Mikhail Trepashkin arrested after establishing the identity of the FSB agent who rented the premises for placing the bomb in the apartment block on Gurianov Street?

Regarding the Dubrovka siege [the taking hostage of the audience of the musical *Nord-Ost*]:

1. Why was the decision taken to begin a gas attack at the very moment when a real opportunity had arisen of negotiating the release of the hostages?
2. Does the fact that the authorities decided to use a slow-acting gas, which would have given time for explosive devices to be

detonated, indicate that they already knew the terrorists had no real explosives on them?

3. Why were all the terrorists, including those who had been incapacitated, killed when they could have been arrested and required to give evidence to an inquiry?

4. Why did the authorities conceal the fact that K. Terkibaev, who, after his name became known, died in a car crash, was an FSB agent who took part in the seizure of the theatre?

5. Why, when the assault was planned, was no attempt made to organise on-site medical assistance for the hostages, a neglect that resulted in the deaths of 130 people?

The only replies were from Irina Khakamada and Ivan Rybkin. She has supported the *Nord-Ost* victims from the very beginning. Altogether, Khakamada is beginning to seem the most normal of the candidates. Everything that she has said so far has been worth listening to. She has been saying that under Putin the country cannot progress.

Irina Khakamada:

I have not studied the explosions in Moscow and Volgodonsk, so I shall reply only to the questions about the events at Dubrovka.

The decision to mount the assault was taken on the third day of the siege. I was inside the building on the first day and am replying on the basis of what happened then. My impression is that on the first day it would have been possible to free the hostages through negotiation. I believe the purpose of the assault was a show of strength, and that saving people's lives was not a high priority.

It remains a riddle to me how it was possible to kill every one of the terrorists, who were situated in different parts of the building and auditorium; and why, after the gas attack, all the terrorists died, while some of the people next to them died and others survived. I suspect they were disposed of because as living witnesses they might have testified in open court that the hostages could have been released. I emphasise that this is a suspicion, because there should be a presumption of innocence.

We in the Union of Right Forces organised an investigation of our own, and came to the conclusion that no thought was given to trying to rescue the hostages. Everything was unplanned and the result was a shambles. The military side was deemed the most important aspect of the operation, and nobody was even appointed to take care of the civilians.

I can add on my own account that after the Dubrovka tragedy Mr Putin misled the whole world. Replying to a question from a journalist on the *Washington Post*, he said, 'These people did not die as a result of the gas, because the gas was harmless. It was harmless, and we can say that in the course of the operation not a single hostage was harmed [by the gas].'

While President Putin and his cohorts were quaking with fear in the Kremlin, not for the lives of their citizens, but of losing power, a number of people were brave enough to try to save the hostages by voluntarily going in to the terrorists in order to attempt to free at least the children. I thank God that I, the mother of two children, had the courage and resolution to go in and negotiate with the terrorists.

In the past I have not made public much of what I saw in the Dubrovka Theatre Complex or, in particular, how the President and members of his Administration reacted to my effort to save lives. I mistakenly thought that President Putin would ultimately help to establish the truth, and would apologise for his order to employ a deadly gas. Putin, however, remains silent and gives no answers to people who have lost those dearest to them. The President has made his choice and decided to conceal the truth. I also have made my choice and will tell the truth. As a result of my negotiations with the terrorists in the theatre on 23 October 2002 and what happened subsequently, I came to the conclusion that the terrorists had not the least intention of blowing up the Theatre Complex, and that the authorities had not the least interest in trying to save all the hostages.

The main events occurred after I returned from negotiating with the terrorists. Alexander Voloshin, the Head of the Presidential Administration, threatened me and ordered me not to interfere further.

Thinking over what occurred, I have come to the inescapable conclusion that this terrorist act helped to reinforce anti-Chechen hysteria, to prolong the war in Chechnya and to maintain the President's high approval rating. I am convinced that Putin's actions in covering up the truth are a crime against the state. I undertake that, when I become President, the citizens of Russia will learn the truth about the blowing up of the apartment blocks, the tragedy at the Theatre Complex, and many other crimes committed by the authorities. Recently, many of my friends have tried to dissuade me from entering the presidential election. In public they state that I am almost betraying the interests of the democrats, who are calling for a boycott of the elections, but in private they warn that I will simply be killed if I tell the truth. I am not afraid of this terrorist regime. I appeal to everybody else not to be intimidated by them. Our children must grow up free people.

Ivan Rybkin also replied:

Both the blowing up of the apartment blocks and the events at Dubrovka are a consequence of the 'anti-terrorist operation' and, more precisely, of the Second Chechen War being waged in the North Caucasus. President Putin rode into the Kremlin on the crest of this wave, promising to restore order. He has proved incapable of doing so. People are dying in terrorist outrages everywhere. The war continues without respite, for which Putin and his immediate entourage are guilty. To this day there is much that is completely unclear and inexplicable about all these tragedies.

Concerning the blowing up of the apartment blocks:

I believe a crime was committed by the security agencies. Even if we accept the claim that [the FSB agents discovered planting explosives] in Ryazan were engaged in 'exercises', all the official rules and instructions were ignored.

How did Seleznyov, the Speaker of the Duma, know? This is not just odd, it is appalling. Having made this announcement, he should face criminal investigation and reveal where he got his information, so that we can see clearly who really ordered and who really carried out this atrocity . . .

The approaches and training which the security forces are receiving in the course of the Chechen War are being extrapolated to the whole of Russia. They are totally brazen and believe that the end result is all that matters. This is extremely dangerous.

On Dubrovka:

All the behaviour of the state authorities points to the fact that when it became clear there was a real possibility of freeing the hostages, they decided to mount an assault. Everyone in Moscow and all over Russia is talking about the fact that the assault was ordered to conceal the real facts about what happened there.

Was the Government in the know? I find it particularly unpleasant to answer this question, because during the events in Budyonnovsk, at a very secret meeting, the security forces contradicted everything the Government has maintained. I was told that this gas and other chemical means could not be used in a bus with hostages because the terrorists would have time to detonate their explosives. As they were losing consciousness they might also start firing at random. As it was used this time, the Government clearly knew there would be no explosions.

The terrorists were shot while unconscious because they would have had a great many interesting things to tell an independent inquiry. The whole of Russia is asking why unconscious people were shot; identified, approached and shot in the head.

The authorities failed to keep [the FSB agent] Terkibaev out of public view, and that is why he was killed. I know how angry people were, because they knew Terkibaev had authorisation from the Presidential Administration. He himself boasted about the fact that he had managed to redirect [the terrorist leader] Baraev's attack from the Duma to Dubrovka.

The lack of assistance to those who suffered during the assault was barbaric, and is wholly on the conscience of those responsible for the final phase. There is an attempt to divert popular anger over the lack of timely medical aid on to the Mayor of Moscow, but it is not the Mayor who is responsible for fighting terrorism; that is the job of the FSB.

The cascade of medals and stars on to the chests and epaulettes of security forces who ought to have been punished for letting Baraev's unit through in the first place confers honour neither on those decorated nor on the individual who decorated them. Again, we need an independent inquiry.

I am not one of those who believe that the time will come when the archives are opened and we discover the truth. That day will never come. We need an investigation now, so that such an atrocity is never repeated, so that there is never a repetition of this appalling mistreatment of our citizens.

Meanwhile, as a result of defections, the United Russia party has gained a sufficient majority in the Duma to change the Constitution. Gennadii Raikov applied to join them today, taking the number of Putin's supporters in the Parliament to 301.

Apathy is ever more palpable; people are certain that nothing good can be expected. The presidential election is discussed on television, but otherwise nobody says a word about it. They already know how it will end. There is no debate, no excitement.

In Moscow the best-known Russian human-rights campaigners this evening celebrated the Old [Russian Orthodox] New Year in their own way. They gathered at the Andrey Sakharov Museum and Social Centre to try to form either a broad Democratic Front or a Democratic Club (as Vladimir Ryzhkov is suggesting), and to do it outside the traditional democratic institutions of the Union of Right Forces and Yabloko.

The most businesslike proposals were made by Yevgeny Yasin: 'If we want a really broad union, we need a very limited programme. We need very few demands, in order to get as many people as possible to join. Our one aim should be to defend the gains of Russian democracy, to confront the authoritarian police-state regime.'

Towards the end of a heated discussion that lasted many hours, tidings from prison were brought to the Sakharov Centre. Karina Moskalenko, a lawyer, arrived direct from Matrosskaya Tishina prison where she had had a meeting with her client, Mikhail Khodorkovsky. She conveyed Khodorkovsky's good wishes to all the champions of human rights and the news that 'the only ideal that enthuses him today is the ideal of defending human rights. If he gets out of prison he is determined to devote himself exclusively to working for the betterment of society.'

They have managed to bring an oligarch to civic consciousness. The activists clapped like children at a Christmas party.

14 January

Moscow's Basmanny Court, as much in the Kremlin's pocket as ever, continues to refine the art of selective justice, where what counts is not the law, but the individual it is being applied to. If that person is an enemy of Putin, the Basmanny judges are pedantic; if he is a favourite, they do not get vexed over legal niceties, or even require him to attend the hearing.

Today Judge Stanislav Voznesensky was considering a claim from Nadezhda Bushmanova of Ryazan Province, the mother of Alexander Slesarenko, a soldier killed in the Second Chechen War. Alexander was fighting in the Armavir Special Operations Unit of the Interior Ministry.

In September 1999, at the very beginning of the Second Chechen War, this unit was included in a special operations group under the command of Viktor Kazantsev, at that time Commander of the North Caucasus Military District. Kazantsev committed an error and Alexander, among many others, was killed. Here is what happened:

Everything began on 5 September, officially the first day of the War, when Putin issued a decree to begin an 'anti-terrorist operation'. There was fighting in villages in Dagestan. At around 1700 hours the fighters occupied the Dagestan village of Novolakskoye on the border with Chechnya, and a unit of the Lipetsk Militia Special Operations Unit found itself holed up in the militia station. It needed rescuing. On the night of 5 September the 120 men of 15 Special Operations Unit were called into action. Among them was Alexander Slesarenko. On 6 September the unit was at the Mozdok Army base in North Ossetia. On 7 September they were deployed to the Dagestan village of Batash-Yurt, and on 8 September to Novolakskoye. At this point the Armavir men came under the command of Kazantsev. He had been placed in overall charge of the operation to clear the Novolakskoye and Hasavyurt regions of Dagestan, and all categories of troops were under his command.

On 8 September, Kazantsev ordered Major-General Nikolai Cherkashenko, his deputy in charge of the Interior Troops, to present a plan to take the adjacent commanding heights in accordance with Kazantsev's general instruction. On 9 September Kazantsev approved the plan, and at 2130 hours Major Yury Yashin, commanding officer of the Armavir unit, received the order to attack and occupy and hold the heights until the arrival of reinforcements, so that fire could be directed down on to Novolakskoye.

The Armavir men did as they were ordered and moved in at top speed, deaf and naked, as they say in the Army, without secure means of communication, using only open-channel walkie-talkies with batteries, which, because there had been no time to recharge them, were flat. How much ammunition they would need had not been calculated, because the Armavir men had not been told how long they would have to hold out. They were expendable, and anyway they didn't even belong to Kazantsev's regular forces.

The war in the Caucasus is very odd. All the federal troops are supposedly on the same side, but the reality is quite different. The soldiers under the Ministry of Defence are at daggers drawn with the FSB, and the Interior Troops are at loggerheads both with their own Interior Ministry and the Army. When officers say, 'The casualties were not ours', that means in Army-speak that the fallen were militiamen or soldiers of the Interior Troops. This is why a battle has been raging for many years over who should head the Joint Command of forces and resources in the North Caucasus. If an Army man is in charge, there is no way non-Army personnel will get the ammunition and walkie-talkies they need.

That is what happened on this occasion. Kazantsev, an Army man, was in command of non-Army men. By 0100 hours on 10 September, 94 non-Army Special Operations troops had occupied the heights without losses. At 0600 hours Major-General Cherkashenko received a confident report from Major Yashin and passed the information to Kazantsev, who immediately drove off, reassured that the hills had been taken. He was absent until 0840 hours, but at precisely 0620 hours Yashin suddenly found himself with a battle on his hands. At 0730 hours Chechen fighters began to encircle the Special Operations troops. Yashin radioed for assistance, but Cherkashenko, left to represent Kazantsev at the command post, was unable to help. He knew that another group of Interior Troops, commanded by Major-General Grigorii Terentiev, had already tried to break through to Yashin's detachment, but had been repelled by stiff opposition. Fourteen men had died and there were many wounded, including Terentiev himself. On the slopes of the heights five armoured personnel carriers were in flames.

Apart from Terentiev's detachment, no others would go to the aid of Yashin because they were Army men and because Kazantsev was asleep. At 0830 hours Yashin shouted to Cherkashenko that they all had only a single round of ammunition left and needed to retreat. Cherkashenko agreed. At 0840 hours Kazantsev, having woken up, burst into the command post. He couldn't understand why Yashin was retreating. He had ordered him to hold the position at all costs.

At this point all contact with Yashin was lost. The walkie-talkie batteries had run out. The Major was 'deaf' and entirely on his own. Yashin divided the unit into groups, headed one himself, entrusted another to Lieutenant-Colonel Gadushkin, and at about 1100 hours, gathering their strength, they began to retreat downhill. This was the only way the unit could hope to survive. Kazantsev was at the command post and observed the movements personally. He then gave orders to bomb the slopes. Why? Because he had his plan and had already reported 'upstairs' the time within which the fighters on the hill would have been eliminated.

At 1500 hours two low-flying SU-25 attack planes appeared in the sky over Yashin's group and delivered a targeted strike at the Interior Ministry troops who were breaking out of their encirclement. The targeter, on Kazantsev's specific orders, was the commanding officer of the Fourth Air Army and Anti-Aircraft Defence Forces, Lieutenant-General Valerii

Gorbenko. As the bombs were dropped, these two heroes, Kazantsev and Gorbenko, were standing at a field observation point and saw with their own eyes that Yashin's group were launching signal flares to indicate where the bombs should not be dropped.

Why was the Armavir Special Operations Unit punished in this manner on 10 September? Because it had been set up. They were sacrificed to protect Kazantsev and his idiotic plan. They were invited to die as heroes rather than escape the encirclement and be potential witnesses, but failed to take the hint. This is the method of our security bosses, later employed many times in Chechnya and elsewhere. *Nord-Ost* was a clear enough demonstration of the same thing. It is a method sanctioned repeatedly by Putin. If you survive, you must be vilified and punished.

The Military Procurator's Office of the North Caucasus Military District is, under our monstrous judicial system, effectively dependent on the commanding officer of its district, in this case Kazantsev, for the allocation of promotions, accommodation and privileges. It considered a criminal case regarding the killing of the Armavir men, brought by their relatives. The court acquitted Kazantsev on all counts. More than that, it depicted him as a hero surrounded by cowards. Here is a quotation from the court records:

> In reality, the Interior Troops were retreating in disarray. The situation was close to critical. Kazantsev took the decision to move to the forward sector himself. He personally halted the subdivisions of Interior Troops who were fleeing in disorder, and personally identified a new mission to them, attempting to deploy the remainder of the Interior Troops' subdivisions to cut off the fighters.

Kazantsev is an Army hero and the Interior Troops are cowards. This is the verdict of the court.

The soldiers certainly were fleeing, but from a death trap they had been put in. They tried to survive the bombing as best they could, which was being directed at them on the orders of imbeciles. They were dragging their wounded, calling for assistance to retrieve the bodies of those who had been killed. Kazantsev observed all this.

The final toll from that single treacherous bombing of the heights at 1500 hours by two SU-25 attack aircraft was eight dead and 23 wounded. Only one soldier was killed in combat with the Chechen fighters.

The overall losses of Interior Troops in the course of Kazantsev's operation of 9–10 September were 'over 80 men', according to the inquiry. No further details are available. The soldiers of Major Yashin's doomed detachment were making their way back to their own lines for several days afterwards. Alexander Slesarenko's body was returned to his home in Ryazan Province two weeks later, in a sealed coffin. The coffins were buried in the graveyards of Russia, and the state stuck into their grave mounds the very cheapest of memorials, an insult to the men who lie beneath them.

Overcoming her grief, Alexander's mother applied to the Basmanny Court, within whose jurisdiction the Ministry of Defence lies. Judge Voznesensky directed the Treasury to pay her 250,000 roubles [£4,700] in compensation. Needless to say, it did not come from the pocket of Kazantsev, who was by then a favourite of the President and Putin's personal representative in the North Caucasus. Kazantsev has been showered with medals, orders and titles by Putin for his part in the so-called anti-terrorist operation, for bringing Chechnya to the state the President wanted it in.

Judge Voznesensky is a young man, dynamic and modern, and doesn't clam up at the mention of administrative interference in the judicial process. He knows exactly what you are talking about. I know him well. He is brilliantly educated and peppers his conversation with Latin expressions, revealing a level of erudition unheard of among Russian judges. Voznesensky did not, however, delve too deeply into the details of Private Slesarenko's death, or indeed bother summoning that 'Hero of Russia', General Viktor Kazantsev, to the courtroom.

So, once again, the taxpayers of Russia uncomplainingly pick up the tab for the Second Chechen War and the idiocies of its generals, plus all the other expenditure on successive military escapades in the North Caucasus.

How long is this going to continue? The tragedy of the Second Chechen War has been the launch pad for the stellar careers of all those implicated in it as comrades-in-arms of the present President. The more blood shed, the higher they rise. So who takes responsibility? It simply does not matter how many people Kazantsev sends to their death; it does not matter how often he collapses drunkenly into the arms of others, including journalists. It is water off a duck's back. The only thing that matters in Russia today is loyalty to Putin. Personal devotion gains an indulgence, an amnesty in advance, for all life's successes and failures. Competence and professionalism count for nothing with the Kremlin. The system that has evolved under Putin profoundly corrupts officials, both civilian and military.

Alexander's mother tells me, 'I shall never reconcile myself to the fact that my Sasha was sacrificed to a general's ambition. Never.'

15 January

In Moscow there is a fuss over a new history textbook. Members of United Russia are demanding that Putin should require that 'pride at the events' of the Russo-Finnish War of 1939 and of Stalin's collectivisation of agriculture should be included. They insist that our children should once more read a Soviet treatment of the Second World War and the supposedly positive role played by Stalin. Putin is going along with this. *Homo sovieticus* is breathing down our necks. Another textbook has meanwhile been banned for including the comment by Academician Yanov that Russia is in danger of turning into a national socialist state armed with nuclear weapons.

Relatives of the *Nord-Ost* victims have a meeting at the Procurator-General's Office in Moscow with Vladimir Kalchuk, a Serious Crimes Investigator running the inquiry into the theatre hostage-taking. They have asked me to accompany them in order to reduce the likelihood that Kalchuk will deceive or insult them. When there are no outsiders present, Kalchuk constantly insults the relatives of those who died, and has never been brought to book for this. He is under personal instructions from Putin to falsify the investigation and ensure that information about the gas used should be suppressed.

'Passports on the table!' Kalchuk barks, signalling the beginning of the meeting. "*Nord-Ost* Association"? What is that? Who has recognised this organisation?'

'Can we talk like civilised human beings?' Tatyana Karpova asks. She is the mother of Alexander Karpov, one of the hostages who died, and she is the Chairperson of the *Nord-Ost* Association. 'How many terrorists were killed? How many managed to escape?'

'According to our data, all the terrorists in the building were killed, but it is impossible to give a hundred per cent guarantee.'

'Why were all the fighters killed?'

'Well, they were, and that's all there is to it. These things are decided by the security forces. They are risking their lives when they go in, and it is not for me to tell them who they should or should not kill. I have my own opinion as a human being, and I have my opinion as a lawyer.'

'Do you consider that a published video tape of a shooting suggests that any of the hostages could have been killed in this manner?' (Tatyana is referring to images from the morning of 26 October 2002 immediately after the assault at the entrance to the theatre complex, which show an unidentified woman in military camouflage aiming a pistol at, and possibly shooting, an unidentified man whose hands are tied behind his back.)

'Nobody is "finishing off" anybody in that clip. Journalists would like to represent it as a killing. We have had it analysed. What is there is a corpse being dragged from one location to another and the woman is merely indicating where it is to be put. We know whose corpse it was.'

'Whose?'

'If I tell you, you will only say it is all lies.'

'Is it the body of Vlakh?' (Gennadii Vlakh was a Muscovite who entered the occupied building on his own initiative to search for his son.)

'Yes, it is. The examination will demonstrate that.'

Kalchuk knows perfectly well that Vlakh's son and his ex-wife have studied this tape carefully, and categorically denied that the person being dragged about is Gennadii. Nothing fits: not his build, his hair or his clothing.

Tatyana continues, 'Do you admit that there was looting in the hall after the assault?'

'Yes. The rescuers, the security forces, were in there and if they saw a purse, they popped it into their pocket. They are only human. It's the kind of country we live in. Their salaries are wretchedly low.'

'Are you investigating instances of looting?'

'Oh, come on . . . Of course not.'

'We desperately want to know the truth about how our relatives died. Are you intending to press charges against any officials for failing to provide [medical support in the aftermath]?'

'If you were all given a million dollars like they do in the West, you would shut up straight away. You would do a bit of weeping and then just shut up.'

Vladimir Kurbatov, father of a 13-year-old member of the *Nord-Ost* cast who died:

'I would not shut up. I would still seek the truth about when and where my daughter died. As it is, nobody knows.'

Lyudmila Trunova, a lawyer present at the meeting:

'How did the body of Grigorii Burban, one of the hostages who died, come to be discovered on Lenin Prospekt?'

'Says who? I don't know.'

Tatyana Karpova:

'Why was the body of Gennadii Vlakh cremated, as if he were one of the terrorists?'

'That is none of your business. Why don't you ask questions about your old man?'

'A question about Terkibaev . . .'

'Terkibaev was never there. Politkovskaya did not help us. (I wrote in my newspaper about FSB officer Terkibaev's role in the siege.) She refused to give us information about him. She just said she didn't know anything.'

'Has anybody been charged in connection with this affair?'

'No.'

Kalchuk is a typical representative of the law-enforcement and security officials of the new era of Putin. They are actively encouraged to treat people high-handedly.

In Magadan, meanwhile, large numbers of conscripts have fallen ill on the way to their units. Putin reacts instantly, calling this 'a criminal way to treat people'. The raw recruits were lined up on an airfield for several hours wearing only light clothing, and more than 80 ended up in hospital with pneumonia. One of the soldiers, Volodya Beryozin from Moscow Province, died on 3 December from hypothermia. Beryozin had been a strong, healthy boy who was selected to serve in the President's Regiment. Volodya's father, like everyone else, is demanding an explanation from the President of how such a thing could occur.

It is already 15 January, and Volodya Beryozin was buried nine days ago, but Russia became indignant only after Putin expressed his anger. Soldiers are dust beneath their officers' boots. That's the way it is here, and Putin, himself the incarnation of a stereotype, accepts it. His anger is a pre-election stunt. No more than that.

16 January

The body of Aslan Davletukaev, abducted from his home on 10 January, has been found showing signs of torture. He had been shot in the back of head. The body was found on the outskirts of Gudermes. Aslan was a well-known Chechen human-rights campaigner. [Despite the intervention of international organisations, the investigation of the murder proved fruitless.]

Glory be to our Tsar! An investigation is under way into the case of the frostbitten soldiers. Their inhuman treatment began at the Chkalov military aerodrome in Moscow Province. The weather was far from warm, and new recruits were crammed for 24 hours into an unheated arms store, sleeping on crates or on the cold floor. They were given nothing at all to eat, either then or on the subsequent journey. They were transported in a cargo plane at a temperature of -30 degrees Celsius, like logs, and were all frozen to the marrow. When they landed in Novosibirsk they were forced out on to the airfield and made to stand in a biting wind at -19 degrees for two hours. At Komsomolsk-on-Amur airfield they spent four hours in light clothing at -25 degrees. In Petropavlovsk-Kamchatsky it became obvious that some of them were seriously ill, but the officers escorting them ignored the situation. In the barracks where they were accommodated after the flight, the temperature was +12 degrees. By now almost 100 of them were ill. There were no facilities to treat them. The Army doctors had only antibiotics that had expired in the mid-1990s, and there were no single-use hypodermic needles. The medics gave them cough medicine.

The Chief Military Procurator's Office has announced that it will shortly be questioning Colonel-General Vasilii Smirnov, head of the Central Logistics Board of the Ministry of Defence, in connection with the case of the frozen soldiers. This is an unprecedented liberty, imaginable only if they have been given the green light from higher up. Twenty-two generals have already been questioned, the first time generals have ever been quizzed over anything that happened to conscripts. It is wonderful to see the President acting as Russia's foremost champion of human rights, but will he be wearing the same mask after the presidential election?

Our democracy continues its decline. Nothing in Russia depends on the people; everything depends on Putin. There is an ever greater centralisation of power and loss of initiative by officialdom. Putin is resuscitating our ancient stereotype: 'Let us wait until our lord the *barin* comes back. He will tell us how everything should be.' It has to be admitted that this is how the Russian people likes it, which means that soon Putin will throw away the mask of a defender of human rights. He won't need it any more.

Where have all the democrats gone? Alexander Zhukov, a former democrat and now a member of United Russia, considers that 'It is a good thing when there is a ruling party in Parliament. The electorate will see clearly who is responsible for everything. In the previous three Dumas that was not the case. It is plain that United Russia is going to encourage a market economy based on reduction of the tax burden, development of free business and reducing the role of the state, reforming of natural monopolies, bringing Russia into the world market, and reform of social welfare, which is not functioning satisfactorily at present. There is no reason to worry about this Duma. Democratic procedures are being observed better than in its predecessors.'

(Zhukov was shortly afterwards appointed a Deputy Prime Minister.)

17 January

Political splits and defections continue. The Russian Revival Party, another of the dwarf parties, this one headed by Gennadii Seleznyov, has decided to support Putin in the election and to dump Sergey Mironov, Chairman of the Soviet of the Federation and leader of the Party of Life, with whom it had an alliance during the parliamentary elections. The decision was taken after analysing the party's showing in the elections. Between them the parties of these two leaders won just 1.88 per cent of the vote.

Television shows Putin reiterating, 'We do not need an argumentative Duma.' The members of United Russia assure the country that their takeover of Parliament is 'more honest' with the electors. It is becoming increasingly obvious that strict military discipline rules within the United Russia party. None of the Deputies is allowed to give interviews to journalists or to vote according to conscience. The party now has 310 Deputies. Deputies are still joining up and swearing allegiance.

The presidential election campaign is really very odd. There isn't actually any need for cunning spin doctors. Everyone already prefers Putin, even those standing against him. The idiot bodyguard Malyshkin has admitted as much. There was an item on television about Malyshkin's mother, who lives in Rostov Province in a house without running water. She says she will vote for Putin because she is very pleased with him. Mironov has even asked in amazement, 'Why are we all standing as candidates? We should all stand shoulder to shoulder with Him.'

Sergey Glaziev, another pseudo-candidate, declares to the people, 'I like Putin. I have a lot in common with him. What I don't like is the way his decisions are implemented.'

The failure of the democrats and liberals to put forward a joint candidate themselves looks increasingly like political suicide.

In Grozny, in broad daylight, Russian troops abducted Khalid Edelkhaev, 47, a taxi-driver, on the road leading to the village of Petropavlovskaya. His whereabouts are unknown.

18 January

The Central Electoral Commission is beginning to receive signatures from supporters of the non-party candidates, but is there anyone left who is actually against Putin? Only Irina Khakamada.

Within the Communist Party there is a conflict between the leaders,

Zyuganov and Semigin, and they have no time left over for a committed political battle against Putin. Rogozin of Rodina says he wants to support Putin. Glaziev is still shilly-shallying.

The deadline for submitting signatures is 28 January, and there are 55 days remaining to the election.

19 January

Committee 2008, an organisation campaigning for fair elections, but hoping to get them only in 2008, has issued a manifesto in which it says it is currently 'repugnant' to live in Russia. As if we didn't know! The chairman of the committee is [the former world chess champion] Garry Kasparov*. He is intelligent and self-reliant, which is a good start.

20 January

During the night, masked gunmen in white Zhigulis without number plates – the trademark of Kadyrov's* forces – kidnapped Milana Kodzoeva from her home in the Chechen village of Kotar-Yurt. Milana is the widow of a fighter. She has two small children. Her whereabouts are unknown.

21 January

Irina Khakamada has made a public appeal for funds to the Russian business elite. Leonid Nevzlin, a friend of Khodorkovsky's, has offered to support her. Chubais refused.

Those who survived the Siege of Leningrad are beginning to receive medals and payments to mark the sixtieth anniversary of the raising of the siege. They are getting between 450 and 900 roubles [£8–17]. The survivors are poor and in St Petersburg people queued for many days to receive it. In all, about 300,000 people were eligible to receive this pittance, but only 15,000 succeeded. The survivors dislike the new medals intensely, which read 'Resident of Besieged Leningrad' and 'For the Defence of Leningrad'. The Peter and Paul Fortress is depicted from an unimaginable perspective, and tank traps that were never there are shown on the embankment. It's all been done Soviet-style. Like it or lump it.

24 January

In Grozny, unidentified persons wearing camouflage fatigues and driving a military UAZ jeep abducted Turpal Baltebiev, 23, from the Hippodrome bus stop. His whereabouts are unknown.

27 January

Putin is in St Petersburg. His election campaign continues against the backdrop of the sixtieth anniversary of the raising of the Siege of Leningrad. He flew to Kirovsk, to the legendary Neva Bridgehead where his father, Vladimir Spiridonovich Putin, fought and was severely wounded. It was from the Neva Bridgehead that, on 18 January 1943, the Siege of Leningrad was lifted. During the siege Putin's elder brother starved to death. His mother barely survived. Between 200,000 and 400,000 soldiers died trying to break through here. The exact number and the names of many are unknown to this day, because most were simply Leningrad volunteers who died before they could be enlisted as soldiers. The bridgehead is one and a half kilometres long and several hundred metres wide. Even today no trees grow there. Putin laid a bouquet of dark-red roses at the monument.

In honour of Putin's arrival, a meeting of the Presidium of the State Council was held. This is a purely consultative but highly ceremonious institution, created by Putin to keep the governors of Russia's provinces happy.

Today's session was devoted to the problems of pensioners, of whom there are more than 30 million in Russia. Some 20 were herded along to a meeting with Putin, wearing old suits and shabby cardigans. They were from Leningrad Province and spoke of their abysmally low quality of life. Putin listened to them all, interrupted nobody and said, 'It is essential for us to consider how we can provide a dignified life in old age. This is a crucial task for the state.' The words 'a crucial task' are heard constantly, but, depending on the audience, it is the welfare of the peasants or improving the health service that is crucial. It is the familiar mimicry of a KGB agent, but the people seem not to notice. This time Putin promised to double the amount by which pensions will be indexed in 2004. The average monthly addition will amount to 240 roubles [£4.50], for which they will be able to buy half a kilo of good-quality meat.

Khakamada has published her manifesto:

During the past four years the state authorities have suppressed all
political opposition and destroyed the independent mass media;
the party of government in the Duma has no programme and no
ideas;
if in four years' time, by 2008, those who support democracy have
not made themselves heard, Russia will slide back irreversibly into
authoritarianism;
I challenge Putin to a debate, because I want to hear from him
exactly what kind of Russia he wants to build;
I have collected four million signatures in support of my candidacy;
I am prepared to be the cork shot from the bottle confining the
genie of the will of Russia's citizens.

Good, effective stuff, but Putin didn't raise an eyebrow at any of the
statements, as if they hadn't been made. Nobody insisted that he should
respond. Our society is sick. Most people are suffering from the disease
of paternalism, which is why Putin gets away with everything, why he
is possible in Russia.

28 January

At 6.00 p.m. the Central Electoral Commission ceased to accept signatures
of supporters of presidential candidates. Putin, Mironov and Rybkin had
already submitted theirs. Khakamada handed in hers at 3.00 p.m. The
entrepreneur Anzori Aksentiev sent in a letter withdrawing his application.
    There are alternatives: Khakamada for Westernisers, Kharitonov for
Communists, Malyshkin for political extremists and hoodlums, Glaziev
for believers in our new superpower status.

29 January

Vladimir Potanin continues trying to position himself as a 'good' oligarch
– that is to say, one not comparable with Khodorkovsky. He is proposing
to reform the oligarchs' trade union: 'Business is a constructive force. We
need a new, meaningful dialogue with the state authorities. Business should
consider the needs of society, should explain who we are.' He also talks

about moderating the ambitions of the oligarchs and says that big business has no need of representation in the country's leading councils.

Potanin was given prime time on television to say all this. Everyone takes that to mean that he had the blessing of Putin himself.

2 February

On television Putin cuts the price of bread by using the old Soviet method of stopping grain exports. Why were we exporting grain anyway, if the country is going hungry? There is nobody to put this question as the opposition has no access to the media. Putin hears reports that in many regions the cost of bread has doubled over the past month, and demands that these uncontrolled price rises should be stopped immediately.

On television he promises to look into the payment of pensions to people disabled in childhood during the Second World War. Zurabov [the minister of Health and Social Welfare] reports to him that he is quite sure the necessary legislation will go through all its readings in the Duma very rapidly. It is as if the Duma had no timetable for other legislation. All that matters are the President's requirements for his election campaign, which seems to consist of constantly doling out money.

At the same time Zurabov reports to Putin on pensions for priests. Putin takes a great interest in the welfare of priests! Zurabov reminds him that before the fall of the USSR priests had no entitlement to a pension at all.

In place of genuine pre-election debates we get yet another episode of the ongoing political soap opera that is the Rodina party: a furious row between Rogozin and Glaziev instead of debates about the future of the country. Rogozin heaps abuse on Glaziev, Glaziev blusters a lot of nonsense in reply, and nobody talks about what it is that Putin might have to offer the country in a second term. Almost none of the candidates who are supposed to be opposing Putin have any ideas at all.

In Moscow, Yelena Tregubova was almost blown up by a small bomb planted outside her apartment block. Was it just hooliganism? She recently published an anti-Putin book, *Tales of a Kremlin Digger*. She was a member of the Kremlin press pool, but then saw the light and wrote a book about the inner life of the Kremlin, which shows him in a highly unflattering light.

[Tregubova was shortly to emigrate from Russia.]

3 February

At about 5.00 p.m. there was a terrorist outrage in Vladikavkaz. A Zhiguli car was blown up just as military cadets were driving past on a truck. One woman died and 10 people were injured. One cadet is in a critical condition.

4 February

In Grozny, unidentified armed men wearing masks and camouflage fatigues abducted Satsita Kamaeva, 23, from her home in Aviatsionnaya Street. Her whereabouts are unknown.

Meanwhile, in Moscow, Putin's election-campaign headquarters are said to have been set up, but they are just as virtual as Putin himself. The address is No. 5, Red Square, only nobody is allowed in. Putin has appointed as leader of his election team Dmitry Kozak, the First Deputy Head of the Presidential Administration in charge of legal and administrative reform. Kozak has the reputation of being the cleverest person in the Administration, after Putin, of course. Like Putin, he is a graduate of the Law Faculty of Leningrad University. He worked there in the Procurator's Office and in the St Petersburg City Hall, and in 1989–99 was Deputy Governor of St Petersburg. In other words, he is one of Putin's Petersburg Brigade.

The League of Committees of Soldiers' Mothers is to set up a political party. In Russia parties are born for one of three reasons: because there is a lot of money somewhere; because somebody has nothing better to do; or because somebody has been driven to desperation. The Party of Soldiers' Mothers is entirely a product of the 7 December parliamentary elections, born in the wilderness of a Russian politics purged of all democratic forces.

'We are mature enough now to found a party,' says Valentina Melnikova, chairperson of the organising committee. 'We have been talking about it within the movement for a long time, but previously we could call on the support of the Union of Right Forces and Yabloko in our campaign for reform of the Army, to help soldiers, for the abolition of conscription and legislative initiatives. Yavlinsky and Nemtsov were still players, but now everything is in ruins. We're standing amidst a political Hiroshima, but we still have problems that need to be resolved. There is nobody left for us to turn to, nobody on whom we can pin our hopes. All the present political parties are a continuation of the Kremlin by other means. You half suspect that the Duma Deputies scuttle off every morning to Red Square to receive their instructions from the Lenin Mausoleum, and then go away to do as they have been bid. That is why we have decided to form a party ourselves.'

The Party of Soldiers' Mothers, then, is a party of desperation, born of the complete political hopelessness that is the sum total of the last four dismal years. In an era when everything is under the Kremlin's control, this is a straightforward grass-roots initiative, which has appeared without the benefit of 'administrative resources', in which Vladislav Surkov, Russia's ubiquitous political fixer, has been allowed absolutely no part.

The decision to create the party was taken very simply: after the Duma elections, women from Miass, Nizhny Novgorod, Sochi and Nizhny Tagil rang the Moscow office of the League of Committees of Soldiers' Mothers. It was the committees in these cities that were the driving force behind the creation of a new political party.

The remnants of Yabloko and the Union of Right Forces are, of course, a sorry spectacle, but a concomitant is the appearance of public initiatives from deeply committed people with an immense dissident potential. Putin wants everything close-cropped, but from his coppicing of the opposition something positive is sprouting. A time for new initiatives is coming. The devastation of the political arena emboldens those who refuse to live under the old Soviet clichés and intend to fight. In order to survive in enemy territory, when no one else will fight for you, you have to summon up your resolve and start fighting for yourself. In the language of the soldiers' mothers, that means fighting for the lives of soldiers against the Army recruitment machine that devours them.

The last straw was an incident involving Ida Kuklina and Putin. Ida has been working for 10 years in the Moscow committee and is now even a member of the Presidential Commission on Human Rights. She had put a lot of energy into getting the pension raised for conscripts who have been reduced to the state of Category 1 invalids (the current pension is 1,400 roubles, or around £26 a month). Category 1 invalids are amputees and those bedridden with spinal injuries or confined to wheelchairs.

Ida Kuklina handed a petition to Putin personally at one of the meetings of his Commission. He wrote a generally encouraging, if not very specific, recommendation on it – 'The question is posed correctly. Putin'– and forwarded it to the Government and the pensions department.

The Deputy Prime Minister for Social Welfare, Galina Karelova, responded tartly that there would be a revolt of the disabled, if the attempt was made to raise the level of pensions for conscripts who had just been crippled to the level of ex-servicemen disabled during the

Second World War, the Afghan and other local wars. That, Karelova opined, would be unethical.

Ida again approached Putin, again received a positive response and was again turned down by the officials. This happened three times in succession. It was at this point the mothers decided that the only solution was to become legislators themselves. The intention is to have Deputies from the Party of Soldiers' Mothers in the Duma after the parliamentary elections in 2007.

'Who will be the leader of your new party? Are you going to invite some clued-up politician?'

'One of our own people,' Valentina Melnikova replies emphatically.

Speaking to the soldiers' mothers about the future, we heard about a fresh atrocity within the Army. Private Alexander Sobakaev was brutally tortured in the Dzerzhinsky Special Operations Division of the Interior Ministry's troops. His family last heard his cheerful voice on the telephone late in the evening of 3 January. Alexander, not quite 20 years old, was in his second year in the Army, already a lance-corporal and dog handler in the sapper battalion. He rang to say that everything was fine. They recalled the day they had seen him off to the Army, and laughed at the thought that they would soon be celebrating his return. That very night, in the early hours of 4 January, if we are to believe the documents that accompanied the zinc coffin, Alexander hanged himself using his own belt, and 'there were no suspicious circumstances'. On 11 January his body was brought home to the tiny forest village of Velvo-Baza, 290 kilometres from Perm. The representatives of his division, who brought the coffin, explained to his parents that 'it was suicide'. There was no coroner's certificate. The parents did not believe this and demanded that the coffin should be opened. The first to back off in horror were his service colleagues. Alexander's body was not only covered in bruises and razor cuts, but the skin and muscles on his wrists were cut to the bone, baring the tendons. A doctor from the local hospital was asked to come and, in the presence of the local militiaman, a cameraman, a CID photographer and officers from the district military commissariat, recorded that this mutilation had occurred while Alexander was still alive.

The parents refused to bury their son, demanding an inquiry. His mother stayed home, but his father went straight to Moscow to the Dzerzhinsky Special Operations Division and to the capital's newspapers. That is how the outrage came to light.

Putin did not react on this occasion. Indeed, if he were to react to every atrocity in the Army he would be doing so almost every day, and the electorate would start to wonder why these occurrences were so common, and why the Commander-in-Chief – i.e., Putin – hadn't done anything about it before.

Accordingly, no attempt was made to track down Alexander's killers. The Military Procurator's Office did everything in its power to ensure that the truth remained hidden. Alexander fared less well than Volodya Beryozin, for whose death from cold and starvation officers will appear in court, thanks only to the fact that Putin's election campaign had just begun and that he got his hands on the story first.

Alexander's death is not being investigated with any urgency. Although his parents refused to bury the body of their son until an independent inquiry made public the truth about his death, this was refused. The family ran out of money to pay for keeping his body in the Kudymkar district mortuary, and Alexander was buried as a suicide. How many more of our sons will have to be sacrificed before a great joint campaign by the public sees this Army reformed root and branch? It is a question that refuses to go away.

Do we see a change in the mood of society, a civil society beginning timorously to emerge from the kitchens of Russia in the same way that, after a purge in Chechnya, people very quietly, very cautiously creep out of their cellars and boltholes?

As of yet, no, although many are beginning to realise what people in Chechnya have realised after being subjected to the 'anti-terrorist operation': you have to rely on yourself if you want to survive; you have to defend yourself if nobody else will. The rampaging of the bureaucracy is more out of control than ever after the triumph of their United Russia party, and there are still far too few public initiatives.

As election day approaches, the television news bulletins increasingly resemble heartening dispatches on Putin's achievements. The greater part of the news is taken up with bureaucrats reporting to Putin in front of the cameras, but without any semblance of independent commentary. Today, Sergey Ignatiev, the Chairman of Tsentrobank, was briefing him on the improbable growth of the gold and currency reserves.

To the accompaniment of a lot of political chatter about the welfare of the people, the Fourth Duma is passing lobbyist-driven legislation even more blatantly than the Third Duma. There is, for example, a proposal for a significant reduction of Value Added Tax for estate agents. This is simply laughable, because estate agents in Russia are millionaires. Nobody raises the matter in the mass media, although they whisper about it a good deal. Journalists practise rigorous self-censorship. They don't even propose such stories to their newspapers or the television stations, certain in advance that their bosses will axe them.

The Eighth World Gathering of the People of Russia has ended. It was touted as the big event of February and almost resembled a congress of the United Russia party, with all the top government bureaucrats turning up. Funnily enough, though, nobody can remember when the Seventh World Gathering took place.

At the Gathering the President's oligarch banker, Sergey Pugachev, sat at the right hand of the Patriarch of the Russian Orthodox Church. Pugachev is one of the Putin oligarchs who replaced the Yeltsin oligarchs, and the Government even goes so far as to refer to him as 'a Russian Orthodox banker'. At Pugachev's instance, the Gathering adopted an odd kind of Ten Commandments for businessmen, called A Code of Moral Rules and Principles for the Conduct of Business.

The Code pontificates on matters such as wealth and poverty, nationalisation, tax evasion, advertising and profit. One of the Commandments informs us that 'Wealth is not an end in itself. It should serve to create a goodly life for the individual and the people.' Another warns that 'In misappropriating property, failing to respect communal property, not giving fair recompense to a worker for his labour, or deceiving a business partner, a person transgresses the moral law, harming society and himself.' Moreover, on the subject of tax evasion, not paying one's dues is 'stealing from orphans, the aged, the disabled and others least able to protect themselves'.

'Transferring part of one's income through taxation to provide for the needs of society should be transformed from a burdensome obligation grudgingly fulfilled, and sometimes not fulfilled at all, into a matter of honour, deserving of the gratitude of society.' On the poor: 'The poor man is also under an obligation to behave worthily, to strive to labour efficiently, to raise his vocational skills in order to rise out of his impoverished condition.' Again: 'The worship of wealth is incompatible with moral rectitude.'

The Code contains allusions to Khodorkovsky, and to Berezovsky and Gusinsky. 'There should be separation of political from economic power. The involvement of business in politics and its influence on public opinion must always be transparent and open. All material assistance given by business to political parties, public organisations and the mass media must be publicly known and monitored. Clandestine support of this nature deserves to be publicly condemned as immoral.'

In that case, of course, the entire election campaign of United Russia was immoral, as is the fact that Putin's oligarch is a Senator.

All this is intended to reinforce the idea that it is right and honourable to be a 'good' businessman in Putin's pocket, but that if you try to be independent you are bad and must be destroyed. The Code is manifestly anti-Yukos. Although it is supposedly voluntary, it is, like everything in Russia nowadays, 'compulsorily voluntary'. You don't have to join United Russia, but, if you don't, your career as an official is going nowhere. Metropolitan Kirill, tipped as the successor of the rapidly declining and constantly ailing Patriarch, conducted the session when the Code was discussed. He said quite openly, 'We will go to everybody and invite them to sign. If any refuse to sign, we shall make sure that their names become known to all.' Some priest!

In any case, who is preaching this morality to us? That same Russian Orthodox Church that gives its blessing to the war in Chechnya, to arms trading and to the fratricide in the North Caucasus. The adoption of this code of moral principles for businessmen is an extraordinary bid by the Russian Orthodox Church, which is disestablished, to involve itself in internal and foreign policy. The RUIE commented that 'The Church itself needs to be reformed. Its own stagnation is the reason why it comes out with such bizarre fancies.'

Viktor Vekselberg, one of the oligarchs rumoured to be next in line for imprisonment by Putin, has suddenly announced he is buying the collection of Fabergé Easter eggs that belonged to the family of our last emperor, Nicholas II. Nobody doubts that Vekselberg is simply trying to ransom his way out of trouble by demonstrating that he is 'on the side of Russia', which the Administration accepts as a coded way of saying 'on the side of Vladimir Vladimirovich'.

Vekselberg insists that 'The return of these treasures to Russia is something personal to me. I want my family, my son and daughter, to have a different understanding of their place in life. I want big business to participate intelligently in public works. I am not seeking advantage, proving anything to anybody, or whitewashing anything.'

The oligarch doth protest too much, methinks.

5 February

In Cheremkhovo, in Irkutsk Province, 17 workers of the No. I Sector Communal Residential Services Office have gone on hunger strike. They are demanding payment of their wages, which are six months in arrears. They are owed a total of about two million roubles [£38,000]. They are following the example of their colleagues in another sector who only had to go on hunger strike at their workplace for three days to get their wages paid.

In Moscow there has been a meeting of Open Forum, an event attended by political analysts; not necessarily the main ones, but reputable people who have been involved as political advisers in all the national and regional elections. They agreed on one important matter: in the four years of Putin's rule, the modernising of Russia has been sidelined by the goal of strengthening the power of one individual. Those associated with him are neither a class nor a party, just people who are 'in step with Putin'. The analysts also agreed that the model of a managed democracy does not work.

6 February

8.32 a.m.: three months after the terrorist attack outside the Nationale Hotel, there has been an explosion in the Moscow Metro, at the interchange between the Paveletskaya and Avtozavodskaya-Zamoskvoretskaya lines. The train was heading into the city centre during the rush hour when a bomb exploded beside the first door of the second carriage. The device had been placed 15 centimetres above floor level in a bag. After the explosion the train's momentum carried it a further 300 metres and a fierce fire broke out. Thirty people died at the scene, and another nine died later from their burns. There are 140 injured. There are dozens of tiny, unidentifiable fragments of bodies. More than 700 people emerged from the tunnel, having evacuated themselves in the absence of any assistance. In the streets there is chaos and fear, the wailing sirens of the emergency services, millions of people terrorised.

At 10.44 the Volcano-5 Contingency Plan for capturing the culprits was implemented, more than two hours after the explosion. Who do they think they are going to catch? If there were any accomplices they will have fled long ago. At 12.12 the police started searching for a man aged 30–35, 'of Caucasian appearance'. Very helpful. At 13.30 Valerii Shantsev, the Acting Mayor of Moscow while Luzhkov is in the USA, announced that the victims' families will receive 100,000 roubles [£1,900] in compensation, and the injured will be paid half that amount.

Terrorists with explosives can move around Moscow without hindrance, despite the extraordinary powers granted to the FSB and militia, and still the people support Putin. No one suggests a change of policy in Chechnya, despite the 10 terrorist acts involving suicide bombers in the past year. Red Square is now almost permanently closed to visitors. The Palestinisation of Chechnya is obvious. An hour after the explosion a statement was issued by the 'Movement Against Illegal Immigration', an organisation created by the security forces. Its leader, Alexander Belov, declared:

> Our first demand is to forbid Chechens to travel outside Chechnya. To this day in the USA and Canada there are special reservations set aside for awkward peoples. If an ethnic group does not want to live like civilised human beings, let them live behind a barrier. Call it what you like: a reservation, a pale. We need somehow to defend ourselves. We can no longer pretend that the Chechens, of whom the majority are linked in one way or another with the Chechen resistance, are citizens in the same sense as Chuvashes, Buryats, Karelians or Russians. For them this is a continuation of the war. They are taking revenge. The Chechen diaspora in Russia, including Chechen businessmen, are a hotbed of terrorism. I am only saying what 80 per cent of Russians think.

He is right. That is exactly what the majority thinks. Society is moving towards fascism.

Only a few members of the state authorities continue even trying to think. General Boris Gromov, the Governor of Moscow Province and a Hero of the Soviet Union for service in Afghanistan, spoke out: 'When I heard about the explosion in the Metro, my first thought was that all this began back in Afghanistan. The decision of the leaders of the USSR to send troops to Afghanistan was irresponsible in the extreme, as was the later decision of the leaders of Russia to send troops to Chechnya. These are the fruits of those decisions. They said they were going after gangsters, but entirely innocent people are now suffering as a result. This will continue for a long time into the future.'

On the state television channels they keep drumming into people that terrorism is a disease of liberal democracy: if you want democracy, you must expect terrorist acts. They somehow overlook the fact that Putin has been in power for the past four years.

Putin, despite the explosion, is having talks with the President of Azerbaijan, Ilkham Aliev, who is in Moscow. Putin merely mentioned in passing, 'I wouldn't be surprised if this were to be exploited in the run-up to the election as a means of putting pressure on the current Head of State. There is a marked coincidence between the explosion and the fact that plans for peace in Chechnya are again being put to us from abroad. Our refusal to conduct negotiations of any kind with terrorists . . .'

What negotiations? Suicide bombers blow themselves up. He was anxious, his eyes flickering around, betraying a hysterical man who does not know what to do next.

In the next few days there is to be scrutiny of the lists of signatures of the non-party presidential candidates: Ivan Rybkin, former head of the Security Council of the Russian Federation; Sergey Glaziev, leader of the Rodina party; and Irina Khakamada. The authorities' actions betray the fact that the person they are most worried about out of these three is Rybkin, even though his opinion-poll rating is virtually zero. The head of the Central Electoral Commission, Alexander Veshnyakov, has stated in advance of the scrutiny that a preliminary check of Rybkin's lists has shown that 26 per cent of the signatures are invalid. Precisely 26 per cent – not 27 and not 24.9, because the law says that if the number of invalid signatures exceeds 25 per cent, they can refuse to register the candidate. People are laughing and saying that at least it's not 25.1 per cent.

Where, actually, is the election campaign? So far there is nothing to be seen. The would-be candidates were in no hurry to stand, and most of them are in no hurry to win. Nobody seems worried by this, neither the candidates nor their supporters. As for Candidate No. 1, he makes no attempt to fight, argue and win. Irina Khakamada is convinced that the Kremlin has succeeded in persuading everybody they can't beat a conspiracy. 'There is no open struggle. Nobody believes it will help.'

The Rodina party continues its internal feuding. They do not want to win the election either. Dmitry Rogozin, who is also the Deputy Speaker of the Duma, has even announced that he will support Putin in the election, not Glaziev, the co-chairman of his own party. They seem a very odd lot. Do they ever give a thought to their supporters? They give the impression that what the electors think is of no concern, and that everything will be decided without consulting them. Rogozin even calls for the presidential election to be cancelled and a state of emergency declared because of the terrorist acts.

7 February

Five new blood-donor centres have been opened in Moscow. There is an urgent need for all blood groups for the 128 bomb victims who remain in hospital.

But where are the explosives detectors in the Metro? Where are the patrols? We Russians are innately irresponsible, always seeing conspiracies against us. We never bother to push anything through to completion, just hope for the best. The militia check passports in the Metro, but no doubt terrorists make sure their documents are in order. The militia catch some hungry Tadjik who can't find work in his homeland and has come to dig our frozen soil because we don't want to do it ourselves. They shake him down for his last 100 roubles and let him go. Where are the security agencies who should answer for the fact that the attack was successful? Where are the security people on the ground? Thousands of half-starved conscripts of the Interior Troops have been brought in to guard Moscow. That's good. At least they will be paid and be able to eat. At least they are not in their barracks.

But 'measures' like these are ineffective, mere reaction. As soon as people start to forget this nightmare, everything will return to how it was. The writer and journalist Alexander Kabakov comments, 'We are still alive only because those who commission these acts are short of people to carry them out. But why those who commission terrorist acts are still alive is quite another question.'

Putin has not sacked Patrushev, the Director of the FSB. He is a personal friend. How many more acts of terrorism have to succeed before Putin realises his pal is no good at his job?

The Memorial Human Rights Centre has issued a statement:

We grieve for those who have died, and sympathise deeply with the injured. There can be no justification for those who planned and executed this crime. The President and law-enforcement agencies are confidently asserting that this was the work of Chechens, although no evidence of this has yet come to light. If their speculation should prove correct, the present tragedy will unfortunately have been only too predictable. The refusal of the country's leaders to take any steps towards a real, rather than a decorative, political settlement of the conflict has only strengthened the position of extremists. These are people who set out no sane political goals on the basis of which compromise might be possible. Over recent years human-rights associations and many public and political representatives have warned repeatedly that the brutal acts of the federal forces in Chechnya spell danger for every person living in Russia. For a long time now hundreds of thousands of people have been living out every day in a lethal environment. They are being forced out, cast beyond the limits of civilised life. Thousands of humiliated people whose relatives and friends have been killed, abducted, physically and psychologically crippled, represent, for the cynical and unconscionable leaders of terrorist groups, a source from which to recruit their followers, suicide bombers, and those who commit terrorist outrages. Peace and tranquillity for the citizens of Russia can be achieved only by a resolute change of policy.

Ivan Rybkin has disappeared. A bit of excitement in the election at last: one of the candidates is nowhere to be found. His wife is going crazy. On 2 February, Rybkin criticised Putin in very harsh terms and his wife believes that did for him. On 5 February, Kseniya Ponomaryova, the co-ordinator of the support group that put Rybkin forward, warned that 'massive sabotage' was being prepared against him. His headquarters have been receiving reports from the regions for a week about unauthorised interrogation of his supporters. The militia visited the homes of people collecting signatures, questioned them and took statements. They wanted to know why they were supporting Rybkin. In Kabardino-Balkaria students gathering signatures were threatened that the militia would inform the university administration and consider whether it was appropriate for them to be allowed to continue their studies.

9 February

No details have yet been established of the type of bomb used in the Metro or of the composition of its explosive. Putin keeps repeating, as he did after *Nord-Ost*, that nobody inside Russia was responsible. Everything was planned abroad.

A day of mourning has been declared for those who died, but the television stations barely observe it. Loud pop music and markedly cheerful TV advertisements make you feel ashamed. One hundred and five people are still in hospital. Two of those who died are being buried today. One is Alexander Ishunkin, a 25-year-old lieutenant in the Armed Forces born in Kaluga Province, where he will be buried. He graduated from Bauman University and went to serve as an officer. On 6 February he was going back home to Naro-Fominsk, where his unit is stationed. He had come to Moscow to obtain spare parts for a vehicle and had taken the opportunity to visit some university friends. That morning, he got on the Metro to travel to Kiev Station, with a change at Paveletskaya. When Alexander didn't return, his mother assumed he had missed the train – just before going to the Metro he had rung to say he would be back at 11.00. His Uncle Mikhail identified his body in the mortuary. He couldn't believe it. Seven years ago Alexander's father was killed, and since then Alexander had been the very dependable head of the family. His mother wept: 'It's as if my soul has been taken from me. He promised me grandchildren.' Even in issuing his death certificate the state can't refrain from dishonesty: the box for 'Cause of death' has been crossed through. Not a word about terrorism.

The other person being buried today is Vanya Aladiin, a Muscovite just 17 years old. The procession of Vanya's family and classmates stretches through half the cemetery. He was a lively, cheerful, friendly boy people called 'Hurricane Vanya'. Three days earlier he had got a job as a courier and on 6 February was travelling to work. On 16 February he would have celebrated his eighteenth birthday.

Rybkin is still missing. Gennadii Gudkov, the Deputy Chairman of the Duma Security Committee and a retired FSB colonel, is letting it be known that Rybkin is safe. But where is he? Does the state have no special obligations towards presidential candidates?

Rybkin's wife, Albina Nikolaevna, insists that he has been kidnapped. The Presnya District Procurator's Office has unexpectedly opened a criminal investigation under Article 105, premeditated murder, but the Central Directorate of Internal Affairs began insisting there is good reason to suppose that Rybkin is alive. An hour later the Presnya office changed its mind about the murder inquiry on orders from the Procurator-General's Office. What is going on?

The political commentators agree that a semblance of competition has been created, saving the election from being a complete farce, as it would have been if Putin's only opponents had been a coffin-maker and a bodyguard. Zero risk, of course, but highly embarrassing. No doubt that is why, in the end, they registered everybody, and decided that a mere 21 per cent of Rybkin's signatures were invalid, even though the day before they had said it was 26 per cent. The only snag is that Rybkin has vanished.

The idea of boycotting the elections, which the liberals and democrats were proposing, has fizzled out. They didn't try very hard.

10 February

In Moscow a further 13 people killed in the Metro explosion have been buried. Twenty-nine people remain in a critical condition. The death toll has risen to 40; one more person has died in the last 24 hours.

Rybkin has been found. A very strange episode. At midday he broke radio silence and announced that he was in Kiev. He said he had just been on holiday there with friends and that, after all, a human being has a right to a private life! Kseniya Ponomaryova promptly resigned as leader of his election team. His wife is shocked and refusing to talk to him. In late evening he flew into Moscow from Kiev, looking half-dead and not at all like someone who has been having a good time on holiday. Rybkin remarked it had been more heavy-going than negotiating with the Chechens. He was wearing women's sunglasses and was escorted by an enormous bodyguard.

'Who was detaining you?' he was asked, but gave no reply. He also refused to talk to the investigators from the Procurator's Office who had been searching for him. His wife, while Rybkin was flying home, gave an interview to the Interfax news agency saying she 'felt sorry for a country which had people like that as its leaders'. She was referring to her husband.

It was later announced that Rybkin might withdraw his candidacy.

Grigorii Yavlinsky's new book on *Peripheral Capitalism* (in Russia) has been launched in Moscow. It has been published in Russian, but on Western money. The book is about the 'authoritarian model of modernisation', which Yavlinsky considers non-viable. In spite of this book, Yavlinsky has effectively given up the struggle against Putin.

In St Petersburg, skinheads have stabbed to death nine-year-old Khursheda Sultanova in the courtyard of the flats where her family lived. Her father, 35-year-old Yusuf Sultanov, a Tadjik, has been working in St Petersburg for many years. That evening he was bringing the children back from the Yusupov Park ice slope when some aggressive youths started following them. In a dark connecting courtyard leading to their home the youths attacked them. Khursheda suffered 11 stab wounds and died immediately. Yusuf's 11-year-old nephew, Alabir, escaped in the darkness by hiding under a parked car. Alabir says the skinheads kept stabbing Khursheda until they were certain she was dead. They were shouting, 'Russia for the Russians!'

The Sultanovs are not illegal immigrants. They are officially registered as citizens of St Petersburg, but fascists are not interested in ID cards. When Russia's leaders indulge in soundbites about cracking down on immigrants and guest labourers, they incur responsibility for tragedies such as this. Fifteen people were detained shortly afterwards, but released. Many turned out to be the offspring of people employed by the law-enforcement agencies of St Petersburg. Today, 20,000 St Petersburg youths belong to unofficial fascist or racist organisations. The St Petersburg skinheads are among the most active in the country and are constantly attacking Azerbaijanis, Chinese and Africans. Nobody is ever punished, because the law-enforcement agencies are themselves infected with racism. You have only to switch off your audio recorder for the militia to start telling you they understand the skinheads, and as for those blacks . . . etc., etc. Fascism is in fashion.

11 February

The *Candidate Rybkin* soap opera continues. Rybkin makes statements each more startling than the last, for example: 'During those days I experienced the Second Chechen War.' Nobody believes him. The jokers are asking, 'Is there a human right to two days of private life in Kiev?'

Before this, Rybkin had the reputation of being a meticulous person, not at all given to wild living, highly responsible, not a heavy drinker and even slightly dull. 'Two days in Kiev' are very much out of character. So what really happened in Ukraine*? And did it happen there? Rybkin reports that after he disappeared he spent a certain amount of time in Moscow Province at Woodland Retreat, the guest-house of the Presidential Administration. He was taken from there and, when he could tell where he was again, found himself in Kiev. He says further that those controlling him compelled him to call Moscow from Kiev and talk lightheartedly about having a right to a private life.

*

So what was going on? What was the motive? There has been no inquiry into the Rybkin affair, so I offer these suggestions:

As we know, Putin refused to take part in public debates, on the grounds that the public supposedly already knew who to vote for. This was clearly an excuse. Putin is not good at dialogue, especially when the topic is one he is uncomfortable with. This has been demonstrated on trips abroad when the Administration is unable to gag reporters; journalists ask questions that the President finds awkward and he flies off the handle. Putin's preferred genre is the monologue, with leading questions prepared in advance.

We have allowed our political firmament to configure itself in such a way that there is now only one luminary. He is infallible and enjoys a sky-high rating, which appears invulnerable to everything except the man himself and his murky past.

But then, out of the rabble of candidates knocked together by the Kremlin, in the week preceding 5 February, Rybkin jumps up and starts hinting at compromising materials that discredit the luminary and his illustrious past, the obvious suggestion being that he is going to reveal some of this. Moreover, Rybkin had the audacity to describe Putin as an oligarch, a soundbite that was completely off-message, since our luminary's campaign is based on showing the people how bad the oligarchs who are 'not on our side' really are.

Rybkin was beginning to give our No. I presidential candidate grounds for serious unease. There was, moreover, the shadow of Boris Berezovsky behind Rybkin. Perhaps he really had something.

In the week before the abduction Rybkin was beginning to look like a loose missile with a warhead of materials that might seriously damage the Kremlin.

But what could they be about? That was why they needed to employ psychotropic drugs, which are now so sophisticated that a person cannot stop himself from blurting out everything he knows. The main source of information was Rybkin himself, not those around him, not his staff, but his brain. That is why they switched it off while they fished around in it. The likelihood is that Rybkin himself has no idea what he told them in those days, or to whom he told it.

There is also Woodland Retreat, a secluded place conveniently closed to outsiders, and Kiev, and the blatant compromising of him after his reappearance when even his indignant wife, talking to an official news agency, was made use of.

Let us look at the detail, the practicalities of the operation. The fact that Rybkin was taken to the Woodland Retreat guest-house is evidence that the Presidential Administration was privy to his abduction, as was the FSB. The President's Secretariat is an outfit that has long been described as a subdivision of the FSB. These two offices are the principal managers of Russia and do not merely work hand-in-glove, but function as a single entity. In addition, the fact that Rybkin had been seen at Woodland Retreat and would shortly return there was blurted out by Gudkov, who had evidently either elicited the information from old contacts or had it leaked to him. Immediately after Gudkov blabbed his mouth, the guest-house administration were able to deny that Rybkin was there.

And indeed he was no longer there. They were already arranging for his return via Kiev. An important detail is that the presidential candidate was secretly smuggled from Russia into Ukraine. (There is no customs or passport record of his crossing the border.) Technically this is quite possible; there are holes in the border, and it is no secret that Ukrainian guest labourers drive into Russia through these holes, which are large enough for vehicular traffic, when they want to avoid unnecessary encounters with officials whom they would have to bribe.

However, what is interesting in the Rybkin case is not the technique of how he was transferred over the border, but the fact itself that he was spirited from the guest-house of the Secretariat of the Administration of the current President of the Russian Federation to VIP apartments in Kiev controlled by the Administration of the current President of Ukraine. Leonid Kuchma* is close to the Administration because he is an accomplice in their political crimes, and in return for that we might well help him out in a similar way, if he were ever to need assistance. This is also the reason why the state wants to develop the Commonwealth of Independent States, but not to make its borders too watertight, so that former colleagues in the KGB of the USSR should be able the better to carry out joint special operations both here and there.

Let us look next at personalities. Who could give the order to shake information out of Rybkin, after first having switched off his conscious mind? *Cui bono?* Our luminary, surely.

We are not talking here about orders, needless to say. Our top cats have only to raise an eyebrow, hinting at their august displeasure, for their serfs to rush immediately to carry out their wishes. In our political Wonderland this eyebrow-twitching even has a name: it is known as 'the Pasha Grachev effect', referring to the time when the former Minister of Defence was apparently thoroughly fed up with the fact that Dmitry Kholodov, a journalist, was unearthing his dark secrets. The Minister of Defence is said to have hinted to his military friends how greatly Kholodov was pissing him off; the next thing you know the journalist was blown to pieces.

No doubt the Grachev effect was in play here, too. Rybkin, thank God, was not murdered, but only because to have the Angel of Death intervening so blatantly in the election would have worked against the interests of Candidate No. 1.

These are the kind of criminal goings-on, complete with psychotropic drugs, that we get when one candidate, who happens to be the current President, is simply incapable of performing in pre-election debates, is incapable of discussion, is irrationally afraid of opposition and, moreover, has come to believe in his own messianism. We are not so stupid as to believe that Rybkin was running away from his wife.

To all appearances, then, Rybkin had relatively little compromising material. The soap opera had no further episodes. Everybody forgot about him, including Putin. The end result, crucially for a society short of alternatives, was that Rybkin failed to confront the regime publicly.

Throughout January, people were being abducted in Chechnya, only for their bodies to be found later. The number of those abducted is comparable to the number killed on 6 February in the Moscow Metro. In Chechnya, everyone is at war with everybody else. There are armed men everywhere, the so-called 'Chechen security forces'. The commonest expression on people's faces is gloom. There are large numbers of half-insane, traumatised adults. Children, who resemble children only in their physical appearance, make their way to school. The armoured personnel carriers plough arrogantly past, and from them soldiers point their sub-machine guns at you as contemptuously as ever. Those they look down on look up, no less unforgivingly, at them. At night there are firefights, 'softening up' by artillery bombardment, battles and bombing in the foothills. In the morning there are fresh shell craters. It is a war in stale-mate. Do we want an end to it, or are we actually not all that bothered?

There has not been a single sizeable demonstration against the war in Chechnya during the entire presidential election campaign. The unbe-lievable long-suffering of our people is what allows the horror that is Putin to continue. One can find no other explanation.

Why has nobody come forward to 'claim' responsibility for the explo-sion in the Metro on 6 February? There are two possible explanations:

Either the intelligence forces were behind the explosion, no matter whose hands they used, which would explain the absence of demands or admissions of responsibility;

Or individual terrorists were involved in an act of personal vengeance for relatives who had been killed, for the trampling underfoot of their honour and their homeland. This is as shameful and depressing an explan-ation as that involving the complicity of the intelligence services.

12 February

Putin is raising the remuneration of those 'working within the zone of the anti-terrorist operation' by 250 per cent. Perhaps this will lead to less looting in Chechnya.

Rybkin is still flapping. He has flown to London to consult Berezovsky. He seems determined to complete his political implosion in full public view. Why is it so easy in Russia to put down democratic opposition? It is something in the opposition themselves. It is not that what they are confronting is too strong, although of course that is a factor. The main thing is that the opposition lacks an unflinching determination to oppose. Berezovsky is a mere gambler, not a fighter, and those who line up with him are no fighters, either. Nemtsov is just playing games, and Yavlinsky always looks as if something has offended him.

Alexander Litvinenko in London and Oleg Kalugin in Washington, former KGB/FSB officers who have been granted political asylum in the West, have suggested that a psychotropic substance called SP117 may have been used on Rybkin. This compound was used in the FSB's counter-intelligence sections and in units combating terrorism, but only in exceptional cases on 'important targets'. SP117 is a truth drug that operates on specific parts of the brain in order to prevent an individual from having full possession of his mind. He will tell everything he knows. According to Litvinenko, 'When somebody is under the influence of SP117, you can do anything you like with them and they will be incapable of remembering in detail or explaining coherently what happened, who they met or what they said. SP117 consists of two components, the dote and the antidote. First they administer the dote. Two drops are added to any beverage and some fifteen minutes after taking it the victim completely loses control of himself, possibly for several hours. The effect can be extended by administering additional small amounts of the dote. When the necessary information has been extracted, the victim is given the antidote, two pills dissolved in water, tea or coffee. After roughly ten minutes he returns to normality. There is a complete loss of memory. He feels shattered. If the drug has been administered over several days, the individual may experience panic and shock because that period of his life has been obliterated from his memory, and he will be unable to understand what has happened to him.'

These statements by Litvinenko and Kalugin will not save the political career of Rybkin. Putin has won this round against Berezovsky, now his sworn enemy, but his great pal in the late 1990s.

Today, precisely one day after the effective removal of Rybkin from the election race and his declaration that he will not take part in debates, is the official start of the presidential election campaign. Each of the candidates is entitled to four and a half hours of free airtime on television, on state channels, and this allowance must be in the form of live broadcasts. The only person with compromising materials against Putin, Rybkin, has voluntarily turned down the opportunity of appearing on live television. Which is exactly what the Kremlin needed.

At 1400 hours Putin had a meeting in Moscow State University with more than 300 of his aides and supporters. He was giving an account of what he has done during his first term. All the press and TV reporters were invited to be present, but, as the main state television stations emphasised when broadcasting the event, 'Putin was speaking as a private individual.' Putin has refused to participate in televised debates, and this speech was as insipid as the reports of general secretaries to Communist Party congresses in the past. His audience in Moscow University woke up as he spoke his last words and clapped like mad.

In the course of the broadcast one candidate for the presidency therefore spoke his way through nine million roubles (£170,000) worth of air time. The official tariff of the Rossiya Channel for 30 seconds of campaign advertising is 90,000–166,000 roubles. Did Putin pay? It was a flagrant abuse of state resources for electoral advantage and a clear violation of electoral law.

Six hundred journalists reported the meeting. They were assembled at the press centre of the Ministry of Foreign Affairs at 9.30 a.m. and registration continued until 12 noon. Everybody was searched before being put on buses. A member of the President's campaign team who looked like, and doubtless was, an FSB stooge, periodically harangued us: 'I repeat once more: nobody will ask any questions! Have you all heard that?' The journalists were transported to the meeting in 23 green buses with a militia escort, the way in Russia we transport children to a pioneer camp. After the meeting the journalists were herded into the buses again and taken back. No stepping out of line! Was this a private meeting between an individual and his friends to seek ways of ensuring a better future for their country?

Olga Zastrozhnaya, one of the secretaries of the Central Electoral Commission, stated that this televising of the President's speech was 'a direct violation of the rules of electioneering, because the broadcast was unquestionably political campaigning rather than informational'. Alexander Ivanchenko, the Director of the Independent Electoral Institute and a previous secretary of the Electoral Commission, commented unambiguously, 'Putin's election campaign falls short of civilised election standards. In technical terms there is a de-legitimisation of electoral procedures. The presidential election should be declared invalid, but the Central Electoral Commission is impotent.'

There was no public reaction to this. Gleb Pavlovsky, a totally cynical individual, the Director of the Effective Politics Foundation and one of the Kremlin's main spin doctors, even stated publicly, 'The electorate doesn't care who gets how many extra minutes on air!'

Television continues its brainwashing through upbeat broadcasts. Today Prime Minister Kasianov reported that agricultural production has risen 1.5 per cent, and that under Putin all the conditions are now in place for the successful development of Russia's agribusiness. 'We are poised to regain our prominent position in the world's grain markets,' Kasianov assured us. It is unlikely that his sycophancy will save him. He will be removed soon. Putin is uncomfortable with politicians left over from the Yeltsin era who remind him of a time when it was he who was a mere puppet, and of the history of how he came to be selected as Yeltsin's successor.

In the course of the election campaign we have heard that we are world leaders in virtually everything, from arms sales and grain exports to space exploration. So far they are not claiming we are world leaders in car manufacture. High-ranking officials' backsides have evidently not yet forgotten the experience of riding in our Zhigulis.

13 February

Does the Duma have any clout at all? Putin wanted it to elect Vladimir Lukin, a former Yabloko man and well-known liberal, as Human Rights Ombudsman before the presidential election. United Russia pulled out all the stops, and although Rodina and the Communist Party said they would boycott the vote, the appointment went through. Lukin was the only candidate in the ballot; the others were simply excluded. He is delighted. 'I very much look forward to working in this area,' he said. But what about those whose rights need to be defended?

(Lukin was to prove a mediocre Ombudsman, lacking in initiative and under the Kremlin's thumb, never straying beyond the bounds of what was permissible. Chechnya, for example, was never one of Lukin's priorities.)

In Qatar, Zelimkhan Yandarbiev, the former Vice-President of Chechnya and colleague of Presidents Dudaev and Maskhadov*, has been killed by a bomb apparently fixed beneath his jeep. He left Chechnya at the beginning of the Second Chechen War. This was almost certainly the work of the Russian intelligence agencies – the Army's Central Intelligence Directorate or the Federal Security Bureau. Most likely, the former.

Ivan Rybkin has announced that he will not be returning from London. A defecting presidential candidate is a first in our history. Nobody now has any doubt that the regime drugged him.

A call to our newspaper's editorial offices, supposedly from 'a well-wisher' in the intelligence services. 'Pass it on to London, as we know you can, that if Rybkin should produce any compromising material against Putin in television debates, another terrorist act will follow. The President will have to distract the attention of the public somehow.'

We passed the message on, but Rybkin has already washed his hands of the election. He is in fear for his life.

Liberal voters seem to be in two minds. Khakamada called a meeting of her supporters in Moscow and I went along. Many people say outright, 'If we don't put forward Khakamada we shall have no option but to vote against all of them, or not turn out at all.'

Rogozin and Glaziev continue to play dangerously on the emotions of those who feel an impaired sense of nationhood.

14 February

A new tragedy in Moscow. The roof of the Aqua Park in Yasenevo has collapsed. It happened in the evening when the celebrations of St Valentine's Day were at their height. Seventy per cent of the dome, an area the size of a football pitch, fell in over the swimming pool. Officially, there were 426 people in the Aqua Park, but unofficially it was nearer 1,000. The building is shrouded in steam. People in their swimsuits leaped out into 20 degrees of frost. In the worst-affected area there was also a restaurant, a bowling alley, bathhouses, saunas, exercise rooms and a family area with a warm pool for children. Twenty-six bodies were found immediately, but there are many body parts. The authorities say it was not a terrorist act.

Officialdom has started making life difficult for the new Party of Soldiers' Mothers. The Ministry of Justice, which is responsible for registering parties, claims it has not yet received any documents from the party; they have not only been handed in to the Ministry, but the Soldiers' Mothers also have an official Ministry receipt for them. The bureaucrats are trying to set all kinds of traps in the hope of tricking the new party into infringing the muddled and onerous laws on forming parties. Then they could simply be got rid of. For now the women are doing all right, checking every step.

Yevgeny Sidorenko, the spokesman of the Ministry of Justice, declared, 'I am not at all sure we shall register such a party. A political party cannot limit its membership to a particular group of the population. What if somebody who is not a soldier's mother wants to join? A soldier's father, for instance?'

He must be a fortune-teller. The fathers do want to join. In our political Sahara, the Party of Soldiers' Mothers is so attractive that many men have joined despite the party's title, and nobody, of course, has any intention of debarring them. Serving officers, moreover, have been phoning the Committees of Soldiers' Mothers asking that there should be a place for them too when the party's structure is being decided. These are honourable officers who refuse to reconcile themselves to the idea of an Army that is little more than a mechanism for taking the lives of our young men. The Party of Soldiers' Mothers is beginning to look like a real means of rescuing the Army and establishing public accountability for our Armed Forces.

15 February

The Sultanovs, the family of the little girl Khursheda who was murdered by skinheads in St Petersburg, have abandoned Russia and gone to live in Tadjikistan. They took a small coffin containing the child's remains with them.

The FSB is to be in charge of investigating the explosion in the Metro. It promptly demanded new powers, comparing the situation to that in the United States after September 11.

Our war of the North against the South continues. Nobody imagines this is the last terrorist outrage, or doubts that the Chechens were behind it. A majority support giving those who live here hell. Seventy per cent of Russians favour kicking out all Caucasians. But where to? The Caucasus is still part of Russia.

Today is the fifteenth anniversary of our withdrawal from Afghanistan. That is seen as marking the end of the Afghan War, but we had already sown the seeds for terrorism to develop. Just like the Americans with their bin Laden: he is what he is today because the Afghan War was what it was.

16 February

Blood-donor centres have been set up for the victims of the Aqua Park disaster. We are beginning to know what to do in these situations.

The shareholders of Yukos have stated that they are prepared to ransom Khodorkovsky from the state. Leonid Nevzlin [Khodorkovsky's right-hand man at Yukos], who fled to Israel, has announced that they are willing to part with their stakes in return for freedom for him and Platon Lebedev [CEO of Menatep Bank, which was the main shareholder of Yukos, serving eight years of penal servitude for alleged tax evasion].

Nevzlin himself owns 8 per cent of the shares of Menatep Group. He says the offer is backed also by Mikhail Brudno (7 per cent) and Vladimir Dubov (7 per cent).

Khodorkovsky has expressed indignation from jail and refuses to be ransomed. He has decided to drain this cup to the dregs.

17 February

The NTV television company is refusing to provide air time for the election campaign and debates of the 'other' presidential candidates. It claims they have a low rating in the opinion polls and nobody would watch the programmes. Perhaps a country gets the candidates it deserves, but they should at least be allowed to speak. There is no doubt that the company's decision was taken under pressure from the Kremlin.

In Moscow the committee supporting Khakamada has met in the fashionable and expensive Berlin Club on Petrovka. Khakamada said, 'I am going into this election as if to the scaffold, and with only one aim: to show the state authorities that there are normal people in Russia who know exactly what they are up to.' That is good. She is trying to show that fear has not yet conquered Russia, which would be an unconditional victory for Putin.

United Russia also held a meeting of 'the democratic intelligentsia' in support of Putin, who, it was claimed, is having mud slung at him by his opponents. Putin's defenders included the veteran singer Larisa Dolina, theatre and film director Mark Zakharov, the actor Nikolai Karachentsev and circus manager Natalia Durova. They were sent a letter asking them to 'defend the honour and dignity of the President', and duly answered the call. It was mentioned in passing that the overall membership of United Russia has reached 740,000, and that more than two million 'supporters' have been registered, although no explanation of what this means has been forthcoming. United Russia emphasised that its purpose as a political party is to support the President. Not policies, not ideals, not a programme of reform: an individual.

The Central Electoral Commission joyfully reports that more than 200 international observers have been officially accredited for the election on 14 March. In all, some 400 are expected.

The Duma contributes its mite to the pathetic attempts to fight terrorism. The powers of the secret police and spies will be widened, and amendments to the Criminal Code have been adopted to increase the penalties for suicide bombers. They will now be liable to life imprisonment! This seems unlikely to deter people who have decided to settle their accounts with life in this way. The Fourth Duma is the collective brain of today's bone-headed Russian bureaucracy.

The Duma is playing up to the intelligence services because that is what Putin likes. There is no mention of the additional three billion roubles [£57 million] the intelligence services were awarded shortly after *Nord-Ost* for the fight against terrorism. Where did all that go, and why has the number of terrorist outrages not decreased? The Fourth Duma has given its legislative blessing to a purely virtual fight against terrorism. The efficiency of the intelligence services is not even queried, and the problem of Chechnya, which is at the root of everything, is not mentioned.

19 February

Sergey Mironov has taken part in the television debates for the first time. Everybody immediately rounded on him, as if he were Putin, but Mironov refused to be a whipping boy.

'Of course you are Putin!' Khakamada said. 'Why, after all the terrorist acts, has Gryzlov been promoted when he should have been sacked?'

'I am not the representative of Candidate Putin!' Mironov replied.

'Then answer as the third person in the hierarchy of power in the state,' Khakamada continued.

Mironov still chose not to answer. That's the kind of debates we have. Nobody takes them seriously. They are broadcast very early in the morning.

The Central Electoral Commission has refused Rybkin permission to take part in live pre-election debates from London. There is no way Rybkin is going to be allowed to dish the dirt on Putin live on television.

21 February

In Voronezh, Amar Antoniu Lima, 24, a first-year student at the Voronezh Medical Academy, has died after being stabbed 17 times. He came from Guinea-Bissau. This is the seventh murder of a foreign student in Voronezh in recent years. The murderers are skinheads.

Zhirinovsky's slogan in the parliamentary elections was 'We are for the poor! We are for the Russians!' It has been taken over by United Russia, and accordingly by the Guarantor of the Constitution himself. And by the skinheads.

22 February

There is increasing speculation that all the candidates, with the exception of Malyshkin and Mironov (and Putin), may withdraw from the election simultaneously. Glaziev has already announced his withdrawal, Rybkin is on the verge of doing so and so is Khakamada. The pro-Putin press says this is a plot to enable them to save political face because they will only achieve tiny percentages of the vote on 14 March.

The real reason is simply frustration at Putin's total absence from all pre-election discussion, putting the other candidates in a farcical situation. In Khakamada's words, 'The campaign is becoming increasingly lawless and dishonest.'

24 February

Putin has fired his Government live on television, 19 days before the election. According to the Constitution, the newly elected President appoints a new Cabinet, and at that point the previous Government retires. The reason for the dismissal has not been revealed. The Government was not blamed for anything, although there would have been plenty of grounds for doing so, and the only explanation being offered is that Putin wants to go to the electorate with an open visor, so that they should know who he will be working with after the election. The sacked ministers speak on television about the joy with which their hearts were filled when they heard they had been sacked. The Kremlin has demonstrated to the electorate that our elections are a complete sham and that the Government is purely ornamental. At any moment of the spin doctors' choosing, it can be done away with.

Does it matter one jot whom Putin appoints as Prime Minister in place of Kasianov, or who is in the Government? No. Everything in the country depends on the Presidential Administration. The sacking resembled a special operation. It was carried out in total secrecy. There were no leaks. It is as if they were carrying out a targeted military strike, not just dismissing ministers. The majority of the Cabinet learned of their sacking from the television news.

The dismissal of the Government in this manner demonstrates the establishment in Russia of Political Oligarchy. With this lot, all the financial oligarchs, who up till now had a finger in the pie, are nowhere.

The official television stations explain that 'The President is optimising the replacement of ineffective ministers so that the Russian people should know who will be in office after 14 March.' As if the election were already over.

Putin's first presidential term has effectively come to an end today. This is the termination of the era of Yeltsin, of whom Kasianov was the last remaining major appointee. Putin will now spend his second term completely distancing himself from Yeltsin's policies.

Yelena Bonner has appealed to the presidential candidates in an open letter from America:

> Once again I call upon the presidential candidates Irina Khakamada, Nikolai Kharitonov and Ivan Rybkin to jointly withdraw from the election. By standing as candidates each of you has tried to make your programme known to the electorate and to demonstrate to Russian society and world opinion the dishonesty of this election. Leave candidate No. 1, Putin, alone with his puppets, and call on the groups supporting you and ordinary electors to boycott the election. Anybody who dislikes the word boycott, may, if they prefer, describe this as a call not to appear on parade. It will then be of no importance what percentage they dream up for the turnout. What matters is that the authorities will know the real figure.
>
> Even more important is that everyone who deliberately does not vote will gain self-respect from not participating in this state-sponsored lie. Most importantly, refusing to participate will clearly indicate your goal, a goal shared for the next four years by right and left politicians and their political supporters. That is the battle to restore the institution of real elections in Russia, in place of the surrogate which is being imposed on the country today. Later, in 2007 and 2008, if you jointly stop elections from being a big lie, a scam, you will once again become political opponents and competitors in the struggle for voters. Right now, however, only your joint refusal to take part in the election and your call to the voters not to participate in it are strategically and morally justifiable.

There was no reaction to Bonner's appeal. No commentaries, no thunder and lightning. Nothing.

26 February

People are beginning to titter about Putin, even on television. He is in Khabarovsk today, looking as pompous and imperial as a king in a folk tale. In the morning he opened the Khabarovsk–Chita motorway. After that he talked to some war veterans who asked him for more money, so he increased the northern supplement for pensions. He spent some time with young hockey players at a new ice-skating stadium. The Commander-in-Chief of the Pacific Fleet, Viktor Fyodorov, had been expressing alarm at the possibility of force reductions, so Putin also announced that the Pacific Fleet would not be trimmed back because 'our Pacific fist needs to be strong'. He also promised support for the submarine base in Kamchatka. (He should try going there to see for himself the conditions in the officers' village at Petropavlovsk-Kamchatsky.) Next, the Acting Minister of Transport, Vadim Morozov, asked Putin for 4.5 billion roubles [£85 million] for a railway link between the Trans-Siberian Railway and the Baikal-Amur Highway, and Putin gave him it. The businessman and Governor of Primoriye, Sergey Darkin, asked for three billion roubles [£56 million] for new ships. The President of Yakutia, Vyacheslav Shtyrov, asked for funds for an oil and gas pipeline from Irkutsk to the Far East, and Putin promised to fix it.

No hint has been given as to who is to be the new Prime Minister. Rumours are circulating.

Some say Putin will appoint himself Prime Minister, others that it will be Gryzlov, or maybe Kudrin.

In the evening, NTV broadcast *To the Barrier!* The duellists were Vladimir Ryzhkov, an independently minded Deputy in the Duma, and Lyudmila Narusova, the widow of Anatoly Sobchak, Putin's teacher and boss. The question for discussion was why Putin had dismissed the Government. Ryzhkov was witty and ironical without being malicious. He mocked Putin, but in a friendly, condescending way. During the programme viewers were invited to vote on whether they supported Narusova or Ryzhkov.

Narusova insisted that the President was always right about everything, but could not explain anything beyond that. This is highly typical of Putin's supporters. The result was a resounding victory for Ryzhkov, who polled 71,000 votes to Narusova's 19,000 for her defence of Putin. Narusova, assuring everyone that Putin was going into the elections with the purest of intentions, was trounced.

27 February

Early voting in the election has begun for those who are on the high seas, in the air, on expeditions, or who live in remote and inaccessible regions. Although the results will be declared only on 14 March, the main ballot-rigging will occur with these early ballot boxes. It is easily done.

29 February

Throughout the weekend we were hearing that the President was consulting the main United Russia figures over whom to appoint as Prime Minister. Most people are sure this is just PR and that nobody is being consulted about anything.

In Moscow, a 'presidential election' by text message has been held. The result was 64 per cent for Putin, 18 per cent for Khakamada and 5 per cent for Glaziev.

2 March

Putin is shown on all television channels talking to the actor and director, Yury Solomin, about the 250th anniversary, in 2006, of the rescript of Catherine the Great on the establishment of theatres in Russia. Putin keeps asking how the occasion should be marked, and goes on being interested for a very long time.

The new Prime Minister of Russia is Mikhail Fradkov*. Nobody has a clue who he is. Apparently, he was an official in the Soviet Ministry of Foreign Trade and worked in various embassies; he occupied various positions in various ministries in the post-Soviet period, and worked in the Tax Police when they were at their lowest ebb. Fradkov, flying back from Brussels, said that he doesn't yet know what a 'technical Prime Minister' is. That is, he doesn't know what position he has been appointed to by Putin. A Prime Minister as clueless as this is, even for us, quite unusual.

5 March

Everything is being reduced to absurdity. The appointment of Fradkov as Prime Minister by the Duma deserves an entry in the *Guinness Book of Records*: 352 votes in favour of a man who, when asked what his plans for the future were, could only blurt, 'I have just come out of the shadow into the light.'

Fradkov is a man of the shadows because he is a spy. We have a truly third-rate Prime Minister. He is even bald. His very appearance tells you he is a political ploy. He has been chosen so that Putin, and only Putin, should be the authority figure. Nothing is going to change. Putin will continue to decide.

So what is the new policy? The answer is: nothing. Fradkov is a modest executive, always ready to carry out the tasks dictated by the Party. No more, no less than that.

Rybkin has withdrawn his candidacy, without giving any clear explanation as to why. He continues to give the impression of being mentally unwell.

Khakamada has travelled to Nizhny Novgorod, Perm and St Petersburg. She appears to the public looking irritated and exhausted, but if that's the state she is in, she would do better not to go there in the first place. Kharitonov is off to Tula. Malyshkin is in the Altai, but can barely string his words together. Mironov is in Irkutsk, but incapable of saying anything without notes.

The main thrust of the television commentaries about the candidates is that it is an outrage for them to dare to compete with our Principal Candidate. There is a gradual atrophy of the organ responsible for the democratic perception of reality. Propaganda is put out to the effect that people voted for a single candidate in the Soviet period, and everything was fine then. Presumably in the next elections we won't even hear these matters debated. There will be one officially appointed opposition candidate, and society will take that in its stride. The country is sinking into a state of collective unconsciousness, into unreason.

8 March

International Women's Day. In accordance with an old Kremlin tradition, Putin assembles token working women. There has to be a tractor driver, a scientist, an actress and a teacher. Words spoken from the heart, a glass of champagne, television cameras.

This is the last moment for candidates to withdraw from the race. Nobody has done so, and six remain on the ballot paper: Malyshkin, Putin, Mironov, Khakamada, Glaziev and Kharitonov. A great deal of television coverage is devoted to early voting by reindeer breeders and those at far-away border posts.

9 March

From today campaigning and the publication of opinion polls are banned, but everybody gave up campaigning after Fradkov was appointed. There seemed no point.

10 March

Putin is on all television channels meeting sportsmen to ask what they need in order to win in the Summer Olympic Games. They need more money. Putin promises it.

11 March

It is 50 years since Khrushchev's campaign to cultivate the virgin lands of Siberia and Kazakhstan. Putin receives prominent public figures at his residence and asks them what they need. They need more money. Putin promises they shall have it. The formation of the 'new' Government is looking unpromising. There was talk about reducing the number of top-level bureaucrats, but the number has actually increased. All the supposedly sacked ministers have been reinstated as deputy ministers in amalgamated ministries, which means we get one new bureaucrat plus two old ones. In total, from 24 old ministries and departments they have created 42 new ones. The Government is just the same, but minus Kasianov. An oligarchic government, controlled by different oligarchs, close not to the Ministry of Finance and the Ministry of Property, but to Putin. Putin is a political oligarch. In earlier times he would have been called an emperor.

12–13 March

Silence and apathy. Nobody can be bothered to listen to the drivel coming from the television. Let's just get it over with.

14 March

Well, so he's been elected. The turnout was, as the Presidential Administration required, very high. The Speaker of the State Duma, Boris Gryzlov, emerging from the polling station, told the assembled journalists, 'Campaigning today is forbidden, but, anticipating your curiosity, I will say that I have voted for the person who for the past four years has ensured the stable development of Russia's economy. I have voted for policies as clear as today's weather.'

In the evening Alexander Veshnyakov, Director of the Central Electoral Commission, informed the Russian people that only a single infringement of electoral law had been noted during the poll: 'Vodka was being sold from a bus near one of the polling stations in Nizhny Tagil.'

In Voronezh, the Central Board of Health issued Order No. 114 to the effect that no hospitals should admit anybody during the period of voting who was not in possession of an absentee vote. All the patients duly turned up with absentee votes in order to be allowed to be ill. The same process was repeated in Rostov-on-Don. In the contagious diseases department of the city hospital, mothers were told they could not see their children unless they had arranged an absentee vote.

In Bashkortostan*, President Rakhimov* delivered 92 per cent of the vote for Putin; Dagestan, 94 per cent; Kabardino-Balkaria, 96; Ingushetia*, 98. Were they running a competition? During the 13 years of our new, post-Soviet life, this is the fourth time Russia has elected a President. In 1991, it was Yeltsin; in 1996, Yeltsin again; in 2000, Putin; in 2004, Putin again. The eternal cycle repeats for Russia's citizens, from an upsurge of hope to total indifference towards Candidate No. 1.

15 March

Now we know the official figures: Putin got 71.22 per cent. Victory! (May it be pyrrhic.) Khakamada got 3.85; Kharitonov, 13.74; Glaziev, 4.11; Malyshkin, 2.23; Mironov, 0.76. Mironov had absolutely nothing to his candidacy other than a dog-like loyalty to Putin. His result reflects that. By and large, the concept of ruling the country by the same methods used in conducting the 'anti-terrorist operation' has been vindicated: *L'État, c'est Putin.*

PART TWO

Russia's Great Political Depression
April–December 2004

From the Re-Election of Putin to the Ukrainian Revolution

A terrible sense of ennui hung over our cities and villages after Putin's re-election. Everything seemed as boring and wretched as it did in the days of the Soviet Union. Even those who had supported the losers seemed unable to rouse themselves to anger. It appeared that people had simply given up, as if to say, 'Who cares what happens now!' Russia relapsed into socio-political hibernation, into a new period of stagnation whose depth can be judged by the fact that not even the tragedy of Beslan, a cataclysm of biblical proportions, could disturb it.

6 April

In Nazran, the capital of Ingushetia, President Murat Zyazikov* has been blown up in his Mercedes, but survived. He is one of Putin's placemen and was 'elected' two years ago in a highly original manner. FSB agents flooded into the republic, not bothering to conceal that they were acting on the direct orders of Putin. He was extremely keen to ensure that even though it had to be by means of a popular vote, power in Ingushetia should be in the hands of someone under his control. Ingushetia borders Chechnya.

Nobody really imagines that the election of FSB General Zyazikov was legitimate, but there was no way of mounting a legal challenge. The republic's courts will not bring actions against Zyazikov any more than the courts in Moscow allow lawsuits against Putin, and when there is no provision for the steam to escape, you get an explosion of terrorism.

Zyazikov survived the attack thanks to his armoured Mercedes. He called it an outrage against the people of Ingushetia. There was not a shred of sympathy for him, but there was interest in what lay behind the attack. One possible motive is that it was provoked by the corruption that has flourished more than ever under Zyazikov and Ruslanbi Zyazikov, his cousin and principal bodyguard. Throughout the winter

97

before the assassination attempt, Ruslanbi was being warned by people who included relatives of the President that he should rein in his misconduct. The same was being said to Zyazikov. When these words produced no effect, Ruslanbi's spanking new jeep was burned out in March in the middle of Nazran right under his nose. Naturally, the destruction of a jeep belonging to the President's main bodyguard was hushed up. Neither Ruslanbi nor Zyazikov made an issue of it. The explanation that it was a warning to officials who had got out of hand is taken much more seriously in Nazran than the idea that it was an assassination attempt.

The second explanation relates to a series of recent abductions in Ingushetia. Under Zyazikov, abductions began occurring in accordance with the pattern established in Chechnya. Victims were seized by 'unidentified masked soldiers' and spirited off to an unknown destination in unmarked vehicles. To date there are 40 names on a list compiled by their relatives. Zyazikov categorically denies state lawlessness on this scale and has imposed a blackout on information about the abductions. They cannot be reported within the borders of Ingushetia, and in the Procurator's Office and the Interior Ministry officials will talk to relatives only off the record.

Naturally, the families are undertaking their own investigations, and this encourages them to take matters into their own hands, just as in Chechnya. Where there is no justice there is rough justice. People lose patience.

There comes a knock at my door. I am in a hotel in Nazran. Outside is a queue of old people. These are the mothers and fathers of the disappeared of Ingushetia. They tell me that people are being slaughtered like poultry. Unidentified detachments of federal troops drive through the streets by day and night. Mahomed Yandiev, a pensioner from Karabulak, has lost his son, Timur. He was a very well-known computer programmer, and accordingly popular with young people. It happened in the early evening. Timur was leaving his office some time after 5.00 p.m. on 16 March when armed men wearing masks and camouflage fatigues pushed him into a white Niva with no number plates and drove off. The Niva was covered by a Gazelle, which also had no number plates. The kidnappers proceeded without hindrance into Chechnya via the Caucasus border post, the main military checkpoint on the border between Ingushetia and Chechnya. There the abductors showed their ROSh passes: they were accredited to the Regional Operational Headquarters of the Counter-Terrorist Operation. These are the findings of the Yandiev family. The law-enforcement agencies did nothing.

'I have been everywhere,' says Mahomed Yandiev, weeping. He has been crushed by what has happened. 'I have asked everybody: the Procurator's Office, the Interior Ministry, the FSB. I have begged them to tell me why he was taken. No matter what he has done, I should know. In reply I get silence. I have many questions. Are those masked people superior to the Ingush agencies of law and order? Who are they? Our Interior Ministry employs six thousand people. That is a great many for a republic of only three hundred thousand people. Can these six thousand really not police the Republic's territory? Or is it they who are allowing individuals who cannot be identified to abduct people? I am outraged that President Zyazikov has never said anything in public about the problem. Since he is saying nothing, he knows where our people are and he is covering up for the kidnappers. They have unleashed a war against their own people. Chechnya is a base for bringing Stalinism back to Russia as a whole; we Ingushes are the next in turn after the Chechens, because we are the people closest to them. I hate Putin and his spawn Zyazikov.'

Mahomed Yandiev leaves and his place is taken by Tsiesh Khazbieva, and her son Islam. On 2 March, right in front of her, 'unidentified masked soldiers' shot her 24-year-old daughter Madina. They were driving that day from Nazran to visit the family's grandmother in the village of Gamurzievo.

'It was just before we reached Gamurzievo,' Tsiesh weeps. 'The cars in front of us began braking and then they blocked the road. We were forced to a halt. We saw masked soldiers drag a young lad out of the front vehicle. They threw him to the ground and shot him on the spot, although he was offering no resistance. Naturally, I started shouting, "What are you doing?!" In reply they shot at us. They hit my daughter in the carotid artery. She didn't even have time to get out of the car. My husband was seriously wounded in the shoulder and leg. He survived, but the doctors were unable to remove the bone fragments. I almost never leave home now, I am so afraid of people. There were no expressions of condolence from the authorities. There wasn't a word about it in any of the newspapers or on television. From what they show on television you would think we lived in paradise. I don't see why my Madina had to die. Who is answerable for shooting her?'

Later I sought out Idris Archakov, the investigator into the murder of this totally innocent girl. Idris had little to say. He was terrified of the truth, and kept shifting about. 'You must understand . . . I want to work . . .' In Ingushetia fear now fetters everybody, from the peasant to the procurator, like a dragon that looks down on everybody from above. I am talking to Idris as if we are at a secret meeting, sitting in a borrowed car with the engine running.

Here is a bare summary of the words of Investigator Archakov, in which there is more cowardice and fear than any desire to carry out the duties of his position: Madina was shot by one of the federal death squads that regularly raid Ingushetia. On 2 March they were engaged in killing Akhmed Basnukaev, a field commander.

'Why did they need to liquidate Basnukaev by shooting at every living thing in the area? Basnukaev was from the moderate wing of the Chechen Resistance. Not only did he not try to shoot his way out when they arrested him, but he had long been living quite openly in Ingushetia and had even, at the request of the pro-Moscow Chechen authorities, tried to mediate between official Grozny and some of the field commanders about laying down their arms voluntarily.'

'It was quite needless, of course, but they take no notice of what we say. The federals do as they see fit. You know yourself, they are scared of their own shadows. It is easier for them to kill than to try to think and see reality.'

'And what are you going to do now? When you know for sure that it was federal troops who were responsible?'

'Nothing. I shall keep quiet like everybody else. Since Putin has won, he has the power, and that means we have to keep our heads down. I will put the case of the murder of Madina to one side. Her parents will cry for a time and then calm down. They are simple people. They're not going to start writing to the Procurator-General's Office. Even if they do, I'll be thanked for not having investigated too closely.'

Archakov's attitude is typical of our times.

The Khazbievs leave and in my room I now have the Mutsolgovs. If there is anything all this can be compared with, it is Chechnya: only there does a journalist instantly attract a queue the length of those we saw in Soviet-era food shops. These are the relatives of victims of extrajudicial executions or, as it is now officially described by the Procurator's Office, of 'targeted force necessary in the struggle against terrorism'. They are the relatives of all those people who have been 'disappeared', dragged off and murdered by 'unidentified masked soldiers wearing camouflage fatigues'. The families can never find those responsible, nor any trace of those who have vanished. They are not to be found in any state institution, whether under interrogation, in custody or in prison.

Adam Mutsolgov is the father of a 29-year-old teacher, Bashir, from the town of Karabulak. His son was shoved into a white Niva outside his house in broad daylight. Adam's two other sons also embarked upon an independent investigation.

(They were later to discover that those responsible for the abduction were agents of the Ingush Directorate of the FSB, under the command of General Sergey Koryakov, a friend of President Zyazikov. General Koryakov was personally involved. The brothers obtained evidence that Bashir had spent the first night after his abduction in the DFSB building in Nazran (or Magas as it was renamed), directly behind the presidential palace. In the morning he was taken in a DFSB vehicle to the main Russian military base of Hankala in Chechnya, but after that they could find out no more. Their informant was himself a member of the DFSB. Those who had seen Bashir Mutsolgov in Hankala also told Adam that his son had been in a bad way, showing signs of terrible torture.)

Adam Mutsolgov hands me the list of 40 names of those who have been abducted in recent months. It is an unofficial list, compiled by their families. The Procurator's Office has refused to accept it. Their only option is to unite and work together. The list, which in late February was rather shorter, was given just before Putin's election to Rashid Ozdoev, the Senior Assistant of the Procurator of Ingushetia. Rashid's official duties were to monitor the legality of the actions of the Ingush DFSB. At that very time he was himself following up what had happened to those who had been abducted, and he too had concluded that extra-judicial executions were taking place with the knowledge of the Republic's security services. Rashid submitted a report to the Procurator-General of the Russia Federation, Vladimir Ustinov, providing evidence of illegal activity, primarily by General Koryakov and the DFSB.

On 11 March, at about 6.00 p.m., Rashid Ozdoev was seen for the last time getting into his car in the car park by the presidential palace in Nazran. Twenty-four hours later his Zhiguli was seen, covered by a tarpaulin, in the courtyard of the Ingush DFSB. Rashid was later observed, as his relatives discovered for themselves, beaten and tortured, in Hankala. They know only that he is no longer there.

'Every day spent not knowing, I bury my son.' Boris Ozdoev, Rashid's father, speaks quietly, hanging his head. He is a judge in honourable retirement and very well known in Ingushetia. He is far from young.

'Did your son tell you what was in his report to the Procurator-General?'

'Yes. He wrote about instances of extra-judicial force being used, and who was guilty of it. I said to my son, "Do not do this. It is a fearsome organisation! Why do you want to take such a risk?" He replied, "If you wish, I will leave this job. But if I am the Prosecutor whose job it is to monitor the DFSB, and if the organisation I am monitoring is involved in murder and abduction, then I am the only person in the republic who has the legal right to demand a return to legality. If I do not use that right now, the Almighty will never forgive me." We discussed it for a long time, and he wondered, "Well, what can they do? Plant drugs on me, weapons? They can't make that stick: I have immunity as a Procurator. Everybody knows I don't take bribes." He didn't consider the possibility that he might be abducted himself. After his disappearance I went to President Zyazikov and I, an old man, a judge, sat in his waiting room for one and a half hours. He kept me waiting, and then simply passed a message through his secretary that he had nothing to say to me. I have no doubt that means he knows who abducted Rashid.'

In the end, the heads of families whose sons had been abducted called a meeting and demanded that Zyazikov should tell them where their sons were, and who was guilty of the abductions. At just that moment, however, Zyazikov was on his way to a meeting with Putin in Sochi to report on how Ingushetia was flourishing and to tell him that 98 per cent of the electorate had voted 'for you, Vladimir Vladimirovich'.

The direct consequence of the parachuting into the Ingush presidency of an FSB general who had worked for the Soviet KGB has been the organising of state-sanctioned lawlessness on a massive scale. Zyazikov is no more trustworthy a guarantor of law than Putin, something that, incidentally, disappointed the hopes of many people in Ingushetia, who were tired of disorder. Instead Zyazikov has presided over a move away from democracy, not just to autocracy, but to state terrorism and medieval barbarity.

I went to my colleagues, Ingush journalists, to ask them how the system of media censorship works in these outlying regions, far away from Putin's Administration in Moscow. Why, for instance, is there not a word in the Republican media about extra-judicial executions, when concealing the problem can only make it worse?

It proved far from easy to discuss. In the first place, nobody would talk on the record. In the second, we could speak only in a car, away from prying eyes, as in the days of the Soviet Union. The person I talked to was in a state of deep depression, which seems to be well nigh universal. This was a Deputy Editor-in-Chief of one of the two newspapers published in Ingushetia.

'Why do we need all these precautions?' I asked.

'If they find out I have opened my mouth, I won't even be able to find a job as a tractor driver,' he answered, a grey-haired, clever man, a professional journalist.

'What would happen if you were to write about the abductions, the corruption, Putin's "98 per cent"? About the massive ballot-box stuffing in last December's parliamentary elections?'

'If I wrote about that, I would be sacked when it reached the censors. Articles of that kind just aren't going to be published, and I would be unable to find work in the future. My relatives would lose their jobs too, even though they have nothing to do with journalism.'

My colleague told me about the censorship mechanism that supports the myth of the 'stabilisation of Ingushetia'. Every column of the newspapers is read personally at proof stage by Issa Merzhoev, the President's Press Secretary. That is the law. He removes anything he considers harmful, anything that might undermine the 'process of stabilisation'. Negative information of any sort is censored if it relates even indirectly to those presently in power. You cannot propose articles about corruption if relatives of Zyazikov are involved. Of the war in Chechnya you may write only about the killing of fighters and the 'voluntary resettlement of refugees'. The death squads are completely taboo, as is all extrajudicial activity.

Exactly the same goes for radio and television. Merzhoev personally checks the programmes from a political angle, and he checks all the topics to be covered in advance.

But why? People have no air to breathe, they are in complete despair. Who can possibly want the Chechen scenario to be repeated here? Nobody in Ingushetia, not even Zyazikov. He is not like Ruslan Aushev, his very competent predecessor. If there is a crisis he will be totally out of his depth. Another Chechnya may, however, be something Moscow needs, and Zyazikov is entirely dependent on Moscow. His rise to the presidency was fixed by Moscow, and the Kremlin set two conditions, which people in Ingushetia know all about: that he would not object if the 'anti-terrorist operation' were extended to Ingushetia, and would deliver the loyalty of his people; and secondly, that he would not demand the return from North Ossetia to Ingushetia of the Prigorodny Region.

And Zyazikov delivers, he and his henchmen. If the media were allowed to reflect reality, it would soon be very clear that the people want proper demarcation of the frontier with Chechnya and the return of the Prigorodny Region, which was taken from them when Stalin deported the entire Ingush population to Kazakhstan in 1944.

'That is why we are under pressure,' the journalist says. 'They need it to appear that everybody in Ingushetia is happy with the Kremlin's policy and with what Zyazikov is doing.'

'Could you disobey Merzhoev?'

'So far none of the Editors-in-Chief have dared to try.'

'Who can resist?'

'Nobody. You can resist only if you leave Ingushetia, or better still if you emigrate from Russia.'

'How would you describe what is happening in Ingushetia today?'

'The Soviet system with a lot of bloodshed.'

Of course, Soviet stability too was a great achievement – the coffins containing soldiers killed in Afghanistan were not allowed to be identified as such; dissidents were imprisoned in labour camps and psychiatric hospitals; the populace voted 99.9 per cent in favour of everything; the party bosses feared only the Party Control Commission; the well-drilled artists of the cinema made politically correct films about everybody having complete faith in the future. The West gave Brezhnev financial support because it didn't want everything to fall apart. That was the reality, disguised as stability. Now, in April 2004, we are back at square one. Reality is tastefully displayed to look like stability, both in Ingushetia and throughout Russia. The West again throws us a crust. We know all about eternal recurrence.

I often wonder why our people are so frightened by even the hint of a threat of repression. If they protest at all, then it is only by anonymously blowing up a presidential Mercedes, not in a civilised, open manner, by opposition in a parliament, or by demanding that the results of a rigged election should be annulled.

It can only be a matter of traditions. The Russian tradition is one of an inability to plan and see through the sheer hard work of systematic opposition. If we are going to do anything, it has to be something we can do on the spot, here and now, after which life will be sorted. As that isn't the way things work, life doesn't get sorted.

I wonder too why Zyazikov, like Putin (because Zyazikov is a mere clone), can't do anything in a decent, human, democratic way. Why, in order to stay in power, do they need to lie, to twist and turn, support corrupt officials, avoid meeting their people, fear them and, as a result, have no love for them?

I think the underlying problem must be that they have not been adequately prepared for leadership. They are appointed to the presidency in the Soviet way, quite by chance. The Party gives its orders and the eager Young Communist replies, 'Yes, Comrade Commissar!' For a time they probably enjoy being President very much, but, after the inauguration and all the celebrations, when the firework displays are over, they find themselves faced with the routine labour of being a president: running the economy, maintaining the water pipes and the roads, coping with terrorists, wars and thieving officials. That is when they realise they are incapable of doing anything except frowning severely, pretending to be Talleyrand, secretively keeping quiet and blaming their failures on enemies who are lurking round every corner.

Zyazikov in Ingushetia copies his big boss in Moscow in all things, but particularly in his basic approach. What matters is not solving the problems, but controlling what gets reported on television; not reality but virtuality; censorship as a way of not having to tackle difficult matters. The downside is that ubiquitous censorship and constant duplicity mean you have no visible opposition with which to debate the issues on a daily basis. Where are the dissenting voices, all those who might criticise and come up with alternative ideas? You can't listen to them because they are not there. Neither in Moscow nor in Ingushetia.

For a long time the only open oppositionists in Zyazikov's republic were Musa Ozdoev and a number of people close to him. Musa used to be in Zyazikov's team, and was even his adviser at one time.

Oppositionist Musa Ozdoev tried to challenge the election results to the Duma. In court he produced records from electoral districts where votes had been written into the record, a bizarre electoral roll in which people with different names had the same passport, or where one person voted several times using the same name, but different passports. Here are a few examples which explain how the opposition came to be 'routed' in the December election and how Putin's party, United Russia, came by its imposing victory.

Electoral Ward 68 is in the village of Barsuki on the outskirts of Nazran, the home village of Murat Zyazikov. This is where his relatives live, and it is here that, on the highest hill, the President's 'Lettuce Castle' is being built. It is a hulking, clumsy great building of feudal aspect, but the green colour works surprisingly well, and he is expected to move there shortly. Naturally, in accordance with the worst Caucasian traditions, those supervising the voting in the polling stations of Barsuki were relatives of Zyazikov, his vassals, those building his castle, its suppliers and staff.

I studied the electoral register, which has been officially certified and bears all the requisite signatures and seals. It tells us who received ballot papers on 7 December in Ward 68. We find that at least three different citizens voted using passport No. 26 01010683: Timur Khamzatovich Balkhaev of 15 Alkhan-Churtskaya Street; Tamerlan Magomedovich Dzortov of Zyazikov Street (a different Zyazikov); and Beslan Bagaudinovich Galgoev of 5 Kortoev Street.

Here again, the same passport No. 26 01032665 apparently belongs to four citizens of Barsuki, three male and one female. Three of them live at 13 Yuzhnaya Street. There are dozens of examples of such double, treble and quadruple voting using the same passport. Next we come across a column of identical signatures in five, six or ten boxes in succession, one under the other, purporting to certify the identities of different people.

Comparing the Barsuki registers for the elections of 7 December and 14 March (when Putin was elected), we find that the same person has two passports. In the register for the parliamentary elections of 7 December, passport No. 26 02098850 is held by Akhmed Tagirovich Azhigov from the farmstead of Tibi-Khi (part of Barsuki), but on 14 March the same person is voting using passport No. 26 03356564. So who is Azhigov? Does he exist? It proved impossible to track him down in Tibi-Khi, a tiny place where everybody knows everybody else and even remembers their parents and grandparents. Nobody had ever heard of him.

There are any number of similar Azhigovs because the electoral commissions were shamelessly creative in their efforts to ensure the right result. The outcome of all this, however, is nothing to laugh about: it has brought about the downfall not only of Russian democracy, but also of Russian society. In Ingushetia, Musa Ozdoev protested about this, and in every town you will find one, or at most two, Musa Ozdoevs. They are usually considered mad. Wiser people pat them sympathetically on the shoulder and say, 'Go on, give it a try. We will watch and see what happens.'

If the town madman were suddenly to kill the dragon, millions would flock to share his glory and enjoy the fruits of his victory. It is an old, deplorable Soviet custom: do nothing yourself, lie still in the mud on the riverbed, and wait for a wonderful new life to float down to you from above.

But to return to the ballot-rigging. Why was it necessary?

The answer is simple: because insufficient people actually voted for Putin on 14 March, or for United Russia on 7 December. The West fervently believes in the results, but the percentages are inflated.

Ingushetia's '98 per cent for Putin' just tells us how desperate Zyazikov was to show off to the Kremlin.

That's all there is to it. That is why Zyazikov's accomplices broke people across their knee, twisted the arms of members of the electoral commissions, perverted, threatened, tortured and ensnared people in a conspiracy of lies. And they went along with it.

Most members of electoral commissions to whom I managed to speak said they were afraid. They had families, children who could be kidnapped. It was easier to add false votes than lose those dearest to you. Who can say we are not returning to Stalinist ways under Putin? A hereditary memory is at work, reminding people how to live if they want to survive. Swim with the tide.

This whole system of thieving judges, rigged elections, presidents who have only contempt for the needs of their people can operate only if nobody protests. That is the Kremlin's secret weapon and the most striking feature of life in Russia today. That is the secret of spin doctor Surkov's genius: apathy, rooted in an almost universal certainty among the populace that the state authorities will fix everything, including elections, to their own advantage. It is a vicious circle. People react only when something affects them personally: old Judge Boris Ozdoev when his son Rashid was abducted, the same as the Mutsolgovs. Until then, if my hut is out of harm's way, why worry? We have emerged from socialism as thoroughly self-centred people.

And that is the background to the attempt to assassinate Zyazikov.

7 April

Today Igor Sutyagin, a military expert and scholar at the US-Canada Institute of the Russian Academy of Sciences, the author of hundreds of scholarly articles on strategic weapons and disarmament, has been sentenced to 15 years' imprisonment for 'betraying the Motherland'. Putin had personal charge of the case when he was Director of the FSB.

Sutyagin was arrested in October 1999. He was accused of passing secret information to foreign intelligence services. In fact, Sutyagin's work consisted solely of analysing publicly available information and drawing conclusions based on non-classified sources. He didn't even have security clearance for access to state secrets. The FSB only demonstrated that, by making use of publicly available data, Sutyagin came to secret conclusions. This was obviously a trial concocted to make an example of someone.

'Making an example' is becoming increasingly common in the courts, as is demonstrating loyalty to the Kremlin. Since the instigator of the Sutyagin case is now in the Kremlin as President of Russia, it was impossible not to find Sutyagin guilty. In addition, the Sutyagin case is being used to instil in the public mind the notion of 'justifiable repressions', that the authorities know better than anyone else who the enemy is, and accordingly have the right to persecute particular individuals even if their crimes are unproven.

Instil it they duly did. Society accepted the idea of justified repressions. Apart from human-rights campaigners, few came to Sutyagin's aid. Some time ago the public demanded that another 'spy', the naval officer Grigorii Pasko, should be released, but he supposedly replied from solitary confinement that he had no wish to be shown clemency. Now, however, with the guilty verdict in this latest, typically Stalinist, show trial, the FSB has won the battle for its own future.

The Sutyagin case revealed another of our problems, trial by jury. In Russia everything civilised seems to become subverted or perverted into its own opposite. Our juries are ordinary citizens who don't mind going without bread so long as 'enemies of the Motherland' get put away for a long time. It was Judge Mironova who determined the length of the sentence, but it was the jury who found Sutyagin guilty despite the absence of any evidence. Why? Because it is etched into their brains that the KGB/FSB is always right. The Sutyagin jury demonstrated the extent to which, as a society, we still carry within ourselves a repressive way of thinking. We have learned nothing. Harshness is more respected than mercy and understanding. It is better to cut down the forest than to worry about the wood chips. It is better to condemn than to think.

Committee 2008 denounced the verdict: 'Trial by jury is becoming purely ornamental, used only to disguise minimally the profoundly undemocratic nature of the state machinery of repression. Today's unjust verdict is an attack by the authorities on the very foundation of a democratic constitutional system.'

That is not actually true. It is a typical little democratic fib. The jury is not a screen: the jury is the problem. The jury is us.

The Duma passed a stunningly draconian law banning all protest meetings in the vicinity of state institutions. That is, they could be held only where nobody other than their participants would hear or see them. Those voting in favour included former trade-union leader Andrey Isaev, who more than once led the people out into the squares in the mid-1990s, but has now become a busy functionary of the United Russia party and interpreter of Putin's ideas on television. In contrast, Alexey Kondaurov, a Deputy of the Communist Party and former KGB general, voted against, describing the law as 'an attack on citizens' rights and freedoms'. The Communists are becoming the most progressive party. How is one to live in Russia between the Scylla of Putin and the Charybdis of the Communists?

(Interestingly enough, Putin waited for the right moment and then said of the law against protest meetings, 'That's going too far! We need something milder.' The Duma promptly reconvened and softened the law, all live on television, under the eyes of the entire nation. It is once again permissible to hold meetings near state institutions and in central squares.)

12 April

I work at *Novaya gazeta*, and published frames from a video made in March 2000 by a Russian soldier in Chechnya, which somehow found its way to me.

The video shows fighters who have surrendered. The assault on the village of Komsomolskoye in February–March 2000 was, after the siege of Grozny in the winter of 1999–2000, the second-largest operation of the Second Chechen War. At that time, retreating from Grozny, the field commander Ruslan Gelaev led more than 1,500 men to his home village of Komsomolskoye.

A terrible siege began, using all manner of military technology and leading to the deaths of most of the people in the village. When Komsomolskoye had been almost completely destroyed, Gelaev and some of his fighters miraculously escaped through the several cordons of besiegers. Those remaining were promised an amnesty if they surrendered; 72 men, as the high command officially announced in March 2000, were given amnesty by the Federal Government.

They were 'amnestied', but immediately arrested. Since then the families of only three of them know where they are: the rest did not return. The video shows these 'amnestied' men being unloaded from two prison vans into a goods wagon at the Chechen railway station of Chervlenaya. The transfer was recorded by officers of a Special Operations unit of the Russian Ministry of Justice.

The video is like a feature film about a fascist concentration camp. This is precisely the way the guards behave, their assault rifles at the ready, lined out down a hill, at the bottom of which is the railway track with the waiting wagon. The soldiers keep their guns trained on those being thrown from the vans. Among the fighters we see two women. They are clothed and, unlike the men, have not been beaten up. They are immediately taken to one side.

The remainder, men and boys (one is clearly 15 or 16 years old), are flung from the vans or themselves jump to the ground. They are all in bad physical shape, some being carried by their friends. All are wounded. Some are without legs, some without arms; the ear of one of them is hanging off, half-severed. The soldiers can be heard out of shot commenting, 'Look, they didn't take that one's ear off properly.' Many are completely naked, barefoot and covered in blood. Their clothing and footwear are tossed out of the vehicles separately. The fighters are completely exhausted. Some do not understand what is required of them and stumble about in confusion. Some are insane.

On the video the soldiers beat them in a routine, automatic sort of way, as if they are doing it only out of habit. There are no doctors to be seen. Some of the stronger fighters are ordered to pull from the vans the bodies of those who have died during the transfer and drag them to one side. At the end of the video there is a mountain of corpses of the amnestied prisoners by the railway track.

The federals do not physically touch the fighters, only using their boots and the muzzles of their rifles. They are plainly revolted by them. They use the toe of their boots to turn the faces of the dead in order to stare at them. This seems to be purely out of curiosity. Nobody is writing anything down, registering anything, recording deaths. No documents are being compiled. At the end there is a discussion between the federals, accompanied by laughter: 'They said there were seventy-two of them, but we've got seventy-four. Okay, never mind, a couple of spares.'

What happened when the frames from this record of our own Abu Ghraib were published? Nothing. Nobody turned a hair, neither the public, nor the media, nor the Procurator's Office. Many foreign journalists borrowed the video from me, and in Poland the headline over the pictures was 'The Russian Abu Ghraib'. In Russia there was silence.

What happens in Ingushetia reflects what happens in Moscow. After Putin's re-election there has been a complete purge of all sources of information, mirroring the purge of the political arena. Now anybody who doesn't want to know doesn't need to know. The majority prefer not to.

14 April

In Ukraine Prime Minister Yanukovych has been declared the successor of President Kuchma. He will be the authorities' candidate in the presidential election. Will Putin really support this Yanukovych? It is beyond belief.

The lawyer Stanislav Markelov was attacked at midnight in the Moscow Metro by five youths. They shouted, 'You've made a few speeches too many!' and 'You had this coming' as they beat him up, stole his documents and his lawyer's ID, ignoring his valuables.

Markelov is a young, very active lawyer. In the case against ex-Colonel Budanov he defended the interests of the Chechen family of Elza Kungaeva, whom Budanov raped and murdered. For this he has been subjected to constant attacks by 'patriots'. He acted for the prosecution in 'The Case of The Cadet', against a federal soldier, Sergey Lapin, whose codename in Chechnya was 'The Cadet'. For the first time in our recent history, an officer was sentenced to 12 years' imprisonment for the abduction of a Chechen in Grozny who subsequently 'disappeared'.

The militia refused to open a criminal case following the attack on Markelov. Who beat him up, and who ordered them to, remains unknown.

16 April

There is new evidence about the abduction of the Senior Assistant Procurator of Ingushetia, Rashid Ozdoev, just before Putin's re-election.

A letter has been sent to the Procurator-General of Russia, Vladimir Ustinov, from one Igor Onishchenko. It was received and registered as Item 1556 by the Secretariat of the Procurator-General's Office for the Southern Federal District on 16 April 2004.

This letter is addressed to you from an agent of the Stavropol Regional FSB. I have been working for the FSB of Ingushetia on a special mission. The period of my commission has ended and I have returned home. I worked as an agent of the FSB for almost 12 years, but never imagined I would be so tormented.

Koryakov, Director of the FSB of Ingushetia, is a dreadful person to have in our system, although he claims to have been sent to work there by Patrushev [the national head of the FSB] and Putin personally. This contemptible louse destroys people solely because they are Ingushes or Chechens. He has some grudge and hates them.

Koryakov forced me and my colleagues – there were five of us working for him – to systematically beat up everybody we arrested, while pretending to be agents of ROSh. Everything was planned: special clothing, masks, false documents, camouflage, vehicles (which usually belonged to those who had been arrested, but with the number plates changed), special passes. While pretending to take the victims away from [Nazran], we would usually circle and return in different vehicles to our building, where we carried on beating the people. All this was done at night. During the day we slept. Koryakov had to report to Moscow that the work was proceeding and to justify the title of general, which he had recently been awarded. For this there was a plan requiring processing of at least five persons per week. In early 2003, when I had just arrived, we really did arrest people who were up to something. But after Koryakov went ape over what he called 'some Procurator', we started pulling in people without any grounds, just going by their appearance. Koryakov said what difference does it make, they are all lice. Personally Sergey and I crippled more than 50 people. We buried about 35.

Today I have returned home. I have been rewarded for irreproachable service because of the last operation to take out the local Procurator, because he had compromising material on Koryakov. I destroyed the ID and personal weapon of the Procurator and broke all his limbs. That night Koryakov gave orders to some different people to get rid of him.

I am guilty. I am ashamed. This is the pure truth. Igor N. Onishchenko.

(Even after this monstrous document was published, nothing changed. There was no popular protest, and the Procurator's Office just let it slide.)

22–3 April

A meeting between Kuchma and Putin in the Crimea. This is the moment Putin decides whether or not to support Yanukovych. So far it looks as though he will not, thank God. Yanukovych was not invited into the meeting, although he was waiting in the wings the whole time.

28 April

At 11.20 a.m., on Staraya Basmannaya Street in Moscow, a hitman shot Georgii Tal at point-blank range. Tal was a fledgling of the Yeltsin nest, the Director from 1997 to 2001 of the Federal Service for Financial Recovery and Bankruptcy. Tal died in hospital this evening without recovering consciousness. His murder is part of a process of destroying those involved in the redistribution of Russia's prime industrial assets through an organised system of bankrupting enterprises. During Tal's years as Director there was a reallocation of ownership, primarily of the oil and aluminium industries, by this means. Under Putin many criminal bankruptcies have begun to be investigated. It is a factor in the Yukos case. The aim of the investigations is to carry out a new redistribution in favour of Putin's supporters.

In fact, the system of bankruptcy under Yeltsin was perfectly legal, and it was exploited by all those who are today the wealthiest people in the country, the oligarchs who made their fortunes under Yeltsin. Putin has a rabid hatred of most of these. Few people doubt that Tal was murdered to prevent him from speaking about the principles on which the Bankruptcy Service operated. He simply knew too much about those who are now highly influential. The murder of insolvency practitioners by hitmen was itself part of the business of bankruptcy in Russia.

Tal was a key professional in the management of the property of bankrupt enterprises. After 2002 he headed a non-profit partnership called the Inter-Regional Self-Regulated Organisation of Professional Insolvency Administrators. The organisation existed under the aegis of the Russian Union of Industrialists and Entrepreneurs, and mainly advised members of the Board of the RUIE on who should be bankrupted and when, so that the enterprise could be put in administration. These are our oligarchs: Oleg Deripaska, Vladimir Potanin, Alexey Mordashev, Mikhail Fridman and others. It is unlikely, however, that Tal's murder was in the interests of these people.

The murder caused no surprise at his own organisation, at the RUIE, among big business or the government bureaucracy. The general population was even less surprised. As if that was perfectly fine.

Late April

We lived through April with the feeling of being constantly deceived, a sensation that suited many, who wanted just that.

We lived also in anticipation of another piece of offensiveness, arranged for 7 May: Putin's second inauguration. You could not exactly say that the air was filled with anticipation. The majority of the population really don't care what sort of inauguration there is, or whether it takes place at all.

On the eve of major official events it is traditional in Russia to pause and reflect on the future. An inauguration might be expected to prompt the main political players to tell us what their plans are for the period between now and 2007.

There is none of this. Total silence from the opposition tells us that it has caved in. The failure to generate any new movements tells us that the 'old' opposition will be in no state to fight for seats in the Duma in 2007, or to put forward credible presidential candidates in 2008. Nobody believes in revolution, either.

The Kremlin's social-survey unit, TsIOM, asked the Russian public, 'If there were mass demonstrations in your region by the population in defence of their rights, would you take part?' Only 25 per cent answered 'yes'. Sixty-six per cent said 'no'. We shall not be having a revolution any time soon.

7 May

Putin's inauguration in the Kremlin. A demonstration of our First Citizen's autocratic power and magnificence, of his separateness and remoteness.

Even from his own wife. During the live television broadcast the commentators actually said, 'Among those invited to the solemn ceremony of President Putin's taking of office is the wife of Vladimir Vladimirovich, Lyudmila Putina.' It is laughable of course, and people did laugh, but not very cheerfully. She stood throughout the inauguration among the VIPs, behind a barrier past which Putin trotted down the red carpet.

He arrived alone, marched past his wife to the podium, then back to the Tsar's Porch to review the parade. All the time alone. No friends, no family. The man is barking mad. It is a sure sign that he trusts nobody, and that is a fundamental characteristic of Putin's rule. The concomitant is the certainty that only he, Putin, knows what is best for the country.

We do not really know what the inauguration of a leader is like in other countries. Is it a time of popular celebration? Or is it, as in Russia, merely an embarrassment?

9 May

Akhmed-hadji Kadyrov, Putin's main placeman in Chechnya, has been assassinated. He had attended Putin's inauguration and yesterday flew back to Chechnya, not disguising his displeasure at the place allocated to him by Putin's entourage. He was in the second hall, not in the first ranks of the most honoured guests, and saw it as a worrying cooling of the First Citizen towards him.

He had good cause to be nervous. Putin was his only hope of power and survival. Kadyrov had presided over the process of 'Chechenisation' of the conflict in his republic, the initiation of a civil war between Chechens, with the Kremlin supporting the 'good' ones who side with Kadyrov and Putin against the ones who are 'not on our side' and have to be exterminated.

Kadyrov was killed while viewing the Victory Day parade at the Dinamo Stadium in Grozny. The explosive device was concreted into the supports beneath the grandstand.

*

There were persistent rumours that Kadyrov was blown up by 'our people'. His security in the last months of his life meant that nobody but 'our people' could get anywhere near him. Whenever he appeared in public, everything was cordoned off far in advance and checked repeatedly for explosives. Those responsible for Kadyrov's assassination were never found, no matter how frequently we were shown on television how hard everyone was trying.

Who are 'our people' in this context? Agents of the Federal Special Operations Units working in Chechnya. State hitmen. Soldiers of the Central Intelligence Directorate of the Army, the GRU; the Centre for Special Missions of the Federal Security Bureau; and secret sub-sections of the FSB for carrying out particularly sensitive missions, which usually means assassinations.

On 9 May it seemed that Kadyrov's death, no matter at whose hands he died, spelled the end of Chechenisation and, with it, of Putin's moronic policy in the North Caucasus. Kadyrov, people supposed, had been removed in order to bring this policy to an end. The surmise was short-lived. On the evening of 9 May the murdered President's psychopathic and extremely stupid younger son, Ramzan Kadyrov*, was illogically elevated to prominence in Chechnya. Ramzan had been in charge of his father's personal security, into which he had brought all the criminal dross of Chechnya, attracting them with promises of immunity from prosecution.

Putin received Ramzan in the Kremlin that evening. He turned up in a bright-blue tracksuit and gave Putin every assurance that he would continue the policy of Chechenisation begun by his father. The meeting was shown on all television channels and seen throughout Chechnya, and made it clear that Kadyrov's gangs were being granted immunity to carry on as before. For some reason Putin's Administration had suspected that, after his father's death, Ramzan would make a run for it into the mountains to join the fighters. Instead he was granted permission to continue to terrorise the population of the Republic.

This led to even more divisiveness and violence in Chechnya in order to underpin the position of the vacuous Ramzan Kadyrov. The armed Resistance was strengthened by an influx of new volunteers after the death of Kadyrov Senior, but people were soon humbly bowing down before the new idiot, and in no time at all he deluded himself that he actually was of real significance.

26 May

Putin has delivered his annual Address to the Federal Assembly. This is how the Russian people are informed of the President's plans for the coming year. He was on top form and in aggressive mood. He talked with total contempt about civil society, claiming it was all corrupt and that the defenders of human rights were a fifth column feeding from the hand of the West. The following is a verbatim quotation: 'For some of these organisations [of civil society] their first priority is to obtain finance from influential foreign foundations . . . When there is a problem with fundamental and basic violations of human rights, infringement of the real interests of the people, the voices of these organisations are sometimes not heard at all. This is hardly surprising. They simply cannot bite the hand that feeds them.'

*

Thereafter, of course, Putin's absurd attack on human-rights campaigners was vigorously taken up by the officials of his Administration, primarily by his chief ideologist and spin doctor, Vladislav Surkov. Human-rights campaigners attending protest meetings against the war in Chechnya subsequently carried placards reading, 'I am the West's fifth column.'

After Putin's 26 May speech, the state authorities started setting up a new variety of 'human-rights associations' under their own patronage. This came to nothing, but the idea was that this parallel civil society, 'on our side', should be financed by Russian business, the oligarchs. They stubbornly refused, no doubt mindful of the fate of Khodorkovsky, who was now in prison for having financed non-governmental organisations.

Why did Putin suddenly mount this onslaught on the human-rights associations? By the summer of 2004, after the collapse of the democratic and liberal parties, it seemed clear that if opposition was going to crystallise anywhere, it would be around the human-rights community, as in the Soviet period. That is why Putin vilified these organisations in his message, why he was so eager to discredit them.

In May the democrats remained quiescent. Ramzan Kadyrov's rise to prominence in Chechnya was the key event of the month, overshadowing the inauguration, but they made no protest. Indeed they made no comment at all.

1 June

Leonid Parfyonov, a brilliant television journalist, has been fired by the NTV television station. In his very popular news-analysis programme, *The Other Day*, he screened an interview with the wife of Zelimkhan Yandarbiev, the Chechen leader murdered in Qatar. It was fairly unexceptional, the widow said nothing particularly startling, but she was inconsolable. The topic, however, was impermissible.

Parfyonov is not an aggressive broadcaster and, if anything, sought compromises between what the authorities wanted and what he wanted to show in his programme. His sacking is political censorship of NTV.

Kakha Bendukidze, an erudite Georgian who is also a Russian industrial oligarch, has been appointed Minister of Industry in the new Georgia. Saakashvili quickly made him a citizen of the Republic.

Bendukidze was persuaded to take the job by the Georgian Prime Minister, Zurab Zhvaniya. He has announced that he intends to introduce 'ultra-liberal reforms' in his old homeland. He studiously avoided all comment on the nature of any reforms that might be needed here, but his departure speaks for itself. There is evidently no place for him as a liberal in Putin's Russia. Even before the Rose Revolution in Tbilisi,

Bendukidze had spoken both in public and in private of his disappointment with Russia's economic development and his desire to get out of business. He was already in the process of selling off his Russian business interests.

In Moscow the Central Electoral Commission is beginning a propaganda campaign to get the electorate to accept the abolition of the right to vote in the Duma elections for individual candidates in constituency seats, rather than for parties through a system of proportional representation. This is a right we fought for stubbornly and it is vitally important in our post-Communist society. The Kremlin's aim is to allow people to vote only for party lists. They also intend to increase the share of the vote required before a party is allowed to be represented in Parliament. In other words, only major parties will be allowed to participate in elections.

Such a system would return us to the Soviet past. It would make it impossible to form new parliamentary parties, and new non-parliamentary parties would be marginalised. The effect would be to enable the Kremlin to deal only with two or three 'old' parties, which have already shown themselves capable of accepting major compromise. The Communist Party, the Liberal Democratic Party and, with some reservations, the Rodina party would operate under the pre-eminence of that bloated party of bureaucrats, United Russia.

The underlying aim is to enable the Kremlin to take away the unpredictability of elections. The planned result will be the actual result. The democratic parties will instantly be marginalised, because support for Yabloko and the Union of Right Forces is below the 7 per cent threshold on which the Presidential Administration is insisting. This proposal was immediately referred to as if it were a done deal by Alexander Veshnyakov, the far-from-independent Director of the Commission.

Veshnyakov explained that elections based on proportional representation could become law in June 2005 by introducing amendments to the law 'On Basic Guarantees of Electoral Rights and of the Right to Participate in a Referendum of Citizens of the Russian Federation'.

*

That is exactly what happened. It was explained that the new system was 'more responsible'. There were no protest demonstrations, and only human-rights campaigners tried to warn the Parliamentary Assembly of the Council of Europe and European leaders that Russia no longer had a democratic electoral system. The Europeans noted that there had been no popular protest, so they accepted it too.

2 June

In Chechnya, Zelimkhan Kadyrov, the elder son of Akhmed-hadji Kadyrov, has been buried. It was well known that he was a drug addict, and he died of a heart attack three weeks after the assassination of his father. Relatives of the Kadyrovs said Zelimkhan was completely opposed to the brutal policies of his father and younger brother and took refuge in heroin.

19 June

In St Petersburg, Nikolai Girenko has been shot dead in his flat. This is a political murder of a well-known human-rights champion and anti-fascist scholar. The murder was carried out by Russian fascists, who made no secret of the fact. It was a show of strength on their part. First they passed a 'death sentence' on Girenko, posted it on the Internet, the state authorities ignored it and then Girenko was killed in accordance with their 'sentence'.

Who was Girenko? He was a St Petersburg academic ethnographer, a prominent research fellow of the Peter the Great Museum of Anthropology and Ethnography of the Russian Academy of Sciences. He was called as an expert witness in the very infrequent court cases brought against fascist organisations. He would analyse the texts of radical nationalist publications and the manifestos of neo-Nazi groups and demonstrate that they were extremist. His forensic analyses were precise and scholarly and were often the basis on which neo-Nazis were convicted. These trials are rare. In 2003, of 72 crimes identified as being racially motivated, only 11 made it to court. The other cases collapsed when investigators were either unable or, more commonly, unwilling to prove racial motivation.

The neo-Nazis hated Girenko because when he was an expert witness, they often received prison sentences, rather than the more usual pardon or suspended sentence. He testified at the beginning of this month at the trial in Novgorod of members of a local branch of the Russian National Unity Party.

Few scholars will today agree to give evidence in open court at such trials. They are afraid of retaliation from the fascists, who enjoy the support of the state authorities and of a significant proportion of the population. They cannot rely on witness protection schemes, because the law-enforcement agencies are themselves shot through with chauvinism and xenophobia. They always have been, but the Putin period and the Second Chechen War have seen an upsurge of hysterical fear of those from the Caucasus.

'When I heard about Girenko's murder, I was sure there would be a wave of social protest,' the writer Alla Gerber, President of the Holocaust Foundation, commented. Until December she had been a long-standing Duma Deputy of the Union of Right Forces. Once again, however, there was no protest, only a wave of social satisfaction as the websites of the nationalistic organisations posted the joyful news of Girenko's murder. 'Nationalists were jubilant to hear the news of the death of this academic!' The Russian National Unity Party announced that they 'heard of the untimely demise of this anti-fascist with a sense of relief'. The Slavic Union (its initials in Russian are 'SS') displayed a poster which, they stated, had been prepared in advance of the shooting. It depicts a young man in the uniform of a nationalist stormtrooper with a pistol. The caption reads: 'In memoriam Girenko'. Nobody stopped them. The Procurator's Office had nothing to say, let alone take the action that the law required. None of the sites was closed. Their owners will face no criminal charges.

At the same time, a list of 'foes of the Russian people' was posted on the website of another ultra-nationalist organisation, the Greater Russia Party. It lists 47 names, including that of Svetlana Gannushkina, Director of Citizens' Aid, the major association assisting refugees and those forced to resettle. Alla Gerber is also there, the President of the Holocaust Foundation, a well-known champion in the fight against anti-Semitism in Russia. So too is Andrey Kozyrev, ex-Minister of Foreign Affairs, for his pro-Western leanings; as are the television presenters Nikolai Svanidze, because he is a Georgian and, incidentally, a relative of Stalin, and Yelena Khanga, because her mother was married to an African. So too is the author of these lines.

The Slavic Union claims: 'It is well known that numerous so-called human-rights associations, generally made up of venal non-Russian human-rights campaigners and surviving on funds from foreign well-wishers, foundations closely related to the CIA, MI6 and Mossad, are compiling dossiers against Russian activists.' Lower down, the leader of the SS, Dmitry Demushkin, openly threatens those on the list: 'The Night of the Long Knives is near!'

There is no doubt that all this vileness has been triggered by the murder of Girenko – which the state authorities were reluctant to disclose, and even attempted to hush up – but also by the example from above of how one should deal with 'venal human-rights campaigners'. In his Address to the Federal Assembly, Putin used almost the same words as the SS.

21–2 June

During the night, the five-year-long 'anti-terrorist operation' reached its apotheosis when fighters took control of Ingushetia.

Some time after 11.00 p.m. I started receiving phone calls from the Republic, where I have many friends. 'Something terrible is going on here! It's a war!' women were screaming into the telephone. 'Help us! Do something! We are lying on the floor with the children!' I could hear the rattle of rifle fire and a lot of people shouting 'Allahu akbar! [Allah is great!]'

The virtual war over the telephone went on until dawn, the whole night filled with a sense of helplessness. At night in Moscow there is nothing you can do to help anyone. The television stations have closed down, the news-service staff have gone home. The law-enforcement agencies have switched off their mobile phones and are sleeping. You can murder if you like, you can steal, but the generals will only give orders in the morning.

That is what happened in Ingushetia. When the fighters began leaving at dawn the soldiers, with whom Ingushetia and the adjacent regions are overrun, finally came out from their 'positions of permanent deployment' and started organising a pursuit. Helicopters thundered overhead, air support appeared.

It was too late. The fighters had left. Bodies lay in the streets, both civilian and uniformed. The great majority of the dead were militiamen from the Interior Ministry of Ingushetia, from the Nazran Office of Internal Affairs and the Karabulak Militia Department. Procurators and FSB agents had also been killed. Middle-ranking officers of the security agencies of Ingushetia had been cut down, vehicles and buildings burned out. It became clear that more than 200 fighters had managed to take complete control of Nazran, and that there had been simultaneous raids in the town of Karabulak and the hill village of Sleptsovskaya. They had set up roadblocks wherever they wanted, and killed anyone arriving at them whose ID indicated that they worked for the law-enforcement agencies, along with others who just happened to fall into their hands.

Witnesses claimed that those manning the roadblocks were Chechens, Ingushes and people 'of Slavonic appearance', all of whom said they were with Shamil Basaev*.

Can Basaev, then, muster a 200-strong group? When all the security agencies, including those in Chechnya, have been reporting to their superiors for the past three years that there are no more than 50 fighters left, and perhaps as few as 20 or 30?

This was a brilliantly organised guerrilla operation of which the intelligence services gave no warning, an operation resisted neither by the half-witted Kadyrov and his regiment (which may scare the Kremlin, but evidently does not scare Basaev); nor by the thousands of Russian soldiers in Hankala; nor even the further thousands in reserve in Mozdok; nor by the 58th Army, based in Ossetia where some of the fighters had come from. There are also more than 14,000 militiamen in Chechnya, and 6,000 in Ingushetia.

So do the intelligence services actually exist? Does Kadyrov's regiment? The 14,000 militiamen plus another 6,000 in Ingushetia? Are Hankala and Mozdok really there?

The raid on Ingushetia proves that, as a genuinely effective security force, they do not. Our system of defence is as virtual as Putin, created purely to make a show of fighting, but not actually to fight. This is precisely why all those thousands of people disappear without trace after encountering 'unidentified masked soldiers wearing camouflage'. Someone needs to send his superiors a new 'anti-terrorist' report. He needs a result. These 'forces' are capable only of furtive abduction and looting. That's all the Russian Army and security forces are good for now.

Those reckless people who left their homes in the night and went to the fighters' roadblocks to ask them to leave discovered that the 'invaders' included just as many of their own people, Ingushes, as Chechens.

When, in the winter and spring of this past year, the abductions began on a grand scale, and young people in Ingushetia began taking to the hills rather than endure it any longer, the authorities brought down thunder and lightning on the heads of those who said openly that this was enormously dangerous and would lead to an escalation of the war. They continued to insist on their own stability. On 22 June that myth cost almost 100 lives. The militiamen who defended themselves and, waiting in vain for help to arrive, died in battle, carried out their duty to the end. But who takes responsibility for the civilian deaths?

The fighters, of course, bear full criminal responsibility for all these deaths, but equally culpable are the so-called state authorities. They never tire of telling us that they 'take responsibility for everything'. The authorities have lied, done nothing, worried only about staying in power, and thereby condemned innocent people to death.

Where was Zyazikov during this night? Zyazikov ran away, disguised as a woman. He dismissed his bodyguard in order not to be identified from his security detail and returned only when the danger was past, when people were searching among the corpses for their loved ones. It was unheard-of behaviour for a man, and not only in the Caucasus. While all this grand nonsense remains in place, with Zyazikov as a condign part of the system, and if Putin does not change his blinkered rampaging in Chechnya, which is entirely without a future, for the tactic of peace, tragedies like that of 22 June are inevitable. Our collective lying over many years about the Chechen War, our failure even to learn from *Nord-Ost*, has brought about these monstrous events in Ingushetia.

We simply must seek a political way out of this dead end.

23 June

Twenty-four hours after the tragedy, while funerals were taking place all over Ingushetia, Alu Alkhanov, Minister of the Interior of Chechnya, announced to the television cameras that he would be standing as a candidate for the post of President of Chechnya. Alkhanov is one of those personally responsible for failing to catch Basaev, but is nevertheless being presented every hour as Putin's preferred candidate. Putting himself forward, Alkhanov said how much he was looking forward to 'peaceful elections on 29 August', and that the main thing now was to consolidate Chechnya's agriculture. He seemed quite oblivious of how objectionable it was to come out with all this one day after the catastrophe in Ingushetia.

1 July

A discussion was held at the Svyato-Danilovsky Monastery in Moscow on the topic of 'Freedom and Personal Dignity: the Orthodox and Liberal Views'. Rostislav Shafarevich was there, at one time a colleague and friend of Andrey Sakharov, but today a terrible reactionary and defender of Putin. Ella Pamfilova was present, the Director of the Presidential Commission for the Development of Civil Society and Human Rights. There were also present Deacon Andrey Kuraev and Archpriest Vsevolod Chaplin. The round table busily set about elaborating Vladislav Surkov's concept of a Russian model for defending human rights: in the first place, it would be funded by Russian business; and in the second, it would be based on Russian Orthodox ethics.

What about those who are not Orthodox? Muslims? Jews? Will they be excluded from defending human rights? The human-rights movement is by its very nature supranational and supraconfessional. In any case, if we are to believe Dostoevsky, the Russian is a 'universal man'.

That, however, is neither here nor there. Putin has instructed the Russian Orthodox Church to flesh out what he was talking about in his Address to the Federal Assembly, to replace 'Western' defence of human rights by 'Orthodox' defence of human rights. In order to prove yet again its loyalty to the authorities, and in return for being made the main state religion under Putin, the Russian Orthodox Church has agreed. Metropolitan Kirill gave a deeply felt speech on the need to find new leaders for the human-rights movement 'who love our country'. He seems to have no inkling that 'finding new leaders for the human-rights movement' is simply not possible. They either are there, generated by life itself, or they are not.

Ella Pamfilova also spoke. At one time she was an enthusiastic democrat who campaigned against the privileges of party bigwigs. Now she enthusiastically supported Putin and his new attitude towards human-rights workers. She said, 'I do not agree that we have a crisis of ideology in the human-rights movement. There can be no crisis of something that by definition cannot exist! There is a crisis in particular human-rights associations whose leaders, who in many ways are still in the last century, are trying to fight a totalitarian state that disappeared long ago. They are accustomed to appealing to the leaders of Western states to try to influence our state authorities. I repeat, we ought not to associate the whole human-rights movement in Russia with five or ten well-known people, most of them from the old days, who long ago confused campaigning for human rights with politics, who still regularly confuse one thing with the other, radically defend positions that have no support among the majority of the population or the informed public. I do not think they represent a great danger for us. I believe that we are now witnessing the birth of a human-rights movement of a new quality in Russia . . . and that there are many young leaders of human-rights organisations who are working in the interests of our people . . .'

There certainly are, but they are not going to gladden the heart of Pamfilova. The radicalisation of young people is an obvious fact. The children of the defeated Yabloko and Union of Right Forces supporters are going off to join the National Bolsheviks, the party of Limonov*.

The final act in the destruction of Yukos has begun. Overnight on 1–2 July the company's accounts were frozen. The extraction of oil has ceased, causing the oil price to jump sharply on the world's markets. Yukos offered a package of shares in the Sibneft oil company to settle their new debts. The state turned the deal down, insisting on the liquidation of Yukos. It is a calamity and amounts to what President Putin likes to refer to as 'kicking the shit out of them'. Nobody cares.

6 July

A meeting in the Chechen hill village of Sernovodskaya to demand the return of the latest group of men abducted by the federals has been dispersed with gunfire. Women from the neighbouring village of Assinovskaya and from the district town of Akhchoy-Martan blocked the state highway with the same demand: stop these arbitrary abductions of their sons, husbands and brothers. Nothing changed. Only human-rights campaigners in Russia itself supported these protests.

7 July

In the Chechen town of Shali there has been a gathering of the mothers of those who have been abducted. The women state that they are prepared to go on hunger strike indefinitely, their patience exhausted by the failure of the law-enforcement agencies to search for the victims. They ask that European human-rights campaigners and international organisations should hear their cry of despair for a simplification of the procedure for according refugee status to Chechens. 'We have been driven out of Ingushetia, we are being murdered and our sons kidnapped in Chechnya, and in Russia we are second-class citizens.' Such is the resolution of the gathering.

That same night federal forces furtively continued taking men from their homes in Grozny, Nazran and Karabulak. There is a flood of letters from Chechnya to Strasbourg.

9 July

The latest atrocious death of a Russian soldier killed by the Russian Army.

Soldiers die in the Army for all sorts of reasons; the Army has made it easy for them to be killed. You may be keen to serve, you may have enlisted before you had to, like Yevgeny Fomovsky, but that will not save you. There will be scum who take a dislike to you, or who don't like your size, or the size of your feet, and they will kill you.

'His schoolfriends were taking their final exams while my son was being buried,' Yevgeny's mother, Svetlana, tells me. She is from the town of Yarovoye in the Altai Region. 'Zhenya took all his exams early in order to be in time for the spring conscription into the Army.'

'Why?'

'In order to get it over with more quickly, in order not to be harassed by the local Military Commissariat, and then to go on to college.'

Things didn't turn out that way. Yevgeny Fomovsky's career in the Army lasted from 31 May to 9 July, less than one and a half months. He arrived at his FSB border-guards unit on the outskirts of Priargunsk in Chita Province on 8 June. On 4 July he swore allegiance. On 6 July this big, healthy Siberian was sent into the hills, to a summer training camp 12 kilometres from Priargunsk. At dawn on 9 July Yevgeny was found hanged using two belts tied together, by the wall of a half-ruined building 100 metres from the training camp tents. At nine o'clock that evening the postman arrived at Altaiskaya Street in Yarovoye with a telegram that read, 'Your son, Fomovsky, Yevgeny Anatolievich, committed suicide on 9 July 2004. Advise place of burial immediately. Date of dispatch of coffin to be notified separately. Commanding Officer of Military Unit . . .'

So what had happened? Yevgeny was strong and well equipped to be a soldier. He was an accomplished sportsman, and by the time he was 18 he had acquired several Army skills. The Army, however, does not need educated conscripts, it wants squaddies. The root of the tragedy is that Private Yevgeny Fomovsky took size-47 boots and was 1 metre 96 tall. He was issued with size-44 Army boots and forced to wear them during a daily five-kilometre cross-country run in 40-degree heat.

Torturing new conscripts is a way of life in the Russian Army. By the day before his 'suicide', Yevgeny was no longer able to walk in anything other than slippers.

'When we went to the mortuary, his longest toe was rubbed down to the bone,' his aunt, Yekaterina Mikhailovna, tells me.

Russia is a big country. When Yevgeny's mother and aunt set out from Yarovoye on the five-day journey to Priargunsk to visit him, they had no idea what was awaiting them. 'We were too late,' his mother weeps. 'We arrived in Priargunsk on 10 July, and on 9 July Zhenya died.' Priargunsk is a town on the remote border of our land with China and Mongolia. The mortuary is a building attached to the District Hospital.

'When we were at the mortuary I saw Zhenya,' his aunt Yekaterina tells me. There was a mark on his neck, apparently from a noose. There were cuts on his left wrist. We were told that Zhenya had first tried to open his veins. His whole body had been beaten, his head was covered in bruises. It was soft to the touch as if there were no bones there, they had all been broken. On the back of his head there was a clear indentation from some heavy object. His sexual organs were swollen and crushed: they were one enormous black bruise. His legs were swollen, just one wound after another, braised as if he had been dragged. His back had all the skin flayed from it, also as if he had been dragged. There was a burn on his foot. There were bruises on his shoulders as if somebody had been pressing down hard on them. I think he was tortured, and then hanged in order to cover up the murder.'

Yevgeny had not wanted to submit to the torment of his undersized boots and had been demanding the proper size. They decided to teach him a lesson in accordance with long-established Army practice: with the blessing of the officers, this is carried out by the 'grandads' – sergeants, soldiers in their second year of service, older servicemen. The officers expect them to 'maintain order' in the barracks.

The fact that Yevgeny was murdered was later confirmed by first-year soldiers who said his tormentors hadn't meant to kill him, just to teach him a lesson so that he didn't try to get above himself. They overdid it and Yevgeny died while he was being tortured. The murderers then decided to pretend he had committed suicide.

The tragedy of Private Fomovsky, 18, killed because his feet were too big, did not cause any particular public outcry at such savagery in the Army. Nobody insisted that the Minister of Defence, Sergey Ivanov, and the Director of the FSB, Nikolai Patrushev, should undertake to ensure the future provision for our soldiers of an orderly environment, with food, clothing and footwear fit for human beings; or that they should accept personal responsibility for the lives of the young men we conscript.

Everything went on just as before, until the next unlawful killing of a soldier.

Late that same evening, Paul Klebnikov, the Editor-in-Chief of the

Russian edition of *Forbes* magazine, was fatally wounded. Klebnikov was a descendant of the Decembrist Pushchin, a friend of Alexander Pushkin; he was an American who had long been researching the development of oligarchy in the new Russia. The murder of Klebnikov was a puzzle, and the suggestion by the law-enforcement agencies that the perpetrators were Chechens taking revenge for a badly written book about the adventurist Hoj-Akhmed Noukhaev is manifest nonsense. They were in a flap because they couldn't solve a crime that caused widespread international outrage. Noukhaev is a strange, contradictory figure. At one time a field commander, he left the Resistance and started representing himself as a philosopher, which he was not. His authority was never great among the Chechens, and it is difficult to imagine anyone carrying out a murder on his behalf.

Mukhamed Tsikanov has been appointed Vice-President of Yukos-Moscow, the holding company of Yukos. A former Deputy Minister of Economic Development, Tsikanov is in reality an emissary of the state inserted to ensure a 'correct' sell-off. Needless to say, Tsikanov is wholly in the pocket of the state authorities. Before this he was engaged in the 'restoration of Chechnya', an enterprise admitted to have been a failure, even though all the money in the budget was spent. The man in charge of all that enjoys his life without untoward consequences, and has even been promoted.

10 July

The last edition of Savik Shuster's *Free Speech* has been broadcast on NTV. The only remaining political talk show anywhere on Russian national television has been axed. The *Personal Affairs* programme has been closed down too, also on NTV. It was a weekly news-analysis programme run by Alexander Gerasimov. Gerasimov was the Deputy Director-General for news of NTV, and he too is leaving. The crushing of all free-thinking and unpredictability on Russian television is a fait accompli.

16–17 July

In the Chechen hill village of Sernovodskaya on the border of Chechnya and Ingushetia, soldiers arrived in armoured personnel carriers and abducted six men: the two Indarbiev brothers, one a major in the militia;

the three Inkemirov brothers, aged 15–19; and the disabled Anzor Lukaev. A protest meeting held by their womenfolk to demand their return was dispersed by warning gunfire. The first to fire were bodyguards of Alu Alkhanov, the 'Chairman of the Public Committee for the Restoration of Chechnya'. He is the leading presidential candidate, a member of the militia and Minister of the Interior – the same Alu Alkhanov who never tires of telling us on television that 'the wave of abductions is declining, we have succeeded in achieving that'. It is easier to make that claim when you shoot at anyone who reminds you that it is not the case.

20 July

At about 4.00 a.m. today in Galashki, Ingushetia, Beslan Arapkhanov, a tractor driver, was beaten up in front of his wife and seven small children before being shot dead. By mistake. The security forces were attempting to arrest the fighter Ruslan Khuchbarov. According to highly secret intelligence, Khuchbarov was sleeping that night at No. 11 Partizanskaya Street.

For some reason, however, the soldiers came and shot the guiltless Arapkhanov at No. 1 Partizanskaya Street. Immediately after the murder, an officer entered the Arapkhanovs' house, introducing himself to the shocked wife as FSB Investigator Kostenko, and presented a warrant to search 'No. 11 Partizanskaya Street'. At this point the error became evident, but Kostenko did not so much as apologise to the grieving widow.

That is the reality of our 'anti-terrorist operation'. What are the seven children of Beslan Arapkhanov going to make of this? What chance is there that they will forgive and forget?

*

Kostenko was not to apologise either to the mothers of the children who died in the subsequent terrorist atrocity at the First School in the town of Beslan, which was directed by the same Khuchbarov whom Kostenko had failed to arrest.

23 July

The team investigating the *Nord-Ost* hostage-taking has been disbanded. In three months' time it will be the second anniversary of *Nord-Ost* and the public have wearied of hearing about it. This is precisely why the investigation has been wound up, even though it had yet to identify most of the terrorists, to establish the composition of the gas with which people were poisoned or say who took the decision to use it.

An inquiry that was of crucial importance to the political progress of the Russian state has been put on ice. Of the entire team, supposedly 'a group of our best investigators working to repay a debt of honour', as our official spokesmen put it, there remains in their empty rooms at the Moscow Procurator's Office only Mr V.I. Kalchuk.

He is meeting those who have suffered – hostages who survived and relatives of those who died – and gives them his findings to read: there was no criminal guilt on the part of any of the personnel of the security agencies, who used a deadly gas to simplify the 'rescue operation', at the cost of 129 lives and the health of hundreds of others.

His findings are shocking in their cynicism. In the document everything is blamed on Basaev:

> Investigator V.I. Kalchuk established: that Basaev after 1995 . . . devised . . . committed . . . selected . . . delegated . . . an international search warrant was issued through Interpol on 5 May 2003 . . . under the pretext of fighting for the freedom and independence of the illegal, self-proclaimed state of Ichkeria . . . in the period indicated, in order to induce the state institutions of the Russian Federation to take a decision to withdraw troops from the territory of the Chechen Republic where an antiterrorist operation is being conducted, did conspire with leaders of an illegal armed grouping and of Chechen separatists not identified by the investigation to cause explosions in densely-populated and socially important places and to take hostage a large number of people . . .

One might reasonably expect the report to conclude that it was Basaev himself who was guilty of leaving the intelligence services no option but to use a deadly chemical. Basaev's guilt, however, is described only in the Preamble. There is not a word about him in the concluding section, which considers the question of blame.

> At various stages of the preparations to commit the terrorist acts, Basaev and other organisers of the criminal grouping selected no fewer than 52 persons, and these became members of the group. To implement the hostage-taking the following were recruited and trained:

A terrorist unidentified by the investigation . . . corpse No. 2007,
A terrorist unidentified by the investigation . . . corpse No. 2028,
A terrorist unidentified by the investigation . . . corpse No. 2036 . . .

Who are they? Heaven only knows. And yet one of the reasons for setting up the inquiry was to attach a first name, patronymic and surname to all these unidentified individuals. Mr Kalchuk does, as we can see from his findings, know the names of one or two of the terrorists. These are the ones whose identity is known to everybody, whose names were published in the newspapers and broadcast on television.

'Faced with a serious threat to the life and health of the large number of people taken hostage, the competent agencies of the Russian Federation decided to conduct a rescue operation.' But who were these 'competent agencies'? We find that the main question relating to *Nord-Ost* – who took the decision to use the gas and, accordingly, who is responsible for these deaths – is completely side-stepped. This only increases the suspicion that the competence mentioned was primarily in concealing what really went on, by killing all the terrorists.

The final conclusion is this:

> The death of almost all the hostages was caused by acute respiratory and cardiovascular failure resulting from a life-threatening combination of adverse factors which arose during the period they were held hostage. The multiplicity of the factors causing death . . . excludes a direct causal link between the effect on the organism of a gaseous chemical substance or substances and death . . . there are no objective grounds to suppose that the use of a gaseous chemical substance or substances might have been the sole cause of death.

How is it possible to say anything about 'objective grounds' if the composition of the gas remained unknown?

These findings, signed by Mr Kalchuk, are altogether very short on fact. The most detailed moment comes when the author tries to explain why all the terrorists, without exception, were killed, even though it was officially declared a major achievement of the operation that they all lost consciousness. Mr Kalchuk is having none of that. 'They actively returned fire using 13 assault rifles and eight pistols.'

Here is the grand finale: 'As a result of a decision taken correctly by the competent agencies of the Russian Federation and the actions of skilled operatives of the intelligence services, the criminal activity of the terrorists was terminated and a much worse catastrophe averted, which might have led to undermining of the authority of Russia in the international arena.'

It is a terrible thing when the citizens of a single state have fundamentally different views on the value of human life. This is what led to the victory of the Bolsheviks and the emergence of Stalin, and this evil feature of our national life is coming relentlessly back into fashion among those who take the decisions on whether we are to live or die.

There is more: 'The application to bring criminal charges against the agents of the special services carrying out the freeing of the hostages is refused. The criminal case in respect of the terrorists who seized and detained the hostages is closed.'

The Government has been granted an indulgence from the Procurator, both for itself and for its Special Operations forces who are there to protect us from terrorists and their attacks in the future. That there will be more of these, few of us have any doubt.

27 July

Igor Sechin, the *éminence grise* of the Kremlin, a Deputy Head of Putin's Administration, has been appointed Chairman of the Board of Directors of the state oil company, Rosneft. Sechin personally oversaw the dismemberment and destruction of Yukos and the arrest of Khodorkovsky. His appointment to head Rosneft, which claims the choicest parts of Yukos, proves the Kremlin destroyed Yukos for its own benefit. Its ideology requires the formation of a 'state economy', supposedly run on behalf of the people. In reality, it is a bureaucratic economy whose principal oligarch is the government official. The higher the official, the bigger the oligarch.

This ideal of state oligarchy appeals to Putin and to an exclusive coterie around him. The underlying concept is that Russia's major revenues come from the export of raw materials, so the state should control natural resources, and '*L'État, c'est moi*'. They suppose they are the cleverest people in the country, know best what is good for the rest of us, and accordingly what those revenues should be used for. In order to service the super-monopolies of Rosneft and Gazprom, monster financial conglomerates like Vneshtorgbank are being enlarged and are conquering new territories with the aid of the Presidential Administration.

These super-monopolies are generally controlled by former secret policemen who are now oligarchs. Putin trusts only these Chekist oligarchs, believing that, because of their common origin in the intelligence services, they understand what is in the best interests of the people. Everything must go through their hands. Putin's immediate circle and, seemingly, Putin himself believe that whoever controls the natural resources markets has a monopoly of political power. While they are in business, they are in power.

There is some truth in this. Many Latin American military juntas remained in power by ensuring that the institutions of repression and the Government – which was part of those institutions – controlled all major business. The detail overlooked by the Putin regime is that such juntas were invariably overthrown by other juntas, and often quite soon.

There is no place in our junta for the youth wing of Yabloko or the young National Bolsheviks. In Moscow 'Youth Yabloko' have mounted a demonstration lasting several seconds outside the FSB building in Lubyanka Square. The young people are increasingly independent of the 'old' democrats.

The demonstration was not officially sanctioned. The young people threw ball bearings with red paint at the memorial plaque on the building depicting Yury Andropov (the new cult of Andropov, as someone who planned to reform the Soviet system without destroying it, is being meticulously fostered by Putin's Administration) and wore uniform black T-shirts with a portrait of Putin crossed out and with the slogan 'Down with Big Brother!' They carried placards reading 'Down with the police autocracy!' They chanted, 'Demolish the Lubyanka and smash the regime!' and 'Down with the power of the Chekists!'

The demonstration was rapidly broken up; there are always plenty of militia around in Lubyanka Square. Nine activists were taken away to the FSB before being moved to the Meshchansky militia station. At about 8.00 in the evening, eight of them were released. Two are in hospital: Irina Vorobiova, 21, and Alexey Kozhin, 19. They were taken away in an ambulance summoned to FSB reception. The chairman of the youth wing of Yabloko, Ilya Yashin, stated that Kozhin had been beaten up during interrogation by FSB Senior Lieutenant Dmitry Streltsov. The activists said that when they began to disperse after the demonstration, they were trapped in the side streets by people in civilian clothes who assaulted them. A number of journalists from NTV, Echo TV and *Nezavisimaya gazeta* were also detained, the militia men threatening to confiscate their cameras. The journalists were released only after everything they had filmed had been taken from them.

*

Youth Yabloko's protest was an all-too-rare example of political resistance to the autocratic police state in Russia. By the summer of 2004, dissidence has been reduced to just two varieties: that of the very rich and that of the very poor. The break-up of Yukos, the brazen devouring of Guta-Bank and the raid on Alfa-Bank have all outraged the business elite, who are moving their capital abroad. The second variety comes from the very poorest, as the Government moves to reduce the social-welfare benefits in kind of the most vulnerable. This too is financially motivated rather than political dissidence.

In July, Russia saw the first, as yet fairly weak, demonstrations against Putin by ex-servicemen incensed at the impending abolition of these benefits in kind. These are essential to survival for the majority of them, but they are also seen as a material token of respect. Some of the ex-servicemen threatened to boycott the celebration of the sixtieth anniversary of victory in the Second World War, which is going to be a very big event. Those disabled by the Chernobyl nuclear accident embarked on a march from Rostov-on-Don to Moscow to protest at the proposal to pay 1,000 roubles (£19) a month compensation in place of the free medicine without which they cannot survive, and which costs well over 1,000 roubles. There are rumblings of discontent from those in the Army, who are also losing benefits.

The social strata between the richest and poorest are asleep for the time being. Anyone who hasn't been hit in the pocket has nothing to say.

1 August

Here is how the Kremlin removes election candidates it disapproves of.

Malik Saidullaev has just been disqualified from standing in the presidential election of the Chechen Republic for having an 'invalid' passport. He was the most serious rival of Alu Alkhanov, whom the Kremlin has already decided is to be the next President, even though the election does not take place until 29 August. Saidullaev has been disqualified on the grounds that his place of birth is described incorrectly in his passport: 'Alkhan-Yurt, Chechnya' should read 'Alkhan-Yurt, Checheno-Ingush

ASSR', since at the time he was born the village of Alkhan-Yurt was in a territory called the CI ASSR.

This is quite correct, except that it was not Malik Saidullaev who made out his passport, but an official in the Balashikhin Directorate of Internal Affairs in Moscow Province when old Soviet-style passports were replaced. 'Of course, I fully expected them to find a way of blocking me,' Malik Saidullaev said in an interview with *Novaya gazeta*, 'but not one quite so ridiculous. When I heard them claim the passport was invalid, I didn't take it seriously.'

'Do you intend to challenge the Electoral Commission's decision?'

'No. Whom should I challenge? That lot? They were acting on orders from Moscow. The same group of five people are back. The ones from the Central Electoral Commission of the Russian Federation who operated in the previous election. They were told to find a way of disqualifying me and that is what they have done, only they have turned themselves into an international laughing stock in the process. The International Helsinki Federation is preparing a protest. They phoned me yesterday. I had a warning that I would not be allowed to stand. When I arrived in Grozny and went to register as a candidate at the Central Electoral Commission, their offices and I myself were surrounded by armed men. About a hundred of them.'

'On the territory of government offices with their own security? Who were they?'

'Kadyrov's troops, OMON* people. They were under the command of Sultan Satuev, the Deputy Minister of the Interior, and Ruslan Alkhanov was there, another Deputy Minister. They demanded that the nomination should be deleted and that I should leave. I went to see Arsakhanov, the Commission Chairman. Armed men threw him out of his seat. He ran away and was replaced by Taus Dzhabrailov [appointed by Ramzan Kadyrov as 'Chairman of the State Council of the Chechen Republic']. Taus said, 'In this place, what we say goes.'

'And what did they say?'

'They told me to leave. There was a heated conversation. They realised they could do nothing with me by force. The gang tried to disarm my bodyguards, but that was impossible, so they had to retreat. They warned me several times they would have my name removed anyway. Three days before the passport saga, I was phoned from the Central Electoral Commission and invited to withdraw voluntarily because, as they said, they would get me out in any case. I refused. This disqualification is the beginning of their falsification of the 29 August election. I also know they have already ordered two hundred thousand extra ballot papers from printers in Dagestan, at six roubles per paper. These will stuff the ballot in favour of Alkhanov.'

'Quite apart from all these electoral games, what do you see happening in Chechnya this autumn and winter?'

'There will be trouble. All these legalised gangs currently rampaging around Chechnya are quite incapable of opposing the forces which carried out that operation in Ingushetia. The population has turned to favour those in the mountains. Those who seized power here have done everything conceivable to make that come about.'

'There is a lot of talk in Chechnya now that a third war is inevitable. People are excavating new cellars and building shelters, taking into account their experience of the Second War. That has been one of the main preoccupations this summer. How seriously do you take that?'

'Very seriously indeed, because I know it is true. After Putin's re-election I said there would be major operations by the fighters unless a stop were put to it now. It's the same thing, only worse. The fighters will not be inactive this summer, especially because they didn't previously have the kind of support they have today. They will force the other side to the negotiating table. That seems obvious to me.'

'What fate awaits Ramzan Kadyrov?'

'He's not worth talking about. He has no serious place in the Republic.'

'It is difficult to agree with that.'

'From a criminal point of view, of course, he matters, but he's illiterate. He didn't receive even an elementary education. If he's lucky enough to survive, and if people forgive his sins, Ramzan should be given good psychiatric treatment and an education.'

2 August

A group of National Bolsheviks entered the building of the Ministry of Health and Social Development on Neglinnaya Street in the very centre of Moscow. They went upstairs, barricaded themselves in the office of the Minister, Mikhail Zurabov, threw his chair out into the street and started shouting their slogans against the reform of welfare benefits from the window. They demanded that Zurabov and Putin should resign.

*

The National Bolsheviks were soon arrested and it was claimed in court that the chair cost $30,000. How come a Minister of Social Welfare has a chair that expensive? At first they were given an unprecedentedly harsh sentence of five years each in a strict-regime labour camp, for political hooliganism. Non-political hooliganism normally attracts suspended sentences. Subsequently the Supreme Court reduced the term to three and a half years, to be spent in the company of murderers and persistent offenders.

It is clear enough what the state is up to, but here is the position of the political prisoners. One of them, Maxim Gromov, said in court: 'It is significant that we heard mention of the name of the terrorist Ivan Kalyaev in the Prosecutor's speech. One hundred years ago, a series of bloody political trials also preceded the appearance of Ivan Kalyaev. The things going on in the state at that time were guaranteed to bring into existence the combat organisation of Boris Savinkov. We are being tried for a political protest under Article 213, but according to this Article all the sycophants in the State Duma should be on trial. Over the course of long years its members have conspired to show their manifest disrespect for society. In the present instance, they have shown disrespect towards millions of disabled people, pensioners and ex-servicemen and women. This is simply a disgrace for present-day Russia, and for present-day civil society, which has had nothing to say about it.'

He is right. The passing of the law abolishing material benefits and privileges provoked no indignation. We heard no demands that Zurabov should resign. The National Bolsheviks are the first to stand up for these groups.

Gromov continued, 'In a police state, trying to fight injustice without ending up in prison is as futile as trying to fire at mosquitoes from a cannon. I am proud to be behind bars at this cruel time, and even more proud that today I am not alone. I have with me my comrades in the struggle . . . Farewell, friends! I hope that sooner or later we shall break through the ice that holds our country in its grip. For the freedom of our Motherland we must go to prison.'

Is there anything I disagree with in this? No, I endorse every word. Today the National Bolsheviks are a group of idealistically minded young people who see an older generation of oppositionists failing to make an impact. Naturally, they are rapidly becoming radicalised.

The most upsetting thing I discovered from talking to them and their parents, who in the main are former supporters of Yabloko and the liberal right, is that the parents say exactly what parents in Chechnya say of themselves and their children. There the young people are also rapidly being radicalised, and this often happens with the best and most idealistic of them.

Here is a recent conversation in Chechnya with the mother of one of those who have just gone off into the mountains, as they call it when young people go to join Basaev and Maskhadov in protest at the 'New Chechen' bandits who have seized power and at the federal troops' atrocities. The mother was an educated woman, a teacher:

'I think the same way as my son,' she told me very emotionally. 'It is better to do something than to be waiting in the night for them to come and drag your children off to who knows where. The federals are occupying troops, and Kadyrov's gangs are brutal collaborators. We don't speak about this openly, but everybody knows and understands it, from great to small. The adults just keep everything to themselves, but the young refuse to put up with it. One day my son disappeared. I was in a panic. I thought he had been abducted and wrote a statement to the militia. Then it turned out that he and his comrades had gone off into the mountains. They had gone to fight for us, their parents. I agree with him completely.'

Lyudmila Kalashnikova is the mother of Ivan Korolyov, a National Bolshevik. She is a Muscovite, a researcher at the Institute of Oriental Studies of the Russian Academy of Sciences. She told me precisely the same thing:

'What is my Ivan fighting for? For us, for his parents.'

It has to be said that Lyudmila is no National Bolshevik, or Communist either. She is an ordinary, metropolitan, educated woman. In the 1990s she supported Yabloko.

'Tell me, is Limonov an idol for Ivan?'

'I wouldn't say that. Ivan is a clever lad, but the position of not reconciling yourself to evil very much appeals to him.'

I had asked the Chechen mother:

'Does he idolise Basaev?'

'No, I've never heard anything of that sort from him, but it was to Basaev that he went. Where else? Boys as idealistic as him are compelled by long years of living in the circumstances we have here, in the midst of all the lying, bloodshed, abductions and murders, to acknowledge Basaev as their commander.'

Limonov and Basaev have become the leaders of young people who cannot reconcile themselves to the existence offered by Putin, a life lived in conditions of total injustice and catastrophic disregard for human life. It is Limonov and Basaev who keep the hope alive in our children that some day they will be able to feel they are decent human beings. It is appalling, but that is how things stand.

People are outraged when I start talking like this. They say it is nonsense, tell me to shut up, say I will attract the evil eye. When I wrote in this vein for my newspaper, the Editor-in-Chief struck out the paragraph because, although he might agree with what I was saying, you can't put it in print.

This is very much our style, closing our eyes to reality until it hits us like a typhoon. Like the majority, I find it appalling that our children have been reduced to this, but I know the way things stand today. So what is it our state authorities want? Are they suicidal? Are they calmly waiting for the appearance of new terrorist Kalyaevs, Zasuliches and Savinkovs like those the Tsars conjured up?

Or are they simply mindless, living for the moment? Today, while they are in power, they have their snouts in the trough and are getting away with it, so let tomorrow take care of itself? Is the main thing to hold on to your place at the trough for as long as possible? Does being in power in Russia really mean no more than having a place at the trough? I think they are mindless.

9 August

In Moscow, the great and the good of the Russian human-rights movement, the flower of the nation, congregated at the Andrey Sakharov Centre. Some years ago they formed a ginger group called Joint Action in order to get together and, at times of national crisis, try to work out a common standpoint.

Today what they are discussing is not the National Bolsheviks' protest and why it came about; the meeting is to consider why the heat is being put on them, the human-rights movement, an exercise in navel-gazing only too typical of our civil society.

Around the table are many of those whom Putin excoriated in his Address to the Federal Assembly on 26 May, calling them a fifth column eating out of the hand of the West, accusing them of being concerned primarily to obtain funds from the West rather than to help people. They debated for a long time, but came to no conclusions. One alarming note was that some of the participants imagine that Putin is being misled, that he hasn't been given the true picture. The Tsar is a good Tsar, but his boyars are bad men. An old, old Russian story.

It is a pity. The activists are no longer active. There is little passion left in them. They have learned too much from bitter experience and have little desire to move forward. Most of them, of course, not all of them.

Apart from discussing their own predicament, they resolved that the human-rights movement should boycott the coming presidential elections in Chechnya, meaning that they would not act as observers.

(Despite the resolution, on which there was a vote, some of those present at the meeting did attend the election in Chechnya, saw what went on and subsequently issued statements.)

Incidentally, 9 August is the fifth anniversary of Yeltsin's proclamation of Putin as Acting Prime Minister – that is, as his successor. A war was brewing in Dagestan. Basaev was wreaking havoc in mountain villages, and the Russian troops allowed him into Dagestan and back out again. Thousands of refugees fled to the mountains, but none of those in Yeltsin's entourage would agree to start full-scale military operations – a Second Chechen War. The first had cost them too dearly.

Well, actually, there was one man who would agree: Putin, the then Director of the FSB, on whose watch Basaev had been allowed to get out of hand and Hattab [a militant Saudi of Palestinian origin] had been free to teach all the young people in Chechnya who came to hear him. Putin sat in Moscow, saw it all – he couldn't but know – and said nothing. He allowed the fruits of evil to ripen.

In August 1999 he decided it was time to destroy the results of his own activities before they were discovered. I believe that it is the sole reason he agreed to begin the Second Chechen War. That is how the rapidly deteriorating Yeltsin came to make Putin first the Acting Prime Minister, then Prime Minister, then President of Russia. Not once since August 1999 has Putin held back from tormenting his fellow citizens and shedding the blood not only of those who live in Chechnya.

It is noon and the sun is shining in Verkhny Tagil, a small, very quiet town in Sverdlovsk Province in the Urals. Beyond it is the impenetrable forest of the taiga. You are deep in the heart of Russia here.

An awkward, half-blind old man in shabby clothes is shifting from foot to foot at the entrance to a tall block of flats. This is Vladimir Kuzmich Khomenko, whose son Igor, an officer in the Parachute Regiment who died in Chechnya, was made a Hero of Russia. The door to Vladimir's ground-floor flat is open. 'Go on in, please go on in,' he says, as if we are old friends. Either Vladimir is very pleased to see us or he is very lonely. In the cramped corridor Lyudmila Alexeyevna, his wife and the mother of the Hero, kisses everybody warmly and shows us through. One whole corner of the room is full of portraits, flowers, icons and candles. It is a memorial to their son.

Captain Igor Khomenko was one of the first to be sent to the North Caucasus under the decree issued by the newly appointed Acting Prime Minister, V.V. Putin. His parachute regiment opened the hostilities of the Second Chechen War, which at that time was still confined to the border between Chechnya and Dagestan. When they arrived they were immediately sent into battle, and on 19 August Igor Khomenko did something remarkable. In order to plot the fighters' firing positions, he took a reconnaissance group to the Ass's Ear, a mountain that was to change hands several times during the fighting.

Khomenko discovered the fighters' positions on the hill, radioed the information back to his regiment, and he and his sergeant remained, covering the group's departure and taking on what they knew to be an unequal battle. That is where they died, having saved the lives of many men. His body was found by his comrades three days after his death, but they were unable to approach it because of the intense fighting. The Captain's Motherland recognised his achievement by awarding him the title of Hero of Russia. At the moment of their son's death, his parents had just become citizens of Ukraine. They lived in a modest wattle and daub house in Dnepropetrovsk Province.

Their history is that of a typical Soviet family. To this day it is often difficult to determine an individual's post-Soviet citizenship. Igor grew up in Yakutia in the Russian Far North, his parents having been sent to build an ore-enrichment factory there after graduating. Completing their prescribed period of service in Yakutia entitled them to an early pension at an enchanced rate, and they decided to return to the warmth, as did nearly everybody in their situation. They chose Ukraine with its wonderful Little Russian climate. When he left school, Igor moved from Soviet Ukraine to Alma-Ata in Soviet Kazakhstan, where there was a prestigious military academy. Graduating in 1988, with the USSR still intact, he was deployed to various hotspots. He was a parachutist, and trouble was forever flaring up. Soon the USSR fragmented, and Igor's parents became citizens of Ukraine while he became a citizen of Russia, because at the moment of the break-up he was attached to a military unit whose headquarters were on Russian territory. The captain died with Stavropol Region (Russia) registered as his place of residence. His grave is there, close to the military unit.

After their son's funeral, Lyudmila Alexeyevna and Vladimir Kuzmich decided to move to live near their son's grave, in Russia. They sold off their hut for the best price they could get, which was very little, but when they arrived in Stavropol the authorities refused even to register them as applicants for permanent residence. They persisted, wrote petitions and for months made a daily round of the offices of the district administration. Finally, the proceeds from the sale of their hut ran out and they were scuppered. The Hero's parents went to Verkhny Tagil in the Urals, where Lyudmila Alexeyevna had grown up and still had some, admittedly very distant, relatives. They were warmly welcomed, but their relatives were also very poor, like everyone else in Sverdlovsk Province, and there was nowhere for them to live.

'We are homeless. We are only allowed to live here through people's kindness.' Lyudmila Alexeyevna shows us the flat. 'We have nothing, nowhere to live, no property. Only that iron is mine, and the sewing machine. And the television. The young people are so kind, they help us a lot. Without them we would have died. It's because of Igor that they look after us, even though none of them knew him.'

The 'young people' standing in a line by the wall look at the floor and say nothing. They are Verkhny Tagil 'Chechens', soldiers and officers who have fought in Chechnya, and they have formed a local association of ex-servicemen.

'Our aim is very simple,' Yevgeny Bozmakov, the chairman of the association tells me. 'It is to help each other to survive. That is our only mission, and it is why we are helping the parents of Hero Khomenko.'

'It was they who managed to get me and father Russian citizenship,' Lyudmila Alexeyevna continues. 'They visited all the offices for us, otherwise we wouldn't even have a pension.' Such are the rules of Russian life. Somebody who is not a citizen of Russia, even if they worked in the USSR for their whole life, is not entitled to a pension.

Lyudmila Alexeyevna begins to cry, quietly and very sadly. Vladimir Kuzmich, moving behind her, strokes her shoulder and she says, now speaking to him, 'No, no, that's right, I know. I'll stop crying. I'll just tell her. What's to become of us?'

She shows us a stack of papers, the correspondence between the parents of a Hero of Russia with various official organisations and the Ministry of Defence. The officials' letters are full of haughty disdain.

As relatives of a Hero of the Russian Federation who died in the North Caucasian Region of the Russian Federation, you are entitled to enhancement of your living conditions drawing on funds of the National Military Fund. At the same time I have to inform you that, consequent upon a dearth of voluntary contributions, the programme 'Homes for Servicemen' is in abeyance. Act. Dir. of the Directorate of Military Welfare of the Central Board of Education of the AF of the RF, V. Zvezdilin.

We send people into the fire of battle, then bury them with great pomp and ceremony, award them posthumous medals – and forget them. It is a Russian tradition to shirk responsibility for our debts. It has never occurred to Putin, at least no one has ever heard him admit it, that he is responsible for those who have paid with their lives for his decision to begin the Second Chechen War.

I have come to Verkhny Tagil with Lyudmila Leonidovna Polymova, the mother of another soldier killed in Chechnya, another mother whom the state forgot after it had taken the life of her son. Lyudmila Leonidovna breaks down when she sees the scene in the Khomenkos' house. 'My own boy died protecting an officer with his body. They gave him the Order of Valour posthumously.' She urges that they should unite their efforts. In Yekaterinburg, where she lives, Lyudmila has already created an association called Mothers Against Violence.

The following day Vyacheslav Zykov, the Chairman of the Ex-Servicemen's Association of Yekaterinburg, another 'Chechen' soldier, takes Lyudmila to Bolshaya Rechka, a little township on the outskirts of Yekaterinburg in which the military cemetery is located. Here are buried the remains of her son, Private Yevgeny Polymov, which she had to find herself in a mountain of soldiers' bodies in Rostov-on-Don. The generals are not going to look for you, nor is anybody else. Parents have to travel to Rostov-on-Don themselves, and look for the remains of their sons in the mortuary of the North Caucasus Military District.

A funeral party advances slowly towards us from the cemetery. They have just buried an officer killed in Chechnya. Through the windows of the bus we see women in black.

'The latest,' Lyudmila Leonidovna comments, and goes off alone to her son's grave. She doesn't ask us to join her. She bears her suffering alone, and tries to help others in the same situation.

Many young men were taken from Sverdlovsk Province to fight in Chechnya, and more than 20,000 'Chechen' ex-servicemen live there now. The region is dotted with memorial plaques and monuments to those who died there. Beside the Officers' Club in the central square of Yekaterinburg they have already added a Chechen section to the Black Tulip memorial, a kind of annexe to the monument to the men of the

Urals who died in Afghanistan in the last war of the Soviet era. This new section already has 412 names etched in gold. There are blank obelisks to either side for those who, we can be sure, are going to die.

How many more such coffins will we tolerate? How many new cripples with arms and legs missing? Every soldier killed or maimed in the Second Chechen War brings the state greater responsibility, when it isn't yet servicing its existing debts. Like a bankrupt, it begins to default, trying to conceal its bankruptcy with measures like this wretched reform of benefits in kind. It removes even those small privileges from the disabled, the 'Chechens', the mothers of soldiers who have been killed, privileges that were some gesture of compensation for its escapade in the North Caucasus.

The number of those to whom the state is now indebted runs into millions, which is why we find Putin and Zurabov saying the number of people with privileges in Russia is artificially high. No other country has so many claimants (happily) and accordingly 'something needs to be done'. The number is artificially high, of course, because of the constant aggressive policies of our state, which produce casualties of war like mushrooms after rain.

'Many of our people end up in jail,' Vitalii Volkov tells me. He is the Chairman of the Verkhnyaya Salda Association of Ex-Servicemen of Chechnya. He has 200 members. 'We are penniless. We can't get work. Many who have come back from Chechnya start thieving, and the next stop is prison. Who is going to come out of our prisons still a human being? If before prison you were in Chechnya, and before Chechnya you were a schoolkid?'

These associations run by Lyudmila Polymova, Vitalii Volkov and Vyacheslav Zykov have been set up when misfortune befell their founders personally. They admit they never dreamed they would become involved in welfare activities or start fighting the state machine. Their organisations have no political aims. They are a product of despair and exist purely to help people survive. Surviving is so hard it leaves no time over for anything else.

How long will people put up with this? That is the decisive question for Russia, as it is also for Ukraine.

29 August

In Chechnya the election of Putin's next President has gone ahead. Needless to say, the Kremlin's candidate came in with an 'overwhelming majority of votes'. Alu Alkhanov may nominally be the new President, but the real boss is the deranged Ramzan Kadyrov, the 27-year-old son of Alkhanov's assassinated predecessor, who in his time was, of course, also elected with an 'overwhelming majority of votes'.

Who is Ramzan? For the past year and a half he ran his father's security detail. After the President's assassination he was, perhaps surprisingly, not dismissed for this lapse, but promoted by Putin personally to the exalted post of First Deputy Prime Minister of the Chechen Government with Special Responsibility for Security. He is now in charge of the militia, all manner of Special Operations subdivisions and the Chechen OMON. Although he has no education, he does hold the rank of captain in the militia. This is surprising, because he is not a militiaman, and higher education is required in Russia before you can become a captain. Be that as it may, he now has the right to give orders to career colonels and generals, which he does. They do as they are commanded, because they know that Ramzan is Putin's favourite.

What kind of person is Ramzan? What kind of qualifications do you need to be a favourite of Putin? To have ground Chechnya beneath your heel, and forced the entire Republic to pay you tribute like an Asiatic bey, is evidently a plus.

Ramzan is rarely seen outside his village of Tsentoroy, one of the unsightliest of Chechen villages, unfriendly, ugly and swarming with murderous-looking armed men. The village is a collection of narrow, winding, dusty streets hemmed in by enormous fences, behind most of which live members of the Kadyrov family and the families of Kadyrov's most trusted bodyguards and soldiers of the 'Presidential Security Service'.

Two or three years ago, those villagers of Tsentoroy whom Kadyrov didn't trust were simply expelled and their houses given to the bruisers of the Security Service. The Security Service is illegal, but well provided with federal armaments. As it is not formally attached to any of the security ministries, it is an 'illegal armed formation', its status no different to that of Basaev's troops, except that it is led by a favourite of Putin. So that's all right.

Kadyrov's men take part in combat operations as if they were soldiers with the Ministry of Defence; they arrest and interrogate people as if they were agents of the Interior Ministry; and they hold people prisoner in their cellars in Tsentoroy, and torture them like gangsters.

No procurator challenges any of this. It is all hushed up. They know better than to poke their noses in. Tsentoroy is above the law, by Putin's will. The rules that apply to other people do not apply to Ramzan. He can do as he pleases because he is said to be fighting terrorists using his own methods. In fact he's fighting nobody. He is in the business of robbery and extortion, disguised as 'the fight against terrorism'.

The capital of Chechnya has effectively moved to Ramzan's estate. Pro-Russian Chechen officials come here to bow down before his fatuous, degenerate countenance either to seek whatever permission they need or when they are summoned. All of them come, including even Sergey Abramov, the young Prime Minister of Chechnya who is supposed to report directly to the Prime Minister of Russia, and who is not supposed to report to Ramzan Kadyrov.

The reality is, however, that Tsentoroy is where the decisions are taken. It was here that the decision was taken to nominate Alkhanov for the presidency, and now he is President.

Ramzan rarely travels to Grozny because he fears assassination. The journey takes one and a half hours. That is why Tsentoroy is such a fortress, with a security 'filtration' system on its approaches that would do credit to the Kremlin: a series of control posts, one after the other. I get through them all and find myself in what the armed men surrounding me describe as 'the guest-house'. I am held there for six or seven hours. Evening falls. In Chechnya this means you should lose no time in finding shelter. Anyone who wants to live hides away in their burrow.

'Where is Ramzan?' I ask. He has agreed to meet me.

'Soon, soon,' the guardian of the guest-house, and now of me, mutters.

There is always somebody with me. Vakha Visaev introduces himself as the Director of Yugoilprodukt, the new oil refinery at Gudermes, the second-largest city in Chechnya. He offers to show me round the guest-house. It is not badly set out. There is a fountain in the courtyard, ugly, but a fountain nevertheless. Bamboo furniture graces an open terrace with pillars. Vakha makes a great point of showing me the labels, which indicate that it was made in Hong Kong. Most likely, he paid for it. People fall over themselves to give gifts to Ramzan, to buy him off. Everybody remembers that the head of the nearby Shali Region, Akhmed Gutiev, didn't pay the required tribute to Ramzan. He was abducted, tortured, and his family had to ransom him for $100,000. Akhmed promptly emigrated, and a new would-be suicide was appointed to govern the Shali Region. I met Gutiev. He was a promising, clever young man who respected Putin and thought his choice of Ramzan was right in the circumstances, given that the first priority must be to drive out the Wahhabis[*]. I wonder whether he still thinks that.

But back to Ramzan's estate. Opposite the main entrance he has a grey-green marble fireplace. To the right are a sauna, a jacuzzi and a swimming pool. The highlight, however, is the two cavernous bedrooms endowed with stadium-sized beds. One is in blue, the other pink.

Everywhere there is massive, dark, oppressive furniture, all with the price tags in full view, denominated in thousands of 'conventional units' (in effect, dollars). There is a price tag on the mirror in the bathroom, on the toilet pedestal, on the towel holder. This is evidently the fashion in Tsentoroy.

The excursion takes in a viewing of Ramzan's modest and very dark study adjoining one of the bedrooms. Its chief decoration is a Dagestani wall rug depicting, in the style of socialist realism, the deceased Akhmed-hadji Kadyrov wearing an astrakhan papakha on his head, against a black background. He is portrayed with a seraphic expression on his face, his chin jutting forwards.

After dark, Ramzan appears, surrounded by armed men. They are everywhere: in the courtyard, on the balcony, in the rooms. Some of them subsequently involve themselves in our conversation, commenting loudly and aggressively. Ramzan sprawls in an armchair crossing his legs, his foot, in a sock, almost level with my face. He doesn't appear to notice. He is taking it easy.

'We want to restore order not only in Chechnya, but throughout the North Caucasus,' Ramzan begins. 'So that we can go any time to Stavropol, or Leningrad. We will fight anywhere in Russia. I have a directive to operate throughout the North Caucasus. Against the bandits.'

'Whom do you call bandits?'

'Maskhadov, Basaev and the like.'

'You see the mission of your troops as being to find Maskhadov and Basaev?'

'Yes. That is the main thing, to destroy them.'

'Everything that has been done so far in your name has been about destroying and liquidating. Don't you think perhaps there's been enough fighting already?'

'Of course there has. Seven hundred people have already surrendered to us and are living a normal life. We have asked the others to stop their senseless resistance, but they carry on fighting. That is why we have to exterminate them. Today we took three. We exterminated two. One of them was a big emir, Nashkho from Doku Umarov's group. He was a big man there. Anyway, we killed him. In Ingushetia. They all rest up there.'

'But what right do you have to kill anyone? Let alone in Ingushetia, when formally you are the Security Service of the President of Chechnya?'

'We have every right. We carried out this operation jointly with the Ingush FSB. We have all the necessary official permissions.' (This later proved to be a lie.)

'Currently, within the territory of Chechnya, apart from your troops, there are Kokiev's troops operating, Yamadaev's, etc.'

'You shouldn't name these troops by their leaders.'

'Why not? Don't you think there are rather a lot of them?'

'What, of troops?! The Chechen OMON is only three hundred men. In other regions the OMON number seven to eight hundred. Kokiev's time is nearly up. His are Army men. They will be withdrawn.'

'In March, just before Putin was re-elected, Khambiev [the Minister of Defence of Ichkeria] surrendered to you. What is he doing now? Is he mustering troops too?'

'You want me to have him brought here? If I give the word, he will be brought here.'

'Isn't it rather late? He's probably asleep.'

'If I give the word, he will be woken. We use him as a negotiator with the bandits. They know him. He was good at that before, with Turlaev, for example. You want me to have Turlaev brought here as well? [Shaa Turlaev was the head of Maskhadov's personal bodyguard. He also surrendered when he was seriously wounded. His leg was later amputated.] Khambiev will not have troops of his own. We will be the only people with troops.'

'In the press Khambiev admitted he was a traitor.'

'That is a lie. They just wrote that. He is not a traitor.'

'How do you personally picture the surrender of Maskhadov: will he come to you and say, "Here I am"?'

'Yes.'

'He can't possibly. The age difference between you is too great. You are a boy compared to him.'

'Perhaps. What choice does he have? If he doesn't come of his own accord, we will bring him in. We are definitely going to put him in a cage.'

'Recently you issued an ultimatum to those who had not surrendered. Was that addressed to Maskhadov?'

'No, that was for seventeen- and eighteen-year-old kids who don't know better. They were tricked by Maskhadov and have gone into the forests. Their mothers are weeping, begging me, "Help us, Ramzan, to get our sons back." They curse Maskhadov. So this is an ultimatum to women to keep a closer eye on their children. I am telling the women to find their children quickly, or else not to blame us . . . Those who do not surrender we shall exterminate. Of course. There are no two ways about that.'

'But perhaps it's time to stop exterminating people and sit down to negotiate?'

'Who with?'

'With all Chechens who are fighting.'

'With Maskhadov? Maskhadov is nobody here. Nobody obeys his orders. The main figure is Basaev. He is a mighty warrior. He knows how to fight. He is a good strategist. And a good Chechen. But Maskhadov is a pathetic old man who is incapable of doing anything.' (He guffaws, neighing like a horse. All present follow suit.) 'He's only got a couple of boys following him. I can prove that. I write everything down. At present Maskhadov has women. I know those women. They told me, "If we refused, we would be killed. We had no work and he gave us money."'

'Are you saying Maskhadov has a women's battalion?'

'No. We have broken Maskhadov. He has other people now.'

'I hear disrespect for Maskhadov in what you are saying, but also clear respect for Basaev.'

'I respect Basaev as a warrior. He is not a coward. I pray to Allah that Basaev and I may meet in open combat. One man dreams of being a president, another of being a pilot, another a tractor driver – but my dream is to fight Basaev in the open. My troops against his troops, with no outsiders. With him in command, and with me in command.'

'What if Basaev won?'

'No way. I will. In battle I always win.'

'In Chechnya there is a lot of talk about your rivalry with the Yamadaevs.' (Brothers from Gudermes. Khalid is a United Russia Deputy in the Duma, while Salim is Deputy Military Commandant of the Chechen Republic. They control powerful troops. Ramzan is thought to work for the FSB, while the Yamadaevs work for the GRU Central Intelligence Directorate of the Army.)

'It isn't a good idea to be one of my rivals. It isn't good for your health.'

'What do you consider to be the strongest aspect of your personality?'

'What do you mean? I don't understand the question.'

'What are your strengths? And your weaknesses?'

'I consider that I have no weaknesses. I am strong. Alu Alkhanov was made President because I consider he is strong and I trust him one hundred per cent. Do you think the Kremlin decides that? The people choose. It's the first time anyone has told me the Kremlin has a say in anything.'

Odd, but that's what he said.

No more than an hour later, Ramzan was saying that absolutely every-thing was decided by the Kremlin, that the people were just cattle, and that he had been offered the presidency of Chechnya in the Kremlin immediately after his father's assassination, but had turned it down because he wanted to fight.

'If you left us in peace, we Chechens would have reunited long ago.'

'Who do you mean by "you"?'

'Journalists, people like you. Russian politicians. You don't let us sort things out. You divide us. You come between Chechens. You personally are the enemy. You are worse than Basaev.'

'Who else are your enemies?'

'I don't have enemies. Only bandits to fight.'

'Do you intend to become President of Chechnya yourself?'

'No.'

'What do you most enjoy doing?'

'Fighting. I am a warrior.'

'Have you ever killed anyone yourself?'

'No. I've always been in command.'

'But you're too young always to have been in command. Somebody must have given you orders.'

'Only my father. Nobody else ever gave me orders, or ever will.'

'Have you given orders to kill?'

'Yes.'

'Is that not terrible?'

'It is not I, but Allah. The Prophet said the Wahhabis must be destroyed.'

'Did he really say that? When there are no more Wahhabis left, who will you fight?'

'I will take up bee farming. Already I have bees, and bullocks, and fighting dogs.'

'Don't you feel sorry when dogs kill each other?'

'Not at all. I like it. I respect my dog Tarzan as much as a human being. He's a Caucasian sheepdog. Those are the most fair-minded dogs there are.'

'What other hobbies do you have? Dogs, bees, fighting . . . and?'

'I very much like women . . .'

'Doesn't your wife mind?'

'I don't tell her.'

'What education have you had?'

'Higher education, law. I'm just finishing it. I am taking my exams.'

'What exams?'

'What do you mean, "What exams"? The exams, that's all.'

'What's the institute called where you are studying?'

'It's a branch of the Moscow Institute of Business. In Gudermes. It's a law college.'

'What are you specialising in?'

'Law.'

'But what kind of law? Criminal? Civil?'

'I can't remember. Someone wrote the topic down for me on a piece of paper, but I've forgotten. There's a lot going on at the moment.'

At this moment Shaa Turlaev is brought to Ramzan, the former head of Maskhadov's security, a major of the Presidential Guard who had been awarded the Chechen orders 'Pride of the Nation' and 'Hero of the Nation'. He is a completely grey-haired man of 32, his left leg amputated to the thigh. He is kept in Tsentoroy under guard, a hostage, but he is not being beaten or tortured. Later, Mahomed Khambiev also appears. Mahomed speaks Russian to me, but Shaa has apparently been forbidden to talk to a journalist in Russian. Ramzan says he can't speak Russian, but later people who knew Shaa told me he used to speak excellent Russian.

Khambiev is brazen and smug, while Shaa seems haunted, but dignified. Khambiev keeps agreeing with Ramzan, while Shaa remains proudly silent. As translated, his words are: 'I fought from 1991. Until 2003 I was in Maskhadov's personal security detail. I haven't seen Maskhadov for a year and a half now. I had a wound in my leg for two years. There was a doctor there and an operating theatre. I could have stayed, but didn't want to, even before the wound, because Ramzan and I had fought together in the past. When Ramzan sent people to me from my village they said, "Follow Ramzan. His is the correct path. Maskhadov is weak. You cannot see any strength in him. He is on his own. He only has twenty to thirty people."'

'Does he have a women's battalion?'

Shaa does not reply. He lowers his head and shakes it. It is not clear whether this means yes or no. The general conversation is unfocused and edgy. Shortly after Shaa's arrival, an older person with a round tyubeteika cap on his head appears and sits at Ramzan's right hand. He introduces himself as Nikolai Ivanovich, at which everybody smirks, indicating that whatever else his name may be, it is not Nikolai Ivanovich. Ramzan orders him to translate Shaa's words into Russian. It soon becomes clear that when Shaa says two or three words, 'Nikolai Ivanovich' spins them into several sentences about how Shaa recognised the ruinous nature of Maskhadov's war.

I complain indignantly about this 'interpreting', and Nikolai Ivanovich, like a dog breaking free from its chain, attacks and insults me. Nobody stops him. Ramzan chuckles, pleased. His real hobby is setting people at each other's throats, and nobody at the table can rival him in this, with his enthusiasm for dog fights.

The conversation becomes more animated. 'You are putting the case for bandits', 'You are an enemy of the Chechen people', 'You should have to answer for this' – all this addressed to me. Ramzan is shouting, jumping up and down in his chair, and Nikolai Ivanovich is goading him on. We are seated round a large, oval table and the scene increasingly resembles a thieves' convention. Ramzan behaves more and more oddly, as if he is the oldest person in the house, though he is in fact the youngest. He laughs at inappropriate moments. He scratches himself. He orders his bodyguards to scratch his back. He arches himself, wriggling, and keeps making irritating, inane remarks.

I try to talk to Shaa, but Ramzan really doesn't like Shaa getting more questions than him. He cuts in and forbids Shaa to say any more. It's time to end. I ask one last question, and it is the only one Shaa answers himself.

'When was the happiest time in your life?'

'There has been no such time.'

Ramzan interrupts even this: 'Did you know that Khambiev voted for Putin?'

Khambiev nods agreement, with the mocking smile of a liar: 'Yes. He is hard. He wants order in Chechnya.'

'What is missing,' I ask Khambiev, 'before there can be complete order in Chechnya?'

'Very little. Yandarbiev has been taken out. If Berezovsky and Maskhadov's men Zakaev* and Udugov are taken out, there will be order. They are pulling the strings. Basaev carries out their wishes. Basaev is not fighting on behalf of the Chechen people.'

'What are you fighting, and living, for?'

'For ourselves. For the people.'

'In what capacity do you see yourself serving it?'

'As Ramzan decides.'

'Why should that be up to Ramzan?'

'He is the first among Chechens. Ramzan is promising to make me President of the Free-Style Wrestling Federation.'

'How old are you?'

'The right side of forty-two.'

'How do you feel about the fact that Ramzan's people abducted your relatives to force you to surrender?'

'No problem. My relatives were at fault, and they were captured.'

'What were they guilty of?'

'They brought me cassette messages from Maskhadov, and bread.'

Ramzan, satisfied, chuckles insolently. He leans backwards smugly, then goes to watch himself on television. He is very pleased about this, and comments on the way Putin walks: 'He's got real class!' He declares that Putin walks like a mountain-dweller.

Outside the windows it is night. The temperature is rising in here and it is time for me to get out. Ramzan gives orders for me to be taken back to Grozny. Musa, a former fighter from Zakan-Yurt, sits at the wheel and there are two bodyguards. I get into the vehicle and think that somewhere along the route, in the dark, with checkpoints every-where, I am obviously going to be killed. But the ex-fighter from Zakan-Yurt is just waiting for Ramzan to leave. He wants to bare his soul, and when he starts telling me the story of his life, how he had been a fighter, why he joined Ramzan, I know he is not going to kill me. He wants the world to hear his story.

*

I understood that, but sat there crying from fear and loathing. 'Don't cry,' the fighter from Zakan-Yurt finally said to me. 'You are strong.'

When argument has been exhausted, and at Tsentoroy they don't understand the meaning of the word, all that is left is tears. Tears of despair that someone like this can exist, that the vagaries of history should have raised up, of all people, Ramzan Kadyrov. He really does have power, and rules according to his own ideas and abilities. Nobody, not a single man present in Tsentoroy, dared to stop him getting out of hand. It was Ramzan Kadyrov who was telephoned from the Kremlin by 'Vladislav Yurievich' – in other words, by a Deputy Head of Putin's Administration, Vladislav Surkov. That was the only time Ramzan stopped misbehaving, scratching himself, shouting and hooting with laughter.

It is an old story, repeated many times in our history: the Kremlin fosters a baby dragon, which it then has to keep feeding to stop him from setting everything on fire. There has been a total failure of the Russian intelligence services in Chechnya, something they try to represent as a victory and a 'restoration of civilian life'. But what about the people of Chechnya? They have to live with the baby dragon. First the Kremlin tried to show the Chechens that resistance to Putin was useless. That more or less worked; most of them gave up. Then it was the turn of the rest of Russia.

1 September

Censorship and self-censorship in the mass media have reached new extremes and increased the probability that hundreds of adults and children in School No. 1 in Beslan, which has been seized by terrorists, will die.

Self-censorship is now the business of trying to guess what you need to say and what you should not mention in order to stay at the top. The purpose of self-censorship is to keep your hands on a large, very large, salary. The choice is not between having a job or being unemployed, but between earning a fortune or a pittance. Any journalist has the option of moving over to Internet publications, which are more or less free to say what they want, while there are still a couple of newspapers that enjoy relative freedom too. Where there is freedom, however, there is low pay, irregularly paid. The big time is the mass media that play ball with the Kremlin.

Television presenters who lie persistently, who keep off the airwaves anything that might upset the state authorities, do so for fear of losing a salary of several thousand dollars a month. They face a choice between continuing to dress in Gucci and Versace, or putting on old, shabby clothes. There is no question of ideological commitment: their only commitment is to their own financial well-being. No journalists have any faith in Putin, nor have had for a long time.

The result is that what the NTV station broadcasts is roughly 70 per cent lies. On the two official stations, RTR and Ostankino, the proportion is a good 90 per cent. The same is true of state radio.

If during the *Nord-Ost* hostage-taking television showed half the truth, during Beslan it broadcast nothing but official lies, chief of which was the assertion that there were only 354 hostages in the school. [The actual figure was apparently closer to 1,200.] This so enraged the terrorists that they stopped letting the children go to the toilet or have anything to drink.

At NTV they knew perfectly well that figure was untrue. The directors of the company suppressed a report from their own correspondent at the scene, who was reliably informed about the real number of hostages. As Leonid Parfyonov, sacked from NTV on 1 June, said later, there was only one word of truth heard on NTV during the Beslan crisis. That was after the assault had begun, when dead and injured children were being brought out, and lumps of human flesh were seen all over the place; the reporter speaking to camera at that moment uttered a resounding Russian swearword, which accurately characterised what was happening.

Beslan was the nadir of this treacherous self-censorship, treacherous because it betrayed people who paid for the lies with their lives. Residents of Beslan attacked state television reporters because their lying, by now habitual in the Putin era, had started costing the lives of women and children they knew. Previously this had been experienced only by people living in Chechnya. Now it was time for others to understand.

3 September

There are 331 fatalities as a result of the hostage-taking in Beslan.

4 September

The Editor-in-Chief of *Izvestiya*, Raf Shakirov, has been sacked. He was a careerist: not a revolutionary, not a dissident, not a champion of human rights. He was sacked for failing on just one occasion to intuit the new state ideology, something that is not supposed to need spelling out. *Izvestiya* published a brutally honest photographic report from Beslan about the assault on the school. The authorities complained that it was too shocking.

Izvestiya is not a state-owned newspaper – it belongs to the oligarch Potanin – but thunderclouds were gathering over Potanin just like those that had gathered over Khodorkovsky. By sacking Shakirov, Potanin must hope he is back in with Putin and the Kremlin.

*

After Beslan there were at least the stirrings of opposition to the authorities' regime of wholesale mendacity and cowardice. Between December

2003 and 1 September 2004 all that had been noticeable was a reluctant, half-stifled dissidence, but after the massacre the emergence of at least some sort of public protest began. Until 1 September nobody chose to recognise that the intelligence services were only interested in sharing out the national loot. After the bloodbath at Beslan on 3 September, many finally realised that they were unprotected. They could either continue to pretend that the President had a high approval rating, or they could have security for their children.

10 September

What is emerging in Russia is not a stabilising middle class, but a new class consisting of parents whose children have died in terrorist acts. They are already almost a party whose manifesto is to demand a genuine and thorough inquiry into the tragedy that occurred in School No. 1.

The first to arrive in Beslan after the catastrophe were the parents of hostages who died at *Nord-Ost*. Muscovite Dmitry Milovidov was among them. In October 2002 he lost his 14-year-old daughter, Nina, at the Dubrovka Theatre. He took to Beslan a handful of earth from *Nord-Ost* in Moscow, and took back ashes from the school. He showed me this mixture in a small transparent box.

'I scooped up some of what is still lying on the floor in the school. You can see there are cartridge cases and dum-dum bullets, even though those are banned, a carefully sharpened pencil, the charred pages of a textbook. All of it is covered in dark-grey ash, and it is as well not to ask what that ash might be.'

'Why did you *Nord-Ost* parents go there? It must have been very difficult for you.'

'We collected money, thirty-seven thousand roubles [£700], and decided to hand it over personally. We thought our own sad experience of how to survive after the death of your children might be helpful. We barely survived, relying solely on our own resources, abandoned by the state.

'There is another reason: just a little over a year ago I was talking to Tanya Khazieva – her husband was a musician in the *Nord-Ost* musical and died, leaving her to look after little Sonya and Tanya. She was the first of us to win a court case claiming material compensation. Tanya said to me then, in June 2003, "I need to know that, if tomorrow one of my daughters were to be taken hostage at school, her life would be so expensive that neither the FSB nor the state could afford to pay me off for letting her die." Do you know, we feel today that we didn't manage to prevent Beslan. I see it as an alternative ending to *Nord-Ost:* "There, just see what would have happened to you if you had been locked in that theatre and we had not used the gas." It is as if they wanted to teach Russia a lesson. We went to Beslan to say to the people there, "Forgive us for not doing enough to avert your tragedy."'

'What do you think the people in Beslan need most right now? Money?'

'No. Understanding.'

'Are there too few psychiatrists?'

'There are enough of them in the hospitals, but it is often young trainee doctors who go round to people's homes. It is difficult to open your heart to them. The problem for people in Beslan is the same as ours was. Many don't want counselling. They want to grieve among themselves.'

'But did you have the feeling that, as people who have been through something similar, you were closer to them than the psychiatrists?'

'Of course. They wanted to talk to us, but not in order to weep with us. They asked what conclusions the *Nord-Ost* inquiry had come to. Had there been a proper answer to the question of how such a thing could have happened? It is already obvious that this tragedy is not just going to go away. There are graffiti on the fences: "Death to the Ingushes", and stronger than that. Nobody cleans them off. Everywhere I heard people quietly vowing to take revenge. There was a meeting of young people while we were there, and that was clearly the theme. They had the darkest things to say about their President Dzasokhov, and what they said about Putin doesn't bear repeating.'

'Is it true that the feeling towards journalists is also bad?'

'Yes. We were the same. In the first months after Dubrovka, at the sight of journalists we would say, "Here come the vultures." It was only much later that we began to see them not as vultures but as dissectors, without whom we would never have heard the truth about the sinking of the submarine *Kursk* or the reality of *Nord-Ost.*'

'Who are people in Beslan now expecting to provide a proper inquiry?'

'They trust only their own families. They expect that an inquiry will come, but, as many say, "from Russia" – in other words, from the state. We have been through *Nord-Ost*, though. We know that isn't going to happen.'

'What is the main impression you brought back from Beslan?'

'We were in Moscow, a big city. Beslan is an entire town in mourning.'

13 September

After Beslan, the security agencies of the North Caucasus, having failed to prevent the terrorist outrage, are now making a great show of fighting terrorism. They are killing or arresting anyone they think might conceivably be involved in terrorism.

How do they go about it? The success or failure of the manhunt is measured primarily by how many 'terrorists' are caught. Human rights and respect for the law go straight out the window. A confession is proof of guilt, and if a suspect has been killed, you don't even need that. It is an exact repetition of what occurred when a 'counter-terrorist operation' was launched after the assassination of the Communist Party leader, Sergey Kirov, on 1 December 1934. Just as then, any attempt to suggest something is wrong and perhaps there should be more regard for the law is treated by supporters of 'radical and effective methods' as a desire to protect criminals.

Representatives of the International Committee of the Red Cross are not allowed to visit the prison cells where 'terrorists' are being held. There is no legal oversight by the Procurator, and certainly no independent judiciary, where these fast-track 'anti-terrorist' cases are concerned. Nobody is going to investigate whether a Special Operations unit was justified in murdering someone. It is an area completely outside the law, incapable of punishing the guilty and acquitting the innocent. The main wave of post-Beslan 'anti-terrorism' has broken over Ingushetia, because there were many Ingushes in the group that seized the school. And, needless to say, over Chechnya.

The predictable result was that throughout the autumn, reacting against this 'anti-terrorism', the real terrorist underground was greatly strengthened. The killing or fast-track sentencing of the innocent leaves the real criminals at large to prepare new crimes, needing only to improve their methods of conspiracy. Moreover, the underground is swollen by those who have suffered unjustly or who seek to avenge their relatives. For others, taking up arms is their personal protest against the lawlessness of the security forces.

You can call this anything you like, but a counter-terrorist operation it is not. It conjures up the most monstrous forms of terror. The true picture is that, after the fighters took over Ingushetia for one night in June 2004, the security forces went on a rampage, murdering and imprisoning a multitude of innocent people they happened to get their hands on, and the result was Beslan.

Meanwhile, Chechen officialdom is celebrating. A few dozen kilometres away they are burying the victims of Beslan, but Alu Alkhanov, the newly 'elected' President, has decided to celebrate the birth of a son to the Prime Minister with a day's horse racing.

In Tsentoroy, behind intense security, Putin's current Chechen favourites are enjoying life. Their retinues indulge them in every way. Rarely does a day pass without some kind of entertainment to demonstrate that peace has come to Chechnya. Even Beslan is not allowed to spoil the fun, and the deaths of all those children, which are on the conscience of the unholy trinity of Kadyrov, Alkhanov and Abramov. It was they, after all, who were assuring Putin and everybody else, right up until 1 September, that there were practically no bandits left in Chechnya and that they would be catching Basaev any minute now. Beslan showed us the real situation.

One of the reasons for Russia's social malaise is this diabolical cynicism on the part of the authorities, who peddle a completely fake reality. Russia's citizens do not rise up against this cynicism. They withdraw into their own shells, becoming defenceless, wordless and inhibited. Putin knows this and employs brazen cynicism as the anti-revolutionary technique that works best in Russia.

The funerals are not yet over, but already Putin is busy. He has informed the Government and the country that in future regional leaders will no longer be elected, but appointed by him. The appointment will need to be ratified by regional parliaments, but if the local deputies twice fail to approve his choice of candidate, the Parliament itself will be liable to dissolution.

There have been rumours for some time about Putin's desire to abolish the direct election of governors, some of whom have a mind of their own. One of the methods for the opposition to remain effective was to reach an understanding in the regions, if this proved impossible with the Presidential Administration in Moscow.

Putin claims that the reason for abolishing the election of governors is the threat from terrorism. Such cynical exploitation of the cataclysm of Beslan to resolve his purely political and practical difficulties is unexpected, even from Putin. There has been hardly a murmur of protest.

16 September

The only reaction came from Committee 2008, who issued the following statement, 'The Threat of a Coup d'État in Russia':

The President of the Russian Federation, Vladimir Putin, has announced that he intends to carry out a coup d'état in Russia. His speech on 13 September 2004 at an extended session of the Government contains a detailed proposal to dismantle fundamental institutions of democracy in Russia.

'Russia is a democratic, federal, law-governed state . . .' according to the first article of the Constitution. The Kremlin is now intending to liquidate all three of those foundations of the Russian state.

Putin's Russia will not be a democratic state, since its citizens are to be deprived of the right to free elections, which, according to the Constitution, are the 'highest and direct expression of the power of the people'. Putin's Russia will not be a federal state, in that its regions are to be governed by officials appointed by and answerable only to the centre. Putin's Russia will not be a law-governed state, because the Constitutional Court of the Russian Federation made a ruling eight years ago that explicitly prohibits any such 'reform', and which will be being flouted.

We call upon the President of Russia, Vladimir Putin, to pay particular note to Article 3, Point 4 of the Constitution, which reads, 'Nobody shall appropriate power in the Russian Federation. Seizure of power or appropriation of the authority of the Government will be prosecuted under federal law.'

The state authorities ignored all that. Nobody protested.

27 September

The authorities are very concerned that human-rights campaigners will again become dissidents, that it is from them, rather than from opposition politicians, that danger threatens. Accordingly, they are constructing a parallel human-rights movement to operate under strict state control. Putin is signing a directive to create an 'international human-rights centre'. The directive is characteristically titled 'Additional Measures of State Support for the Human-Rights Movement in the Russian Federation'.

The driving force behind this directive is Ella Pamfilova, Chairperson of the Presidential Commission on Human Rights. She is loudly insisting to anyone who will listen: 'I completely reject the scurrilous allegations that one of the tasks of the International Human-Rights Centre is to

introduce centralised control of the human-rights movement. This directive is a great help to us. It will be easier for the leaders of human-rights
organisations to find each other (in the Kremlin? – AP). We shall be able
to extend the reach of our expertise. This idea is the initiative of human-
rights campaigners themselves. I have had phone calls from the representatives of many human-rights associations, people have rung in from the
regions. They are all in favour. They say it is a small victory for us. First
and foremost, we need to guarantee the rights of defenders of human
rights themselves to help people effectively.'

Hardly anyone believes Pamfilova's invariable protestations of the
benign nature and democratic credentials of Putin.

Yelena Bonner had this to say in an interview with *Yezhenedelnyi
zhurnal*:

> There is the philosophy and outlook of defenders of human rights,
> and there is the philosophy and outlook of those who represent
> governmental power. They have different aims and different
> missions. The aim of the human-rights movement is to defend
> society from the state authorities and to form a civil society. The
> aim of any state authority is to consolidate its own power. I am
> upset to see many well-known human-rights campaigners falling
> for this. If they do, they effectively cease to be defenders of human
> rights. They want to cosy up to the state authorities. This testifies
> to a crisis in the human-rights movement.
>
> What today is called the human-rights movement in Russia, and
> the politicians whom we call the opposition and who for many
> years have been sitting between two stools, have missed the boat.
> We have missed the opportunity of acting by legal means. Today,
> exploiting the Beslan tragedy, attempts are being made to destroy
> the independence of the courts. What does that leave open to
> society? Only revolt and rebellion.
>
> I am not calling for revolution. I see no leaders capable of leading
> it, and no readiness for it in the country. Accordingly, Russia will
> follow the path outlined for it by Mr Putin. What else can it do?
> Local elections have been removed, the right to referendums has been
> taken away, the accountability of the electoral institutions to the popu-
> lation was done away with long ago. I see this directive as another
> trick. The state is creating a parallel human-rights movement.
>
> I see no ways of returning to a democratic path at present. I am
> not saying that we had a democracy, but there was a tendency in

that direction, which might have developed, given the existence of free mass media. We needed a proper electoral system; the last thing we needed was for it to be destroyed. The elections have long ago been turned into a fraud, and elections are the institution fundamental to any democracy.

All three branches of power in Russia, the executive, the judiciary and the legislature, have been made over to suit the President. We have ceased to be a democratic or, I would say, even a republican state. Formally, presidential elections are to take place (in 2008). If, of course, the country as it is being constructed by Putin survives that long. All channels for a legal and peaceful alteration of the situation in a democratic direction have been removed. Accordingly, this sealed boiler will heat up until it explodes. This can occur in a number of different ways.

*

Putin's 'International Human Rights Centre' never got off the drawing board. Funds were allocated from the budget, and somebody no doubt got their hands on them, but nothing else happened.

Putin's authority rests solely on the fact that there is no alternative to him within his entourage, which he has made faceless and dull. His supporters call this 'the loneliness of Putin'. There is nobody in his team who could replace him in an emergency. They are all pygmies with Napoleon complexes, or not even that.

Is a new, liberal, pro-Western party in the offing? Vladimir Ryzhkov could be its leader. He has matured a great deal. Such a party might succeed in completing the liberal-democratic revolution. The problem of our political elite, however, both of those in power and of those in opposition, is that they would prefer just to let things carry on, or at least crawl on, as they are.

28 September

Putin has not kept us waiting for long. Without any political debate, he has submitted to the Duma amendments to the electoral law abolishing the direct election of governors. The electorate are being bombarded with assurances that they are not yet sufficiently mature to choose the right local leader. Does that not mean they are also not yet mature enough to elect Putin?

29 September

A number of Duma Deputies have written to the Chairman of the Constitutional Court, Valerii Zorkin, asking him to review the President's actions as a matter of urgency.

*

Zorkin chose not to. The Deputies subsequently received a purely formal reply. The sense of hopelessness was as profound as in the final years of the USSR.

5 October

In Grozny the laughable inauguration of Alu Alkhanov, the President foisted on the people of Chechnya by the Kremlin, has taken place. They erected a marquee inside the fortified government compound and Alkhanov took the oath there, speaking in bad Chechen. He looked out of sorts, with heavy blue rings under his eyes. The security measures were unprecedented, as if they were expecting Putin, who didn't show up, but sent greetings. In the interests of security, three locations had been prepared and until the last moment nobody knew exactly where it would be.

What sort of peaceful life does that suggest? Alkhanov showed the whole of Chechnya how afraid he is of dying. Nobody will take him seriously now.

6 October

Joint Action, an association of the main human-rights organisations, has also issued a statement entitled 'A Coup d'État in Russia', calling for the convening of a Citizens' Congress that would evolve into an independent national forum involving the human-rights, ecological and other public associations, free trade unions, democratic parties, scholars, lawyers and journalists.

It is a peculiarity of Russia that the defenders of human rights – of whom several, like Lyudmila Alexeyeva, Sergey Kovalyov and Yury Samodurov are former Soviet dissidents – are far more resolute and progressive than the parties and politicians. They are urging the politicians: for heaven's sake, do something!

A serflike psychology has once again taken hold of the country, and rounds on anyone less servile. How malevolently Russian television rants when Yushchenko makes a mistake in Ukraine, and as for Saakashvili, he is the Kremlin's *bête noire*. Georgia is our main enemy among the countries of the former USSR.

7 October

In Vladimir, a first criminal case has been got up against the Committees of Soldiers' Mothers. The Chairperson of the Vladimir Committee, Lyudmila Yarilina, is accused of 'complicity in evasion of military service', an offence carrying a three- to seven-year prison sentence.

What is the basis of the accusation? Through her persistent defending of conscripts and soldiers, Lyudmila has made herself thoroughly unpopular with the local Military Commissariat and Military Procurator's Office. She agrees that a great many soldiers are found unfit for Army service in Vladimir Province. The area is notorious for alcoholism. It is a place where people drink more than they work, so the health of their children is poor. Half of them are invalids, but the Military Commissariat goes to extraordinary measures in order to get its quota of conscripts, falsifying health certificates and cheating the young men in other ways.

Between 400 and 500 people consult the Committee each year: conscripts, soldiers and their parents. Most of them want to be rescued from the brutal bullying of the 'grandads', older soldiers; from death and disease and a state machine that has no interest in investigating abuse.

When Dmitry Yepifanov came to the Committee he had already served several months in Chechnya and been wounded and burned in a tank. He was given leave and, back home in Vladimir, complained to his parents of constant stomach pains. He had suffered from these before going into the Army, but the conscription commission decided they posed no problem and sent him off to fight in Chechnya.

Dmitry came to ask how he could get into hospital during his leave. That was all. The system in Russia is quite absurd: if a soldier on leave is ill, he will not be admitted for diagnosis at the nearest military hospital, but must return to his unit, where an orderly or military doctor will decide whether to hospitalise him or whether he is malingering. If, however, a soldier can present a written diagnosis, he can be admitted to hospital locally.

Lyudmila began ringing round doctors she knew, and one, an endoscopist at the Vladimir Cancer Clinic, agreed to see Dmitry and, if necessary, conduct a gastroscopy. This duly revealed an ulcer, and he was admitted to hospital. Subsequently, Dmitry was sent from Vladimir to a hospital in Moscow, and from there to an Army commission. The military doctors in the capital discharged Private Yepifanov from the Army on the grounds that he had a duodenal ulcer.

The way this is presented in the materials of the criminal case is:

> L.A. Yarilina, being the Chairperson of the Vladimir regional section of the Committee of Soldiers' Mothers, on the pretext of providing assistance to obtain exemption from military service, with the assistance of medical workers of various hospitals in the City of Vladimir, connived at creating in citizens subject to conscription for military service, and also serving military personnel, a fictitious (feigned) illness, namely a duodenal ulcer, for which she received remuneration.

Of course, they never produced any evidence to support the allegation about receiving money, which was completely untrue, but the case proceeded nevertheless and the imagination of the investigators of the Military Procurator's Office proved boundless. Captain Golovkin, Assistant Military Procurator of the Vladimir Garrison, described the process by which the 'feigned' duodenal ulcer had been produced with Yarilina's complicity:

> With the assistance of an endoscopist, Yarilina assisted in conducting a biopsy on the bulb of the duodenal intestine with subsequent thermocoagulation of the site for the purpose of creating a post-cautery scar there, which a subsequent conscientious endoscopic investigation assessed as post-ulcerous – that is, a fictitious ailment, namely an ulcerous condition of the duodenal intestine.

It is Stalin's Doctors' Plot all over again, with dissidents as their accomplices.

'The materials of the case seem to be saying that you assisted the endoscopist.'

'Of course I didn't. I only asked him over the telephone to examine the boy,' Lyudmila replies.

So was Yepifanov malingering? Nobody is charging him with evasion of military service. Did the doctor deliberately harm him? Nobody is trying to prosecute him, either. The only person under criminal investigation is the human-rights campaigner Lyudmila Yarilina. Fabricating criminal cases against those who cause trouble, or are just too active, is part of life under Putin, both in Moscow, where Khodorkovsky and Lebedev are in prison, and in the provinces like Vladimir.

The 'good' defenders of human rights are those who try to help people by collaborating with the authorities rather than through constant confrontation, people like Pamfilova. For the bad ones, the technique is to try to marginalise them and, if necessary, use 'themocoagulation' to destroy them.

The method of thermocoagulation starts with an enervating, objectionable investigation. This leads to a trial followed, for the most intractable, by prison.

20 October

Dmitry Kozak, Putin's representative in South Russia, has appointed Ramzan Kadyrov as his security adviser for the entire Southern Federal District. If, before this, Kadyrov Junior was able to trample underfoot the law and the Constitution only in Chechnya and Ingushetia, now he will be able to share his experience and advise the directors of the Security Services throughout the North Caucasus region on how to behave similarly, and will supervise the atrocities they commit on behalf of Mr Kozak.

This is going to cost many lives. Ramzan is virtually brain-dead, and is in his element only where there is war, terror and chaos. Without them he literally does not know what to do.

Ramzan's promotion continues the suicidal policies that lead inexorably to future terrorist acts, and the consolidation of power in the hands of people who appear to want to do everything they can to ensure that the bombing of the Metro should be followed by the hijacking of aeroplanes, and after that the seizure of a school.

There is no special meaning to be found in this act by Putin. He has no idea what needs to be done next. It is Russia's familiar tragedy of having top political leaders who are incompetent, having landed their jobs through the operation of blind chance, and in turn promoting nonentities to positions of great power.

23 October

In Moscow a major demonstration has taken place to protest against the war in Chechnya and commemorate the victims of the terrorist acts. The meeting was held at 5.00 p.m., and from 10.00 a.m. there was a line of demonstrators on Pushkin Square. Those who suffered in the *Nord-Ost* siege were there for the first time, because today is the second anniversary of the hostage-taking.

The meeting was not 'official'. After Beslan a wave of officially organised anti-terrorist meetings rolled over the country on the initiative of the Presidential Administration. The Central Moscow authorities had agreed to a demonstration of up to 500 people, but around 3,000 turned up and the authorities warned that this was more than had been permitted. The second reason was that the slogans on banners were not only anti-war, but also anti-Government. But then, who is conducting the war?

A lot of those attending arrived in expensive cars, members of the middle class who don't usually attend such meetings. A cold, heavy rain was falling, but people came and stayed, which is significant. As Boris Nadezhdin, a member of Committee 2008 and Co-Chairman of the Union of Right Forces, said: 'This is a demonstration that people do not want to be held hostage to an ideologically generated fear, which is being imposed on them after Beslan . . . Chechnya is a terrible wound, which has caused both *Nord-Ost* and Beslan. In 1999 Russia was offered a physician who promised to cure the country, and he was elected President. He has not succeeded. Today, when we have no free mass media or parliament in Russia, there remains only one way of putting pressure on the state authorities; and that is good people coming out to demonstrate.'

The good people stood in the square in the pouring rain, bearing placards reading, 'We are the West's fifth column!', alluding to an interview by Vladislav Surkov in *Komsomolskaya pravda*, in which he had the gall to say that the opposition was a section of society 'irrevocably lost as partners'; that Russia was under siege; that the liberals and nationalists were a fifth column financed by the West; that there was no such thing as Putin's Russia, there was 'only Russia', and that anybody who didn't believe that was an enemy.

This is no longer a neo-Soviet ideology: this is the Soviet regime pure and simple. No sooner has the Communist elite got rid of hindrances such as the decayed Party Central Committee, and gained limitless opportunities for self-enrichment, than it has started resurrecting the ideological frameworks of the past. Surkov is regarded nowadays as Putin's chief ideologist.

It is the autumn of 2004, but a political winter has already set in that makes your blood run cold.

25 October

The magazine *Itogi* asks the Governor of St Petersburg, 'Could Russia be a parliamentary republic without a president?' Valentina Matvienko, a close ally of Putin, replies, 'No, that wouldn't work for us. The Russian mentality prefers a master, a tsar, a president. In other words, a leader.' Matvienko is capable only of repeating what she hears in Putin's immediate entourage.

The Human Rights Association has responded:

> We are outraged by this pronouncement, which is an insult to the national dignity of the Russian people. The sense of these words is clearly that the Russian people are serfs who cannot do without a master, craven subjects who cannot get by without a tsar. The addition of the word 'president' only makes it clear that the new ruling elite sees the head of state not as a democratic leader, but as an authoritarian potentate. This assertion of the innate servility of the Russian people is racist. In effect the Governor of St Petersburg has expressed her disagreement with the Constitution's premises of inviolable democratic freedoms ... The notion of our national inferiority and the innate servility of the Russian people is at the heart of the main Russophobic theories. It was such doctrines that the ideologists of German Nazism used to underpin their aggressive attitude towards Russia. It is particularly reprehensible that such views should come from the person in charge of the Heroic City of Leningrad. We demand the immediate resignation of Valentina Matvienko.

Nobody thought it necessary to reply. The new ruling elite no longer consider it necessary to conceal their true attitude towards the majority of their compatriots and the principles of constitutional democracy.

28 October

A very public split in the Yabloko party. The youth wing are being shown on the main television stations taking issue with Yavlinsky.

Meetings in support of Putin, organised by United Russia, are taking place in many cities. The largest is in Moscow, and it was there that the leader of the youth wing of Yabloko spoke out.

Students and pensioners are the mainstay of protest meetings organised by the opposition. For the first time, the Communist Party, Yabloko and the Union of Right Forces are uniting to conduct anti-Putin protests.

29 October

The state authorities remain on course for the abyss, taking all of us with them. The Procurator-General, Vladimir Ustinov, announced in the Duma that, in the opinion of the main institution charged with supervising citizens' rights, and of himself, it is necessary urgently to adopt a law regulating action to be taken in the event of a terrorist attack. His main proposals are that fast-track court proceedings for terror suspects be introduced; that relatives of terrorists be seized as counter-hostages; that the property of terrorists be confiscated.

The prospect of having a video recorder, television or even their Zhiguli confiscated seems unlikely to deter those going off to commit suicide and slaughter other people.

The Procurator-General's idea of fast-track court proceedings for terrorist suspects is a straightforward revival of what were known under Stalin as 'mass purges'; or more recently, to use the language of the 'anti-terrorist operation', 'cleansings'. All these simplified procedures are only too familiar in Chechnya and Ingushetia, where they have been in use for five years and more. The security agencies (all of them: the Interior Ministry, FSB, the Army's Central Intelligence Directorate and others) arrest whomever they want, sometimes after receiving operational information, but more often without it. They beat, cripple and torture as they see fit, extracting confessions of terrorist activity or at least of sympathy with the terrorists, although in reality they don't really even need the confessions.

There are two possible outcomes: if their victim has been seriously mutilated, they kill and bury him; or if the family has managed to raise a bribe, they put him in court. Nobody has the least interest in evidence. In the 'zone of the anti-terrorist operation', fast-track court cases are the only kind they have. Gotcha! You are a member of an illegal armed grouping: 15 or 20 years. The presence of a lawyer and procurator at the trial is purely decorative, to give a veneer of legality to the statistics of terrorists condemned and terrorist acts averted. The lawyers usually do no more than persuade the accused to confess to everything; the task of the procurator is to tell the family that complaining will only make matters worse.

Our Procurator-General's stated plans would effectively abolish the presumption of innocence. In the 'zone of the anti-terrorist operation', in Chechnya and Ingushetia, there has been a presumption of guilt for several years and in future that will extend to the rest of Russia. For the past five years most people had supposed that the horror of extra-judicial lawlessness on the part of state institutions would affect only far-away rebels, which was nothing to worry about; the rest of Russia would somehow be immune. Unfortunately, miracles do not happen. At some point the practice was bound to spread.

The Procurator-General's proposal to seize relatives as counter-hostages is undoubtedly innovative. He explained to our Duma Deputies that we would seize the terrorists' relatives, demonstrate what might happen to them, and the terrorists would then free their own hostages and surrender.

This method has also been used in Chechnya, particularly during the Second Chechen War when Kadyrov's forces became powerful. Torturing relatives in order to make those they are seeking surrender has become their trademark. Kadyrov-style hostage-taking has, however, also been practised on the state's behalf with the blessing of the Directorate of the Procurator-General in the North Caucasus, and with complete disregard of the law and Constitution by the procurators.

We now find ourselves in a disastrous situation. For five years the Procurator-General's Office has been encouraging a wave of terrorism in the North Caucasus, carried out in accordance with the wishes of the President of Russia. It has not only condoned this by averting its eyes: procurators have often been present during torture sessions and executions, and have then issued assurances that everything has taken place within the framework of the law.

What kind of arguments can now be found to persuade people like that? How can someone who is in reality an anti-Procurator-General be made to withdraw his bloodthirsty innovations from the Duma? The Procurator-General's Office is interested solely in its own institutional survival, in ranks and rewards, in concealing the truth about what it has been complicit in. The state authorities hold on to their power at the price of our lives. It's as simple as that.

The Procurator-General's speech to the Duma was interrupted – by applause. Our Parliament thought it was all a great idea. President Putin, sworn to protect the Constitution, did not remove a Procurator-General who was proposing massive violations of the law.

The year 1937 marked the height of Stalin's terror. Today Chechnya's 1937 is developing into another 1937 for Russians generally, whether we attend meetings at the Solovki Rock memorial to Stalin's victims or not. Any of us might now go out to buy bread and never return. Or return 20 years later. In Chechnya people say their farewells before going to the bazaar, just in case.

On 29 October 2004, as ever, the Russian people remained silent, hoping it would be the neighbours they would come to get.

3 November

The Soviet of the Federation has rubber-stamped the abolition of the local election of governors.

6 November

Mikhail Yuriev, a former journalist who now works in the Kremlin, has placed an article on behalf of the Presidential Administration in *Komsomolskaya gazeta*, helpfully advising on how to differentiate between someone who is helpful to the President and someone who is an enemy of Russia. The false antithesis is blatant and deliberate. According to Yuriev, an enemy of Russia is anybody who criticises Putin. Those who spoke in favour of negotiations during Beslan, or against using chemical weapons in the *Nord-Ost* assault, are enemies; as are those who attend protest meetings against the war in Chechnya, or who organise them. Likewise those who call for peace talks on Chechnya and cessation of the civil war.

The Committees of Soldiers' Mothers have formed their own political party, as they said they would back in February. Their founding congress is no random event. It results from the complete devastation of our political landscape after the Duma elections, when those Deputies they could rely on to lobby for military reform and the interests of conscripts all lost their seats. As their Chairperson, Valentina Melnikova, said: 'Our party programme sets out our basic goals as being to ensure that the state takes a responsible attitude towards human beings, and to create a secure framework for life in Russia. Bringing about a democratic transformation of the Russian Armed Forces is only a part of that larger task. In economics we are a party tending towards liberalism, and as regards the state's responsibilities towards society we incline towards socialism.'

The Party of Soldiers' Mothers is the first political organisation in Russia to state that it will fight to protect our lives. The Russian electorate doesn't really have that great a choice. Our politicians might slip us a hundred roubles before election day, but they have no time to fight for the issues that vitally affect us. They are far too busy fighting for their own place in the sun.

The founding congress took place on board the steamer *Konstantin Fedin*, moored for the winter in the furthest corner of Moscow's Northern River Port. Why was it held on a steamer? Because nobody would give it house room for fear of the regime's reaction.

The party was established by 154 representatives from more than 50 regions, all of them part of a movement that has saved the lives of thousands of conscripts and new recruits since its foundation in 1989. The movement began back in the USSR. In the late 1980s, women trying to protect their sons from the bullying of the Army's grandads and from universal conscription began forming themselves into committees. In 1989 they were successful in persuading Gorbachev to release 176,000 soldiers from the Army ahead of time so that they could continue their education. In 1990 he also issued directives 'On the Implementation of Proposals from the Committee of Soldiers' Mothers' and on state insurance benefits for conscripts. In 1991 the Committees were successful in having Yeltsin grant an amnesty to soldiers who had deserted, and in 1993–4 their persistence ensured an inquiry into the deaths from starvation, disease and torture of more than 200 sailors on the island of Russkoye. Between 1994 and 1998 they were the first of Russia's human-rights organisations to demand immediate cessation of the war in Chechnya, got President Yeltsin to pardon 500 soldiers who had conscientiously objected to participating in the First Chechen War, forced an amnesty for all who had participated on either side in the Chechen War, and managed to get a ring-fenced item included in the state budget for seeking and identifying the remains of soldiers killed in Chechnya. Since 1999 the Soldiers' Mothers have demonstrated against the Second Chechen War, conducting a public campaign against falsification of the true numbers of casualties, and compiling and publishing lists of those who had died and disappeared without trace.

Their main goal became putting an end to the slavery of conscription and replacing it with a fully professional army. All the democratic parties supported them and, with time, the idea of a professional army was accepted by top officials and successive Ministers of Defence, whose speeches were often taken word for word from their flysheets. But in the implementation everything was twisted: contracts were signed on a 'compulsory voluntary' basis, wages were not paid, the war continued and recruits were sent straight to Chechnya. After last December's elections there was nobody left in Parliament to lobby for democratic legislative projects.

In late January 2004 the Soldiers' Mothers decided it was time to create their own party. Ten months passed, because creating a new party involves a huge amount of bureaucracy and is extremely expensive. During this period they were stigmatised as a fifth column, supported by the West to undermine Russia's combat capability. That is, they were 'enemies within' in a period of military extremity.

Their political strength, and the thing that will ensure their survival, is that their policies come from the heart. Until now people here have become politicians at the dictate of their minds. Party passions simmered primarily over who was to be top dog, rather than what could be done for the electorate. In 2003 the state authorities played on this very successfully and sordid compromises undermined what trust people still had in the opposition. In the end no democrats or liberals made it into the Duma.

The Soldiers' Mothers greatest strength is their passion to defend our children, and our trust that they will do this to the best of their ability. They have no other political capital. Their maternal urge sweeps all before it, as was evident within two minutes of talking to any of the delegates outside the conference hall (and, indeed, inside it). We soon found ourselves discussing the fate of some particular soldier who urgently needed help: 'Look at what is happening in our region,' Lyudmila Bogatenkova from Budyonnovsk said, pulling from her bag a stack of soldiers' testimonies about the most appalling treatment. She has brought them for the main Military Procurator's Office.

'For as long as there is conscription, the soldier in the Army is a nobody,' Lyudmila Vasilievna says indignantly. 'He can be used for anything. He can be used as an unpaid labourer. Millions of our people are slaves today, and our mission is to bring about the abolition of this slavery. There can be no compromise about that!'

The main discussion at the Congress concerned the wording of the manifesto. Should they campaign for the abolition of conscription, or leave it to one side for the time being? More generally, should the new party follow the usual Russian path of cocking a snook when no one is looking, saying that you are against conscription, but leaving it out of the programme so as not to upset the Presidential Administration and making it easier to get the party registered? Or should they be completely honest and worry only about gaining the respect of the Russian people?

In this major matter of principle, the second approach won. Passionate conviction is impossible without total honesty. Abolition of conscription went into the manifesto. They will fight for it, and thank God for that, because being trusted by the electorate will be their main asset. If they start trying to strike 'sensible compromises', they will be cheated by the authorities, who know how to manipulate compromise-mongers, and the voters will desert them.

'Yes, it's important that our women should get into the Duma,' Lyudmila Bogatenkova explains. 'Otherwise it would be impossible to push through the abolition of conscription. If we are in the Duma it will also be simpler to help soldiers and conscripts in particular situations, and to prevent the authorities from stonewalling when a crime has been committed.'

One of the few remaining ways to exert influence, after the resurgence of the bureaucracy, is the parliamentary question. A Deputy's question can produce rapid and significant results, and speed is often essential. Most of the cases where soldiers have been saved have required prompt investigation and action. When a story gets publicity and a Deputy gets through to the Procurator-General's Office, somebody in the closed world of the Army has a chance of surviving. The lack of that opportunity often means death.

One of the first toasts proclaimed after the creation of the party was: 'To 2007! Look out Duma, here we come!'

The Party of Soldiers' Mothers has a lesson to teach the world. It will have to create its own future with the sincere passion that the women in their Committees live by. For a long time we have been told that the more cunning a democratic politician, the more effective he is. This has proved to be untrue. Our people do not care for cleverness and cunning, or for those who lack passion. That's the kind of people we are. First the passion, then clear-headed, straight thinking. Never the reverse.

9 November

The Kaluga branch of the Yabloko party has demanded a referendum on retaining benefits in kind for retired workers, victims of Soviet repression, and those who worked on the home front during the Second World War. The benefits concerned are free travel on suburban buses and free medicine. The Kaluga Province authorities were planning to abolish all benefits in kind in return for a derisory monthly supplement to pensions of 200–300 roubles [£4–6]. So far, officialdom has paid no attention to protests, but a referendum might force a rethink. This is a very sensitive matter. Who will be entitled to benefits after 1 January 2005? The 'monetarisation' of benefits was intended to reduce the number of claimants, which we are told is currently half the country. There is certainly scope for rationalisation.

*

Nothing came of the idea of a referendum. The democrats abandoned it because they thought the resistance was too great.

11 November

Crisis in Karachaevo-Cherkessia. A crowd has occupied the office of Mustafa Batdyev, the President, and is demanding his resignation. The reason is a case involving the abduction, murder and destruction of the bodies of seven young businessmen in which Batdyev's brother-in-law was involved. He has already been arrested.

The authorities are in an unenviable position. If Batdyev is thrown out, there may be a chain reaction. Next in turn will surely be Murat Zyazikov in Ingushetia. Batdyev ran away from trouble, just like Zyazikov did earlier in the year, but was sent back by Kozak, Putin's representative in the Southern Federal District. It was Kozak who came to talk to the people in Cherkessk, and a few hours later the television stations were announcing the good news that the 'coup' had failed. Kozak had persuaded the crowd to leave Batdyev's office, he would return and his administration would continue as before.

It was another disaster for Putin's human-resources policy. The Kremlin-controlled local leaders are incapable of leading, or taking any responsibility at all. At the least sign of danger, they run for their lives. The authorities, meanwhile, react to a mob. Kozak would have gone nowhere if the mob had not seized Batdyev's office by force. If people had requested a meeting with him, they would have had to badger him for a good six months, no matter how serious the issue.

26 November

It is a year now since Khodorkovsky was arrested. The authorities ignore the anniversary. In the days of the Soviet Union the mediator between society and the state was the KGB, which provided the authorities with distorted information about what was going on, and this ultimately led to the collapse of the USSR.

Today's FSB also seriously distorts information going upstairs, but Putin distrusts all other sources. The aorta will duly be blocked again. Let's hope we don't have to wait 70 years this time.

11 December

What speed! The President has already signed the law abolishing the election of governors. It has been our fastest ever passage of a law, and all so that from 1 January Putin should not have to discuss matters with the governors or worry that they might be uncooperative. A Tsar should have serfs, not partners. Some of the children massacred at Beslan have yet to be identified and buried, but that's not the priority. The parents are increasingly being left to sort that out themselves. What is really important is to change the structure of the state into something more amenable to Putin.

As for Beslan, the town is quietly going out of its mind. The autumn that began on 1 September is over now, and the onset of winter certainly hasn't made anyone feel better. Certainly not the families whose children have yet to be found, who have no child, no funeral, no grave where they can mourn. Zhorik Agaev, Aslan Kisiev, Zarina Normatova, all junior pupils born in 1997, and 11-year-old Aza Gumetsova have yet to be found. Zifa, the mother of second-year Zhorik Agaev, almost never leaves home. She stays in waiting for him.

'What if he came back and I wasn't here! What sort of welcome would that be?' Zifa says, smiling somewhere inside herself. Her mouth is twisted: she was wounded at the school. 'I know people in this town think I am crazy, but I'm not. I am just certain that my Zhorik is alive. He is being held somewhere.'

Families whose children are listed as missing divide into two groups. Some, like Zifa, believe they are being held hostage. Others believe they are dead, and that their remains have been buried by somebody else by mistake.

Zifa's strangeness has several causes, which God grant you may never experience. She is the hostage who let the children in the gymnasium drink from her own breast. She gave her breast to all who were sitting near her. Later she squeezed the life-giving liquid out, drop by drop, into a spoon that the children passed round.

'Zhorik will come back and everything will be the same again. Do you know, on 3 September it was very quiet in the hall. The terrorists had gone off somewhere, there were very few of them with us. We were already crawling over the trip wires, we didn't care about anything by then. I began hallucinating, imagining I was in a coffin. Then I imagined I heard a terrorist calling, "Agaevs, some water has been brought for you, take it!" I must have frightened Zhorik, because he crawled away from me.'

Suddenly Zifa was blown out of the window by the blast of an explosion. Everybody who had been sitting near her was burned to death. Half her face was mutilated; she has had operations and there are more to come. Four pieces of shrapnel can't be removed.

'All these scars and fragments don't matter. What matters is Zhorik. When he comes back we will celebrate his rebirth,' she says again and again. 'How I'll shout, "Look everybody! Zhorik has come back!" I won't let him go away ever again . . . I won't let them bring any of their bags into my house. Zhorik is alive!' By now she is in desperation. 'Zhorik in a bag? Never!'

A 'bag' is Beslan newspeak for human remains brought from the Rostov-on-Don military mortuary after identification. Zhorik's remains haven't been identified, although there are unclaimed remains of boys of approximately his age. What is going on?

Zifa by now is quiet and calm, her voice just that of a mother devastated by the loss of her child: 'When Zhorik comes back, I will take him to President Dzasokhov and President Putin and say, "Look! This is the angel you made no attempt to save!"'

Then, in a whisper: 'I shall never eat raspberry jam again. For those first two hours we were so afraid. When Zhorik shouted, "He's killed him!" I said, "It's just a film they're making." Zhorik said, "But why is it so real? And what is this running towards us?" I said, "It's just raspberry jam, Zhorik."'

Marina Kisieva is 31 and lives in the village of Khumalag, a 20-minute drive from Beslan. She lost her husband, Artur, and her son Aslan in the atrocity. Aslan was seven and a pupil in Class 2A. Marina now has only her daughter, five-year-old Milena, who is serious beyond her years and never asks where Aslan has gone. She simply refuses to go to nursery, and she used to faint whenever the women in their apartment block began wailing.

Aslan's teacher, Raisa Kambulatovna Dzaragasova-Kibizova, would later say that Artur 'was the best father in the class'. It was he who insisted that Aslan should go to the best school in Beslan, and it was he who did the driving, although he had a job and was also studying. Marina shows me his last piece of coursework, 'Creating Rights', for the Law Faculty of the Pyatigorsk campus of the Russian University of Commerce and Economics. Just one day before 1 September, Artur came back from Pyatigorsk in order to take his son to school himself. Marina was intending to go too, and stayed at home quite by chance.

'Why did I stay behind? I would have got him out of the gymnasium! Aslan was a loppy-eared, thin, funny little boy. Everybody loved him. He was very timid,' Marina says, furrowing her eyebrows, trying not to cry in front of Milena.

Artur was killed almost immediately. They shot him on 1 September when the terrorists took the men away to work on fortifying the building and hanging out explosives. Apparently Artur said, 'Do you think I'm going to kill children with my own hands?' and they killed him.

Aslan was left in the gym without his father. He crept over to his teacher, Raisa Kambulatovna, and stayed close to her almost to the end, constantly asking, 'Where is Artur?'

Raisa Kambulatovna is 62. On 1 September she had been a school-teacher for 40 years. 'Could I have imagined that I would spend my anniversary not receiving flowers, but under a hail of bullets?' Like many experienced teachers, Raisa Kambulatovna sits very upright and holds her head high, even now when a campaign has started in Beslan – deliberately fomented by the intelligence services and agents from the Procurator-General's Office – to seek 'the killers' among the teachers who survived.

'Yes, they're trying to shift the blame on to us, as if to say, "They can't have done their duty towards the children if they survived and the children didn't." Don't imagine anyone could have done anything to save anyone. There was nothing to be done, either before the explosion or after it. The duty of the teachers in there was to be an older friend, to set an example and give the children strength. That's exactly what they did until the explosion. After that there was nothing anybody could do. By 3 September everybody was completely dazed, having hallucinations. I tried so hard to protect Aslan, but at the very end I was unable to save him.

'On 1 September we had been among the first to be herded into the gymnasium because our class, 2A, was at the front of the procession, near the school doors. I sat down in the hall in front of my class. At my back were pupils and their parents. The explosives were hanging above me. Artur Kisiev was with his son, like everyone else. The fighters said, "All the daddies come to the front, please." Five minutes later they shot them in the corridor. That's how two of my pupils lost their fathers, Misikov and Kisiev. I said to my children, "They won't shoot children."

'Aslan was lying at my feet and said he was hungry. I did everything I could to feed him. The first evening there was a young mother next to us with a little child who kept crying. She was rocking him, but he wouldn't stop. At first a fighter pointed his rifle at her as if ordering her to keep him quiet. Then he gave a deep sigh and took out a bottle of water. "This is my water. Give it to the child. And here are two Mars bars. Get him to suck them through a cloth." The mother was afraid it was poison, but I said to her, "We're not going to get out of this alive anyway. At least let the child quieten down now." She broke off a piece of one of the bars and gave it to the child to suck through some cloth. The remainder, one and a half of their Mars bars, I hid behind my back. I broke off a big piece for Aslan and quietly gave the rest to the children from my class.

'The second night, when everybody was terribly thirsty and they weren't letting any of the children go to the toilet, I said, "Just do it on the floor." They relaxed and started doing as I suggested. The boys were given cut-off bottles to pee in. I told them to drink from them. The children didn't want to, so then I drank some of the urine of the oldest pupil, a boy in the sixth grade who had been in my class in the primary school. I didn't even hold my nose, so that the children should see it wasn't that bad. After that they started drinking it, Aslan too. On the morning of 3 September Karina Melikova, a girl in the fifth grade, unexpectedly asked to go to the toilet. They let her out and her mother, who teaches one of the primary classes, told her to pull some leaves off the house plants in the office, because they let them go to the toilet in the office where they had broken a hole in the floor. Karina managed to pull off some leaves, hide them between the pages of a notebook and bring them back to the hall. We gave the leaves to the children, and Aslan ate one that second day. Karina and her mother were both killed. Whose fault is that? I lost Aslan at the very last moment.

'Immediately before the assault many people were feeling very ill. Some were lying there unconscious and being trodden on. Taisya Khetagurova, the teacher of Ossetian language, wasn't well. I crawled over to pull her to the wall, to stop her being trodden on, and left Aslan for a moment. And that was it. I didn't hear the explosion or the shooting. The world simply disappeared. I came to when Special Operations troops trod on me. They just walked over our bodies and they walked over me too. I began to be able to feel again and started crawling out. There were bodies beside me, piled one on top of another. Why did I survive and not them? Why did seven of my second-grade pupils die, when I, who am already sixty-two, didn't? And where is Aslan? I see him in front of me every night, creeping towards me like a little mouse. His mother is half-dead, I know. I have met her.'

Marina leafs through Aslan's school books. That has been her main occupation this autumn. She went to the school, rummaged through everything in the office of 2A and found Aslan's books from his first year, and those, unwritten in, that Raisa Kambulatovna had prepared for her pupils entering second grade. For hours Marina reads and rereads the five lines from the only annual dictation test her son was destined to sit: 'The eighteenth of May. In the garden a wild rose is growing. It has lovely, fragrant flowers . . .' Behind Marina's back as she gazes at these books is a bed on which Artur's favourite things are laid out: an open pack of cigarettes, his student record, his registration card, his course work. And his portrait. He looks very stern, but has thoughtful eyes. Milena is completely silent when she moves in front of the portrait.

'For the first two months I was completely numb. I didn't go out. I neglected the house. I wanted nothing to do with my daughter. I was completely isolated. I couldn't bear to turn the tap on, I couldn't bear to hear the sound of running water. Why didn't they let the children drink? It angered me that people went on eating and drinking after 1 September. I was going crazy. I still am.'

Marina shows me a letter that was brought to her home together with a new satchel, charity for Aslan 'from the schoolchildren of St Petersburg'.

'Why did they have to do that, when everybody knew our son had died?'

There is a letter 'from Irusya, 14'. It reads, 'You survived those terrible days. You are a hero!' There follows an invitation to be pen-friends.

'How could our address have got on to the wrong list?' Marina asks, crying from the hurt caused by this dreadful act of carelessness. 'The satchel was unbearable. It was just the opposite of what we needed. I understand now that nobody is going to help me. Where is that Putin? Too busy with some drivel to give orders for all the bodies to be identified as soon as possible, those that can be. Then at least some of the parents could be at peace and have a grave to tend.'

Sasha Gumetsov and Rimma Torchinova are the parents of Aza Gumetsova. Sasha is beside himself with grief and self-torment. He cannot sleep at night, blaming himself for failing to save his daughter. He has black rings under his eyes and hasn't shaved for many days. Sasha and Rimma are heroically going round Beslan from house to house, trying to persuade mothers and fathers who have buried their children to have the bodies exhumed.

'At first, of course, we believed that Aza was being held hostage. Gradually we had to recognise that was not the case. On 4 September parents were "identifying" their children by the pants they were wearing, because you couldn't identify them from anything else. They only took charred bodies for DNA identification at the forensic medical laboratory in Rostov, but there were so many that a lot were just left here, unidentified. People took them back to their homes. This is a small town, we don't have any smart boutiques, and many of the children had identical clothes from the bazaar. That's how everything got muddled up. We could see how it happened as we went round the mortuaries ourselves, looking into every bag, examining every little finger.'

'How could you bear do to that?'

Not a muscle flickers on Rimma's face.

'I told myself, "Nothing could be worse than what the children went through in that school. I have no right to pity myself." And I don't. Now the only question for us is how to bury our child, how to perform our last duty to Aza. In the mortuary there is the body of an unidentified little girl of a similar age to ours, but she is not Aza. That means that somebody else has our daughter in a grave. It might be the parents of the little girl in the mortuary. We realise, of course, that the chain of who belongs to whom could turn out to be very long. We are only too aware of that.'

'The chain of exhumations?'

'Of course. On the list we were given by the Procurator's Office there are 38 addresses of people who might have buried the wrong child. Thirty-eight girls of roughly the same age and build died. The main thing is that we are on the right track: if the total number of remains in Rostov and the number of those missing are the same, then it is simply a matter of errors in identification. They have all been found, only they've been mixed up.'

On 1 September, Aza went to school alone for the first time, without her mother, without flowers, as she and her best friends from Class 6G, who were beginning to grow up, had agreed. One was Sveta Tsoy, a Korean girl, the only child of Marina Park: Sveta the dancer,

Sveta the fantasist, Sveta the star of the Theatre of Children's Fashion, Sveta who was identified only on 27 September by DNA analysis because her legs had been blown off and her body was unidentifiable.

Another friend, Emma Khaeva, was brimming with energy. She would make up impromptu poems. When she was running to school in the morning, she always found time to say good morning to all the neighbours and to ask the old ladies along her route how they were feeling. Her parents were lucky. She was killed too, but could be buried in an open coffin.

And then there was Aza, the only, adored daughter of Rimma and Sasha. Rimma didn't go out to work. She gave Aza every opportunity that Beslan had to offer: dancing, singing, languages, societies. 'I used to tell myself the three of them were people of the twenty-first century,' Rimma continues. 'They were not like us. They had a positive attitude towards life. They wanted a lot. Aza had her own opinion about everything. She was a philosopher.'

All we now know is that Emma, Sveta and Aza were at first separated in the gym, but on 3 September managed to move towards each other. They decided to celebrate the birthday of Madina Sazanova, another of their classmates, and were last seen sitting together right under the window where the wall was blown in to make an opening for the children to escape.

'I haven't heard of anybody sitting by that part of the wall who survived,' Rimma concludes. 'All that is left now is for us to bury Aza. We go round the addresses, working down the list, as if it were a job. We try to talk people into agreeing.'

What respect can anyone have for a state machine that dementedly replicates these cataclysmic events for its citizens: first *Nord-Ost*, then Beslan. The state refuses ever to admit responsibility for anything, and furtively shuffles off all its other duties too. Should there be exhumations? Leave it to the most vulnerable to worry about that. We will set them against each other, the families who have buried their dead and those who have no dead to bury, and everyone will forget to protest against Dzasokhov and Putin. They won't demand a genuine inquiry for a long time. They will have other things to worry about.

The state has distanced itself from everything that happened at Beslan, abandoning the town to madness in its isolation. Nobody else in Russia wants to know.

12 December

In Moscow, the National Citizens' Congress has brought together delegates from every part of Russia. There were hopes that it would turn into a front of national salvation, but that hasn't worked out. The reason is simple: Georgii Satarov and Lyudmila Alexeyeva, who organised the event, don't want to tread on the Kremlin's toes. Accordingly, sitting up there in the presidium, they quash 'excessive' criticism of Putin, with the result that, by the end of the sessions, almost nobody is left in the hall. When Garry Kasparov, one opposition leader who actually is beginning to make a mark, came to the rostrum, people shouted, 'Kasparov for President!' The organisers were so put out by this that they sidelined Kasparov for the rest of the Congress.

Centre stage was taken by the same old dears, and they reduced everything to a talking shop, shaping a Congress in their own image.

The question is: can an extra-parliamentary democratic opposition exist at all at present? If it should come into being, will it be able to keep its head above the water in a corrupt society where only those who can lobby the authorities can raise funds from 'sponsors'?

Who could sponsor it anyway? Only oligarchs, and given that it is open season for hunting oligarchs there are no takers, apart from Berezovsky. A financial link with him would send voters fleeing in the opposite direction.

There is another problem. Hatred does not work as a platform for parliamentary elections and political struggle in Russia. The democrats cannot build their campaigning on hatred.

What can they build it on, if they have no positive ideas? Well, they damned well should have positive ideas! The average life expectancy in Russia is 58 years and six months. Why not make the main plank in your election platform a demand to let people live at least to 70!

The liberals and democrats are approaching the New Year of 2005 as political sleep-walkers. In the year since they were trounced in the parliamentary elections they haven't even managed a realistic assessment of why they were defeated.

The dissidents and the democrats both tried to fool the people for too long into believing that Yeltsin, of all people, was a real democrat. There came a time when that fairy tale became unsustainable and 'democrat' became literally a dirty word: people changed the word '*demokrat*' to '*dermokrat*' (shitocrat). It became current not only among fanatical Communists and Stalinists, but among the majority of the population.

The 'dermocrats' had given Russia hyper-inflation, made them lose the savings they had carried forward from Soviet times, started the war in Chechnya and presided over the Russian Government's currency default.

People didn't elect Yeltsin in 1996 because they believed in him, but simply as the lesser of two evils; not because they believed in his prescription for taking the country forward, but because they feared what might happen if the Communists got back in. Government resources were shamelessly exploited, national television stations broadcast only in favour of Yeltsin and were in effect his campaign cheer-leaders. People turned away in disgust when they saw how the 'democratic' parties kept silent about this travesty of democracy. A number of democrats even stated openly that it was reasonable to sacrifice the truth in order to save democracy.

This enthusiasm for sacrificing the truth caught on, and became the main force propelling Putin to power after Yeltsin proclaimed him his successor. The Kremlin took control of all television news coverage, with independent stations allowed only to provide entertainment, even when hundreds were being killed in Chechnya.

And that was the end of that. The election was based on trickery, fraudulence and state coercion. The democrats kept mum, trying to cling to their vestiges of power in the Duma and locally. They forfeited whatever was left of their authority, and the Russian people are now profoundly indifferent to all things political. That is the terrible legacy of 13 years of Russian democracy.

[10–14 December

An incident in Blagoveshchensk involving three masked militiamen and the owners of a local casino, against whom the mayor had a grudge, led to a grotesque overreaction when the Deputy Minister of the Interior of Bashkiria* sent in a 40-strong militia Special Operations unit. Armed with truncheons and rifles, they descended on the main street and started dragging out and arresting any man they found in the cafés and gaming establishments. Those arrested were photographed, fingerprinted, beaten and forced to sign blank statement forms.

After being searched in public, girls were taken to a room on the first floor of the city's Internal Affairs Directorate. The Special Operations troops queued at the door, and witnesses state that half a bucketful of used condoms were subsequently brought out. Over the next four days a great many men were beaten up and women raped. Local taxi drivers report that the troops sent them for vodka, and that the screams of girls were to be heard coming from the local swimming pool. The attacks later spread to neighbouring villages.

There followed a massive official attempt to intimidate witnesses and cover up the reality of what had happened.]

14 December

A group of students and school pupils belonging to the National Bolshevik Party entered the reception area of the Presidential Administration in Bolshoy Cherkassky Lane, barricaded themselves into a ground-floor office and began shouting slogans out of the window: 'Putin – *you* get out!', 'Putin, sink with the *Kursk!*' and the like. Forty-five minutes later, through the joint efforts of OMON and the Federal Security Service, they were all brutally restrained. Lira Guskova, 22, ended up in a prison hospital with severe concussion; Yevgeny Taranenko, 23, had his nose broken by the soldiers; and Vladimir Lindu, 23, who has dual Dutch and Russian citizenship, suffered leg injuries.

PART THREE

Our Winter and Summer of Discontent

January–August 2005

Russia after Ukraine,
by Way of Kirghizia

The Ukrainian Orange Revolution* of December 2004 put an end to the Great Russian Political Depression. Society was shaken out of its torpor: everybody so envied them their Maidan Square. 'For heaven's sake, why aren't we like they are in Ukraine?' people asked. 'They're just the same as us, only . . .'

Everyone had their own arguments to prove that we and the Ukrainians are as alike as peas in a pod. A vast number of people living in Russia are either pure Ukrainian or half- or quarter-Ukrainian. In the Soviet Union there was no city closer to Moscow than Kiev, and everything in our way of life was so intertwined there was no way we could ever be pulled apart. Even after the break-up of the USSR, most Russians were certain Ukraine would remain an adjunct and a semi-colony, and that Moscow would decide what was best for Kiev.

Only, it all turned out differently. While the former imperial capital continued to delude itself that its ex-colony would stay in line, the ex-colonials underwent a remarkable transformation and developed into a nation.

The political passions of the Orange Revolution did not, however, sweep like wildfire over Russia; they gave a boost to the spirit of protest. They got people off their sofas to at least think of demonstrating; but that was as far as it went in January 2005. Millions took part in demonstrations against the law to replace the extensive system of benefits in kind with token monetary compensation which came into effect on 1 January. There were hopes of a revival of democratic opposition.

*

January was nothing but protest meetings. The sick lost their right to free medicine. Soldiers lost their right to send letters home without paying postage, a monstrous deprivation because they have almost no money. If their parents could not afford to give them money, there would be no letters home. Expectant mothers lost the right to paid leave, which is hardly the best way to go about raising our abysmal birth rate.

[In the summer of 2004, when the reform was passed by the Duma, Anna was in Yekaterinburg in the Urals. She wrote at the time:]

Here, in Sverdlovsk Province, live 20,000 ex-servicemen who have fought in the Chechen War. Almost all of them qualify for benefits in kind as former participants in the 'anti-terrorist operation'. They see the Government's benefit reform as a crusade against themselves.

The 'Chechens' here in the Urals can barely make ends meet. Nobody wants to employ or teach them, and many become alcoholics, junkies or thieves and end up in prison. In the village of Repino they have actually set up an Association of Ex-Servicemen of the Chechen Wars inside the prison. It has 200 members.

They are not welcome in free institutions and hospitals, and usually have no money to pay privately for the services they need. They are driven like lepers out of hostels, become outcasts and gravitate into their own groupings, 'Chechen' communities and associations. Most of them see the material privileges as a token of at least some kind of respect and gratitude from society, as compensation for lives broken at the very outset. Abolishing these privileges and replacing them by a cash pittance is seen as a final kick in the teeth from the state to which their comrades sacrificed their lives and they sacrificed their health.

The wounded and disabled will simply die. Many will lose jobs they were barely managing to cling to. The few who, in spite of everything, were studying will lose educational privileges extracted from the state only with immense effort.

Ruslan Mironov is a young man with Category 2 disability. He has a friendly, open smile untypical of a 'Chechen' ex-serviceman. He behaves undemonstratively, wears no medals on his chest. He would be an ordinary lad, but for the obvious consequences of a severe head injury. Half his face is twisted and he has problems with his arms, which had to be pieced together after he was wounded.

We are sitting in a small room in the Yekaterinburg premises of Arsenal 32, one of the largest Sverdlovsk associations for disabled ex-servicemen.

'Ruslan, you are plainly self-sufficient. How do you do it? What do you stand to lose as a result of the reform?'

'I am losing everything,' Ruslan answers, 'and that hurts. I am disabled, but I didn't just collect my pension and burden others with my problems. I do a little business and make around a hundred thousand roubles (£1,900) a year. I fought to get the tax exemption ex-servicemen are entitled to but now I shall have to give away 48.5 per cent of my income.

That is a loss of forty-eight and a half thousand roubles, almost half. My business ceases to make commercial sense. I am going to be poor.'

In addition to that, Ruslan had a financial incentive to take on disabled workers, to support his own 'Chechen' comrades whom other employers were reluctant to take on. They have a reputation for working badly and causing problems.

'If a disabled worker was paid, say, eight thousand three hundred roubles [£160] a month,' Ruslan explains, 'he paid no tax. This privilege is also being withdrawn. He will have to give the state four thousand roubles in tax; in other words, twice the two thousand roubles he will receive in recompense through monetarisation. This is not a sensible policy towards disabled people who do not want to be a burden on society. You would think they would do everything they could to support us, enable us to develop by individual initiative, so we aren't just lying around at home or sprawling drunk in gateways. But now they are forcing us on to the scrapheap.'

Ruslan continues: 'I had a right to half-price air and rail travel in the autumn and winter. That was a great boon, because my parents live in Anapa on the Black Sea and my mother-in-law is in Novosibirsk. I used that privilege a lot. Again, the right to free false teeth has been taken away. That matters. We nearly all came back from Chechnya without our teeth. There is an enormous queue in the hospital. And now? The "social package" for someone who is disabled is two thousand roubles [£40]; for those who took part in combat it is one thousand five hundred [£29]; families of those who died get a total of six hundred and fifty [£12.50]. It will be impossible to get your teeth sorted.'

Sergey Domrachev, born in 1976, has a punctured lung. Part of his skull has been replaced by a titanium plate. Nevertheless, today Sergey is a typical representative of the Yekaterinburg middle class. He confidently drives the streets in his modest Zhiguli, wearing a smart suit and carefully chosen tie. He is well groomed, sleek, self-reliant. It's a pleasure to look at him and listen to him. He is married to an independently minded, literate and beautiful woman. He likes his work, has completed a first degree and is studying for a second.

'Of all the people I know who took part in combat operations, only one in ten got back on their feet after the war. The rest of them drink, or do nothing. They live with their parents and sponge off them. We scare people. That is why most "Chechens" work as security guards. They are mainly employed by "Afghan" ex-servicemen in private security firms. The Afghans take us lot, but even they aren't keen.'

'But many "Chechens" who don't find a place in civilian life go back to Chechnya under contract. You don't feel an urge to do that?'

'I can do without going back there,' he laughs.

'But why do others do it?'

'It's perfectly clear why. You can do whatever you please. You shoot whoever you want to. There are no laws. That's what they like.'

'How did you manage not to sink to that level?'

He laughs again: 'I declared independence from the state. There came a moment after I had come back from the slaughter in Chechnya when I realised I could either choose to sink with all the others or start all over again. I never wear my Order of Valour medal. I have survived only because I pretended to forget everything and started living as if none of it had ever happened.'

He would have reached the front of an accelerated queue for state accommodation in 2005, but now they have abolished the privilege.

'I have always known you should never rely on our state authorities. They always cheat you,' Sergey says. 'Of course, it's a shame that I'm losing all these benefits, especially the priority for housing. It will be a pity if everything collapses.' Sergey shows me the tiny flat that he and his wife are renting. 'I can't afford to buy an apartment yet. I work hard, but I recognise that I'm not up to holding down several jobs simultaneously. I don't expect to be able to do that in the future, either. At the moment at least I am working, but the plate in my head needs to be changed. I need money, I need to earn it and put it aside for the time after the operation.'

We live in a most unusual state. It just loves driving people into a dead end, even those who are capable and really want to make their own way. The question is: what kind of citizens does such a state prefer? A mass of drunken idlers, or people who are looking to live an active life? Today the state is deliberately impoverishing those it should be helping to get on their feet. It forces into penury even those who have managed to raise themselves, while proclaiming that combating poverty is the President's new priority. The benefits reform may be the last straw for people whose lives have been broken by these same authorities. Many of the 'Chechens' say they will find it difficult to swallow this. 'Survival of the fittest?' It's not the ideal approach to social welfare. Are the weakest supposed just to die?

Nadezhda Suzdalova locks her son Tolya in when she goes off to work at the village boiler-house. He is 28, an ex-serviceman with Category 1 disability: paralysed from the chest down; a talking head with arms, his elbows the only support for his body. They live in the remote village of Karpushikha in the dense taiga of the Urals. The regional centre is Kirovgrad, 38 kilometres along a track through thick forest. It is from places like this that boys are sent to fight in the Caucasus. Their mothers do not throw themselves on the rails to save their sons.

It is to such dire places that they return from the war. Karpushikha today is the 'sink estate' for all the antisocial elements who, unable to adapt to the new times, have been expelled from Yekaterinburg for rent arrears run up over many years. By the entrance to the block of flats where the Suzdalovs live there is a heaving mass of drunks, tramps and junkies. They stagger about yelling, swearing, grabbing each other by the hips and kicking. They steal what little there is to steal: washing bowls, brushes, teapots, jugs. It is on account of the 'neighbours' that Nadezhda has to lock Tolya in. He would be unable to stop their thieving.

There is very little, but if they stole a bowl or unscrewed a tap, there would be no way it could be replaced. Tolya and his mother live on disability benefit of 1,200 roubles [£23] a month. Nadezhda has not been paid her wages for more than six months.

Tolya's story is typical: 'He cries in the evenings.' As she tells me this, Nadezhda too begins to cry. She is worn out looking after her bedridden son. 'But what can you say? I used to tell Tolya to fight back, to stop drinking, but now it's too late. That's all behind us.'

Tolya left school as a naive, good-looking boy and was immediately sent to Chechnya. He returned a complete mental wreck, as they all do. Without any kind of rehabilitation, he was sent straight back to Karpushikha, where the only rehabilitation is alcoholism and drug addiction.

Shortly afterwards Tolya went berserk and wrecked a trading booth in Levikha, the neighbouring village. In court the traders said the odd thing was that he didn't steal anything or hit anyone. So he landed in jail, like more than half the 'Chechens' in Sverdlovsk Province. He was released under an amnesty, and started drinking again. Before long he became paralysed. The doctors told his mother not to make a fuss. He wouldn't last five days. Their diagnosis was 'severe neurological infection'.

'In fact he has lived more than a year already,' his mother says, seating herself on a low bench by the bed. There is happiness in her eyes. 'At first only I could feed him, but he has even started feeding himself.'

Nevertheless, Tolya's illness is as severe as it is incurable. He has been diagnosed with HIV. Where he picked that up from, whether in

Karpushikha or in hospital, there is no telling. The only thing his country is honour-bound to do is to allow him to live out his life in dignity. The room in which he lies is clean, but the smell of a sickroom is ineradicable. Urine flows into a bag attached to the bed frame. Tolya is covered in bedsores and infections, which his immune system cannot fight.

'How could it? What do we eat? His catheters are brought by a girl who was in his class. She works at the cancer clinic and steals them for him. We can't afford to buy them ourselves,' Nadezhda says.

A disabled veteran can count on getting only a pathetic selection of irrelevant medicines, and for the ones that are essential he has to pay. The cost of those Tolya needs exceeds the 'social package' many times over. 'And then there are the catheters. They are constantly getting clogged. He needs a mattress to prevent bedsores. I don't know what to do.'

'No money will ever reach us because it never does,' Tolya says. 'I don't believe a word the Government says.' In his calm eyes there is a readiness for death.

It is difficult to believe that Karpushikha is in the same country as Moscow, or even as Yekaterinburg. Not a single care worker has visited Tolya in the year and half that he has been bedridden. The wheelchair issued to him at the disabled ex-servicemen's hospital in Yekaterinburg stands unused in the corner. There is nobody to help him down from his first-floor room to get a breath of fresh air.

It is good to write uplifting stories about people who have fought their way to a decent future in spite of the hopelessness and brutality of life in Russia; but the truth is that there are thousands more like Tolya, weak people at the bottom of the pile, who can only survive in the remote, provincial scene of their last days if they are given social support. Withholding the full cost of necessary medical treatment for the likes of Tolya is equivalent to sentencing him to death. The state machine becomes an agent of natural selection.

It is the middle of the working day. A stunted, drunken man with a black eye and with his pants pulled down grabs a hefty, dishevelled woman in a skirt short enough to reveal her swollen thighs. A crowd of bystanders is guffawing under Tolya's window, but nobody looks up. Here you are either a fellow drunk or you are of no interest to anybody. Here, in the remote jungles of Russia.

Revda is a small town on the Yekaterinburg–Moscow highway. It is difficult to like the place. It is a territory of extreme politics where the idol is Zhirinovsky, our cunning holy fool who makes big money out of all the losers longing for the good old days of Soviet Russia. Dust, drunkenness and drugs. Prostitutes loiter by the roadside, aged 12–56, and costing between 50 and 300 roubles [£1–6], according to a pugnacious man with a skull pendant. This is Andrey Baranov, Deputy Chairman of the Revda Section of the Sverdlovsk Provincial Union of Ex-Servicemen of Local Conflicts. Baranov is no Tolya.

'I look out for myself,' Baranov boasts. 'I chucked my Work Registration Record out. What use is it? Nobody gives us work. A lot of us have head injuries, we are unpredictable. People are scared of us.'

'Probably not without reason. Are you aggressive?'

Baranov is not standing for that. 'No, we just see injustice before other people do. Half of us are in prison for that. Seventy per cent have become alcoholics. It takes a heroic wife to put up with our boys, but some do. I don't trust the state for an instant. I trust Zhirinovsky.'

'How do you earn a living?'

'We have got ourselves organised and escort freight. Straightforwardly, without any Work Registration Records.'

'You are into protection, then?'

'Why do you immediately think that? It's just that the Government is totally useless. Why work for it? Anyway, protection rackets are old hat. We help people to do business.'

Baranov and the 'Chechens' in Revda are an outlaw private taxation department. Among their clients, to put it politely, is the local taxi firm. We are talking in its decrepit little office at Revda railway station. The whistling of the locomotives underscores the edginess of our conversation, the confusion in the damaged minds of the 'Chechens' sitting around, Baranov's rage at the rest of the world, and the fact that he believes he is fighting for justice on his own terms.

'Do you make use of welfare benefits?'

'Never. We look after ourselves. On the train to Yekaterinburg I organise my own free travel. I get on the train, show my military card, which makes it clear that I took part in combat operations, and the ticket inspector moves on. They steer clear of me.'

'Would it be worthwhile getting an education?'

'What for? No thanks.'

I ask them to find me at least one sober 'Chechen' to talk to. Time passes. In the evening in Revda there are none. Valerii Mokrousov, a friend of Baranov who fought in the Afghan War and is the Chairman of the Ex-Servicemen's Association, walks in and out. He is constantly distracted by telephone calls. As our conversation at the railway station is ending, he mentions, 'I just tried to get through to Oleg Donetskov, but his wife told me to bugger off. He is lying there dead drunk. He fought in both the Chechen Wars and has concussion.'

'Concussion? He shouldn't be drinking!'

'Well, what do you expect?' Baranov returns to the fray, hurling his words straight at me. 'You have a choice: either hit the vodka, or go back to Chechnya. I went back there under contract.'

'What for?'

'For a holiday. To get away from your civilian way of life. I know where I stand there. Here it's nothing but problems. All our lads are looking for the truth and not finding it. When you come back from there you see things clearly. Everything here is rotten. Brother abandons brother. It's complete shit. There everybody is honest: we are here, the enemy is there – fight and shoot!'

Vyacheslav Zykov, Chairman of the Sverdlovsk Province Ex-Servicemen's Association, served as an ambulance driver in the present war. He confirms what Baranov is saying.

'Seventy per cent of our guys try to go back to fight again. Out of desperation. But only about thirty per cent get selected as contract soldiers.'

'Have you heard that benefits are being abolished?'

'Who cares. That won't save them.' This prognostication comes from another individual wearing a skull pendant. 'We are for Zhirinovsky. We'll get a patriotic movement going; take kids off the street and put them in patriotic soldiers' clubs. If we show them the ropes, things may work out in the end.'

'Work out how?'

'With a strict monarchy.'

'But how can you teach anybody if you aren't well yourselves?'

'I lost three hundred and sixty lads in the assault on Grozny. Only you're not allowed to write about that.'

'Why not?'

'Because something like that "couldn't happen". Everybody lies about Chechnya. I took part in the "cleansings" after the assault on Komsomolskoye, know what I mean? But we're the ones who have to deal with that. That's why we are fighting for justice.'

'Why did you go back to Chechnya? If you know that it only makes things worse, for you and for everyone else?'

The question goes unanswered, thank God. If anyone in Russia manages to stir up this community of 'Chechens' to political action, it will be the end.

1 January 2005

In the Chechen town of Urus-Martan, three boys have gone off to fight for the Resistance. They left notes for their relatives explaining that they could no longer put up with the lawlessness and could see no other way to get back at the failure to punish evil-doers.

9 January

Another four young men from Urus-Martan, aged between 25 and 30, have left to join the Resistance. January has seen a record number of recruits. This is in response to the large-scale, brutal cleansings of the last six months.

12 January

On 12 January Ramzan Kadyrov, the lunatic Deputy Prime Minister of Chechnya, set off with a column of between 100 and 150 jeeps to sort out the Dagestanis. When they arrived at the border between Chechnya and Dagestan, the Dagestan militia on duty fled in terror. In Hasavyurt in Dagestan, Kadyrov's troops detained and then released the regional Chief-of-Police.

This was a typical piece of bravado in retaliation for the brief detention of Kadyrov's sister in Dagestan on 10 January.

14 January

Aslan Maskhadov, President of the Chechen Republic of Ichkeria, has announced a one-month, unilateral ceasefire. He has ordered all his armed groups to take a break until 22 February.

What does it signify? Winter weariness? An attempt to foster goodwill on the basis that both sides are fed up with the carnage and should just stop it? Or is he testing his authority? One must suppose there's a bit of all three. In announcing the ceasefire, Maskhadov is first and foremost testing himself, and very courageously so because he is doing it publicly. It is no secret that many people shrug when they hear mention of Maskhadov and ask whom he actually controls.

The reasons for this lack of confidence are obvious enough; Maskhadov stays very deep underground. For many years he has refused to see journalists, fearing the fate of Ahmad-Shakh Masud of Afghanistan, the Pandsher Lion blown up by journalists who had been specially sent for the purpose. For the time being Maskhadov's public self-examination is not going well. The use of landmines against the federals is not decreasing, and whoever is planting them is paying no attention to his ceasefire.

This is also a test for a Kremlin not noted for courageous responses.

The first to raise his voice against the ceasefire was, naturally, the Kremlin-appointed 'President of Chechnya', Alu Alkhanov. He announced that he would not negotiate with Maskhadov, but was prepared to negotiate with fighters about a unilateral surrender of weapons. The Kremlin simply disdained to react to the ceasefire at all. If you are not for peace, you are in favour of war.

To underline its stupidity, the Kremlin decided to announce that when it got its hands on Maskhadov and Basaev, it would arrest both of them. The charges against Maskhadov include the fact that 'there is evidence that Basaev instructed the Beslan terrorists to include among their demands the opening of negotiations with Maskhadov' (Nikolai Shepel, Deputy Procurator-General).

15 January

The mothers of soldiers killed in Chechnya have sent back to Putin their monthly 'compensation' of 150 roubles [£3] in protest at the withdrawal of benefits in kind.

Before 1 January, mothers whose sons had been sacrificed in the North Caucasus escapade were entitled to free medical treatment, free travel on public transport, a half-price ticket each year for train, plane or steamer; they also paid half-price for their telephone and television service and had the right to a one-off loan on preferential terms and to a free plot of land.

That was entirely just. In most cases the state uses the sons of poorer families to fight its war in Chechnya. Often the mother is a single parent. Well-off people with any influence at all ransom their sons from the misfortune of Army service, and certainly from service in Chechnya.

Anti-monetarisation demonstrations are snowballing. Every day people turn out in their thousands. Political causes do not produce anything like the response to a policy that hits people's pockets, and Putin has little to fear. He will throw them some money, the Russian people will fail to sweep him from power, and their aggression will be directed against whichever stranger happens to be in the vicinity.

17 January

Russia's first Internet referendum is under way at www.skaji.net [*Skazhi net!* means 'Say no!' in Russian]. It is a classic grassroots initiative. Some students from the Higher Institute of Economics got together and decided to invite citizens to vote on the Net on two issues:

1. Law 122 (abolishing benefits in kind);
2. No confidence in the Government.

I was phoned by Alexander Korsunov, the leader of the team, who asked for support.
'But who are you?' I asked. 'What party are you from?'
'I am nobody. We are just doing it.'
The students who had thought up the project belong to no single political party, although their initiative has subsequently received formal support from Yabloko, Rodina and the Communist Party.
The students wrote:

We regard Law 122 as an insult to our old people in the year when we celebrate the sixtieth anniversary of victory in the Second World War. The Government has discredited the sound idea of monetarisation of benefits. The sole legal means of protecting our rights today is a referendum in which we can express our protest. Students have always been the most socially active part of the population, reacting effectively to events in Russia. We call on you to join us.

Millions of our people voted online against the law and the Government's policy, but where do these and other millions disappear to when they cannot hide behind anonymity? Fear makes them invisible.

Protest demonstrations are particularly strong in St Petersburg, Tver, Tyumen, Samara, Perm and in Khimki in Moscow Province. People are coming out on to the streets, blocking the roads, picketing buildings and threatening the authorities with more to come. The reason is that Law 122 is beginning to hurt.

In St Petersburg the police tried to arrest members of Yabloko and the National Bolshevik Party. After the meeting an old-age pensioner was arrested, taken away and brutally beaten up at a militia station. In the morning the militia arrested Vladimir Soloveichik, a member of the Joint Action Committee, which has been co-ordinating the protest demonstrations. They also subsequently arrested eight members of the National Bolshevik Party who had taken part in the demonstration at Gatchina.

19 January

If the protests against Law 122 continue at their present level, it is clear there is going to be an increasing overlap between the interests of the protesters and those of the militia sent in to pacify them.

Most of those working for the security agencies are also losing benefits. Their wages are traditionally low – militiamen get no more than 3,000 roubles (less than £60) per month. These protests are taking place in large cities and most of the militiamen will live in the suburbs. Until this month they enjoyed free public transport. There have been reports of mass resignations in the Moscow militia. One militiaman shot himself while on duty in the centre of Moscow, guarding the offices of the Directorate for the Struggle Against Organised Crime; he had told his colleagues that he could no longer feed his family. The Ministry of Defence has officially notified the Soviet of the Federation that a survey conducted this month showed that 80 per cent of officers feel dissatisfaction over the law on benefits, and only 5 per cent of officers consider their material situation to be satisfactory.

I suspect the state authorities are starting to take notice because they know that, apart from the security forces, nobody supports them. They have begun offering subsidies and handouts in order to head off unrest. They saw that militiamen were refusing to beat demonstrators, and it reminded them of the Orange Revolution in Ukraine when the security forces refused to fire on their own people and changed sides. That was the decisive moment.

In Moscow, a coalition of voluntary organisations has been set up: Social Solidarity (SOS). It promptly called for demonstrations throughout Russia on 10 and 12 February, 'Nationwide Days of Joint Action' against the authorities' antisocial policy. SOS is a pro-Communist organisation, the democrats having missed the boat once again. It is demanding the repeal of Law 122, the doubling of pensions, reform of the tax system in favour of the regions and low-income groups of the population, the sacking of all United Russia Deputies and resignation of the Government.

Nobody wanted to make a fuss about this last summer and autumn. It was only when the benefits were actually withdrawn and pensioners were unable to get on to public transport by showing their pension books that the protests took off.

22 January

This Saturday too saw mass demonstrations. Further January opinion polls say that 58 per cent of those who formerly enjoyed benefits in kind support the protesters. The survey was conducted by the state-owned Channel One television station.

In Krasnoyarsk, more than 3,000 people protested against a rise in electricity prices. From 1 January a customer can use only 50 kilowatt-hours a month; anything over that will be charged at double the rate. In most of the apartment blocks in Krasnoyarsk the central heating is extremely inefficient and, as Siberia is a cold place in winter, people have no option but to leave their electric fires on. There is no way they can use only 50 kilowatt-hours in the winter months – surveys suggest that the average citizen uses two to three times that amount.

In Ufa almost 5,000 people attended a rally in the city centre demanding that President Murtaza Rakhimov should either repeal monetarisation in Bashkiria by 26 February, or resign. After the meeting, pensioners wearing orange clothing blocked one of the main streets. Bearing the orange flags of the Ukrainian revolution, they began collecting signatures for a referendum on the direct election of mayors in the cities of Bashkiria.

In Moscow, ten activists of the Vanguard of Red Youth have been arrested for 'attempting to march to the building of the Presidential Administration', although they were arrested near the Byelorussky Station, which is two or three kilometres away. There had been an anti-monetarisation rally at the station organised by the Communists and attended by 3,000–4,000 people. Many young people and the National Bolshevik Party also took part. Their slogans were 'Free travel for employees of the militia and servicemen', 'Stop robbing the pensioners', 'Hands off the law on ex-servicemen', 'Down with the Putin regime!', 'Down with the El Puta clique!'

The formal reason for detaining the Vanguardists is that permission had been granted for the Communists' meeting, but not for a procession afterwards. All 10 of those arrested were beaten up.

Street protest is becoming increasingly left-wing and nationalistic. Democrats attend protest meetings, but behave as if they are doing everyone a favour. They are not popular.

According to the January social survey by the Kremlin's TsIOM polling service, the slogan 'Russia for the Russians' is wholly supported by 16 per cent of the population, who consider that 'this should have been done long ago'; 37 per cent consider that 'it would not be a bad thing to implement it, but within reasonable limits'. 16 + 37 = 53 per cent fascism, because this policy cannot be implemented 'within reasonable limits'.

The only ray of hope is that 25 per cent oppose the idea. They believe that 'Russia for the Russians' is a fascist idea.

The same survey shows a very Russian reason for wanting ethnic minorities driven out. It is because, in the opinion of 39 per cent of respondents, they live better than Russians. Only three regions of the Federation – Moscow, Tyumen Province and Tatarstan – have a standard of living comparable with Europe's.

23 January

The authorities are waking up to the fact that they need to do something about these protests. The state television channels have started putting out propaganda to explain why the new monetarisation law is good, and old-age pensioners say how pleased they are with everything.

Alexander Zhukov, the First Deputy Prime Minister, is the chief apologist. Here is an example: 'There are protests where the payments received from the regional budgets are less than the real cost of the abolished benefits. When this law was passed, however, it was agreed that regions that have sufficient resources can make higher payments if they so choose.'

This is the main aim of the central government authorities: to shift the blame on to the regional authorities, even though 80 out of 89 regions are totally dependent on the subsidies they receive from the federal budget. Zhukov relies on the fact that most people are simply unfamiliar with how the financing works.

Mikhail Zurabov, the Minister of Health and Social Development, is forever urging people not to worry. 'Additional sums are being allocated from the federal budget. In 2004 expenditure on benefits was one hundred billion roubles [£1.92 billion], but in 2005 we are allocating three hundred billion roubles [£5.8 billion]. We're just working out the details. The decision will be taken either today or on Monday.'

Zurabov claims that Law 122 was introduced in order to regularise the delivery of benefits. He says that although people had benefits in kind, no finance was allocated for them. 'We need to make people free and independent of the state, and for that we need to improve their financial situation.'

This is poppycock: the new system is so onerous and over-administered that to talk about freedom is casuistry. Old people have to stand in queues for hours in order to get the cash for a month's bus travel! The next month they will have to start all over again. No doubt the old social-welfare system was cumbersome and had many faults, but the new system is worse and, moreover, is causing great financial hardship to millions of people.

Another constant claim on television is that all the protest meetings are being organised by the mafia who control chemists' shops and the transport system. The opposition is said to be exploiting the situation in order to score political points. The democratic opposition, on the contrary, is making no attempt to score points, although it could and should.

25 January

The Steering Committee of the National Citizens' Congress holds a meeting at the Journalists' Club in Moscow.

Everything at this festival of democracy degenerates into a fruitless discussion about who is the most important person.

Boris Nadezhdin tries to mount a takeover bid for the Union of Right Forces. The Yabloko supporters try to behave like the owners of the enterprise. There is a lot of shouting, but no sign of action. Lyudmila Alexeyeva in the chair gets cross. Garry Kasparov says how fed up he is with everything, and rightly points out irregularities in the procedure for adopting resolutions.

Kasparov leaves before the end of the meeting. He stands outside in the corridor for a long time, complaining that the democrats are again missing the boat. The boat is already transporting the people of Russia to a different landing stage and the orchestra waiting to greet it there is not the Citizens' Congress.

Only St Petersburg has managed to corral all the opposition parties and movements into a consultative assembly called the Petersburg Citizens' Resistance. Even more amazing is that it is in action every day.

Demonstrations in St Petersburg are the most energetic and outspoken in the country; Putin is least loved in his native city. Petersburg Citizens' Resistance is demanding restoration of the election of governors, dissolution of the Duma, abolition of Law 122, resignation of the President and Government, the raising of pensions and the abolition of censorship on state television.

27 January

Demonstrators in St Petersburg formed a living corridor at the entrance to the city's Legislative Assembly on St Isaac's Square. As the Deputies arrived they had to pass along this corridor to shouts of 'Shame on United Russia', 'Shame on this dull, grey Duma', 'Putin out!' One of the protesters burned her United Russia membership card at the door of the Legislative Assembly.

28 January

We are discussing what is going on at the Citizens' Congress with Lyudmila Alexeyeva. She admits that she does not have high hopes of it.

'Then why waste time?'

'Who knows – it might work!' she replies.

30 January

From the Internet: 'Right, and now Comrade Deputies, all those who voted in favour of the election of Vladimir Vladimirovich as Tsar may put their hands down and move away from the wall.'

A year ago no jokes like this were circulating. It was the era of the Great Political Depression. People were afraid of the high-and-mighty Putin, who had broken the opposition.

Whenever there is an acute crisis, Putin waits in the wings, and only when the dust has settled does he come out with some thoroughly grey utterance. Is he now seen as a joke? Or are people resigned to him, anticipating a return to the Period of Stagnation, and to laughing, as they did at Brezhnev, in the privacy of their kitchens. Revolution from above seems to be what we favour, when something prevents those at the top from being able to carry on in the old way.

1 February

An opinion poll by the Yury Levada Analytical Centre, commissioned by the People's Verdict Foundation, finds that 70 per cent of respondents do not trust the law-enforcement agencies and view them with apprehension. Seventy-two per cent believe they might suffer as a consequence of their lack of accountability. Only 2 per cent stated that there is no problem of arbitrariness in the law-enforcement agencies.

2 February

The Duma has granted permission to the Army to conduct operations inside the country. What efforts were made in the Yeltsin period to ensure that the Armed Forces could not be turned against Russian citizens! Now we are back to the situation as it was in the USSR. An amendment to Article 10 of the federal law 'On Defence' reads: 'The Armed Forces of the Russian Federation may be employed to counteract terrorist activity using military resources' (Addendum to the law 'On Defence'). This is included in the so-called 'Beslan anti-terrorist package' of laws. The only group to express concern that the Army could be put to improper use, if this amendment was passed, was the Communists. They were brushed aside.

The Government has quelled the wave of anti-monetarisation protest by throwing money at the regions.

The Islamic underground, however, is growing in strength. Non-official Islam is becoming increasingly attractive to young people because of the short-sighted religious policies of the Kremlin. After Beslan, the Kremlin decided to revive Soviet methods of containing Islam. The FSB took over responsibility for dealing with it, just as its former incarnation, the KGB, had in the days of the Soviet Union. The intelligence services will foster 'tame' Muslims, and put the rest in jail. The result will be the same as it was under the Communists: the formation of underground religious groups.

This morning, 48-year old Yermak Tegaev, Director of the Islamic Cultural Centre of Vladikavkaz (the capital of North Ossetia, some 20 kilometres from Beslan), found himself in jail under Article 222 of the Criminal Code, for 'harbouring explosive materials and related components'.

'At about six o'clock in the morning, soldiers broke into our flat,' his wife, Albina, tells me. 'My husband was reading the Koran before doing namaz and I was in the bathroom. When I heard noises, I partly opened the door and found a rifle pointed at me. There were people in masks and helmets all over the flat, about twenty of them. They dragged me out of the bathroom almost naked and didn't let me dress for a long time. For us that is not permitted. My husband was lying on the floor with three people sitting on top of him. I started shouting for the neighbours – I thought robbers had broken in – but they didn't allow them to come in and started searching. My husband told them they couldn't conduct a search without a lawyer, but they had brought their own "witnesses" and started with the toilet. Three or four times they looked there in exactly the same place, and I suspected something bad. We have been searched several times recently and have feared this.

'I tried to keep an eye on them the whole time to prevent them planting anything, but then they grabbed the keys to our car and ran out to where it was parked. They told my husband to get dressed and ordered him out. We refused to approach because we knew they had already planted what they needed to. They opened the boot and said there were explosives there. They telephoned somewhere and a person appeared with a video camera who started filming us. Then they took my husband away.'

His family and friends and Suleiman Marniev, the imam of the central mosque in Vladikavkaz, are convinced that the explosives were planted. The authorities want to jail the Chairman of the Islamic Cultural Centre, preferably for a long time, in order to neutralise an unofficial leader of the Muslim community whose existence does not suit them. His only crime is his popularity among his fellow believers, especially the young, and the fact that he won't collaborate with the Republican Directorate of the FSB.

What kind of collaboration are we talking about? And what is the Islamic Cultural Centre of Vladikavkaz, that its leader should face such major unpleasantness?

Formally the Centre is only one of the public associations of North Ossetia. It is a religious club whose status is identical, for example, to that of the Religious Board of Muslims of North Ossetia. On paper, the Centre and the Board are exactly the same. Not, however, in practice. The Board enjoys the financial support of the state authorities, and openly admits that it collaborates with the FSB. The Centre keeps its distance. That is the root of its problems.

'After Beslan, the authorities, or more precisely the Directorate of the FSB who hold power in the Republic nowadays, wanted complete subordination of Muslims,' I am told by Artur Besolov, the Centre's Deputy Chairman. 'The FSB is keen to control the life of Muslims through the Religious Board, through the Chairman, who is an official mufti of the Republic, Ruslan Valgasov. We are quite certain that Valgasov was appointed a mufti by the security agencies, which is categorically forbidden in Islam. The only place that sort of thing went on was in the Soviet Union. The majority of Muslims in North Ossetia (who comprise thirty per cent of the Republic's population) oppose such appointing of religious leaders. Tegaev was offered appointment as a mufti, but refused, precisely because he feared pressure from the regime. Nonetheless, it is Tegaev who has the greater authority. Valgasov, on the other hand, has only old men around him. The authorities simply decided to resolve the situation by jailing Tegaev.'

Everybody can see that there has to be an accommodation with the Muslim world, but nobody in Russia is opening negotiations. They are pressing ahead with the old Soviet methods: if you can't abolish the Koran, then at least everything should be under control; no jamaats, and if muftis and emirs are unavoidable in a country with 20 million Muslims, then they had better be on our side.

Today all this jiggery-pokery is embedded in the state's approach to the fight against terrorism, an approach that is above the law. What has happened to Tegaev is simply one of its manifestations. They jail him, send in their report and think the problem has been solved. In reality, it has merely been made worse. Persecuting Islam throughout Russia has led to a predictable Islamic backlash, which we have been seeing throughout 2004 and 2005 across the North Caucasus.

In January, the security forces stormed a flat in an ordinary five-storey block in Nalchik, Kabardino-Balkaria. They believed a terrorist group was inside, or at least that's what they claimed afterwards. However, those in the flat were simply Muslims who were 'not on our side'. Among them were Muslim Ataev and his wife Sakinat Katsieva, a young married couple involved in the Islamic underground. They and their friends, another young Islamic family not under state control, were shot.

Muslim and Sakinat had a six-month-old daughter, Leyla. The bodies of the adults were returned to their families after the assault, but Leyla had vanished. There was no body, no baby, no information; all attempts by her grandparents to find their granddaughter were in vain.

They had, of course, also shot the baby. People in the neighbouring blocks saw the soldiers carry out a small body swathed in a blanket, but, since the murder of an infant would have been too shocking for the public, they did not return her remains. How does the murder of Leyla differ from the deaths of the children killed during the assault on the school in Beslan?

The more intense the pressure, the more committed the adherents of non-official Islam become. Islamic communities reluctant to exist within a system of 'religious boards' are becoming ever more isolated, closing themselves off from the outside world and thereby becoming less comprehensible. Needless to say, Orthodox or Catholic Christians or anybody else would behave in the same way under the same circumstances. The situation is no different in Chechnya where 'FSB Muslims' fight Muslims who do not enjoy official sanction, exploiting the long-established religious boards, or 'departments of religious affairs' as they were called in the USSR. These were to be found even in the Communist Party's Central Committee, and in provincial and district Party committees.

Today many Soviet-era officials are still in the same jobs. Rudnik Dudaev, a general of the KGB and now of the FSB, was for many years Kadyrov's Director of the Security Council of Chechnya and, before that, was also for many years one of the heads of the religious boards of Muslims in Soviet times.

Dudaev 'ran' Akhmed-hadji Kadyrov from the moment he entered a madrasseh in the 1970s. Working for the KGB, he monitored Kadyrov, Djohar Dudaev and Maskhadov, and now keeps an eye on Kadyrov Junior. And what good has it done? Are there fewer jamaats now in Chechnya? Or emirs aged between 15 and 17 who are completely out of control? What good has come of these religious boards? Has the authority of the official mufti of Chechnya been enhanced? Or the authority of emirs who are 'not on our side' diminished?

Mufti Valgasov will benefit to precisely the same extent as Shamaev, the former Mufti of Chechnya, and as Mirzaev who has replaced him. The state authorities may like their malleability, but the charisma and respect enjoyed by religious leaders do not derive from their closeness to the FSB. The fight against Islam, using Soviet methods, leads to the opposite of what is intended. In Chechnya and Dagestan, in Ingushetia,

Kabardino-Balkaria and in Karachaevo-Cherkessia, Islam is going underground.

3 February

The Presidential Administration swings into action. In Tula the clowns have organised a meeting in support of Law 122. This is the new approach of the Presidential Administration: meetings populated with 'their' people. Old folk are paid a fee to attend – how much depends on the circumstances, but money changes hands. The corrupting of our people continues, and our people are wholly willing to be corrupted.

The meetings are organised by local authorities after a co-ordinating phone call from the Kremlin. Putin's 'line management' is alive and well. At these 'anti-protest meetings', governors who have grown fat from bribe-taking waddle on to the platform accompanied by their bureaucratic entourage. They promise, as they have been told to, that social-welfare payments are on the point of being increased and that everything will again be exactly as it was before the law was passed. Day after day these meetings are the lead item on the television news.

In Tula too we see the Governor on stage with a pack of his apparatchiks. The meeting has been organised by United Russia. The Governor announces that everyone receiving a pension of less than 1,650 roubles [£32] will be issued with free season tickets for the city's public transport system (of which there is virtually nothing left). On the other hand, from 1 February a ticket on Tula's private transport system has gone up from six to seven roubles.

Bewilderingly, the people rejoice and give thanks for the season tickets.

10 February

So far, people on the periphery of the empire are not giving in. In Abakan, Siberia, in 36 degrees of frost, some 30 people picket the building of the Khakassian administration with placards reading 'No to the anti-social policy'. In the town of Kyzyl, the capital of Tyva, in 45 degrees of frost, 56 people attend a demonstration against Putin's policy. In Khabarovsk, in the Far Eastern strom wind, a handful of people stand in the central square with a banner reading 'United Russia disgraces Russia!'

12 February

In Yuzhno-Sakhalinsk the local Human Rights Association has performed a piece of street theatre called 'The Funeral of Democracy'. On a life-sized dummy representing youthful democracy the campaigners hung 15 or so heavy accusatory placards about the recent unconstitutional actions of the state authorities, Law 122 and the abolition of election of governors. Eventually, under the weight of these woes, democracy collapsed and was placed in a coffin covered with stickers proclaiming its demise. Bearing wreaths, to funereal music, the demonstrators nailed down the lid of the coffin and bore it away on a catafalque. The performance took place by the building of the provincial administration, watched with interest by bureaucrats from the windows.

In Tula, a meeting organised by the Communists attracted around 1,000 protesters. In Abakan too they held a meeting and almost 300 people were present this time: it wasn't quite so cold. It was a result of sorts, but a Nationwide Day of Joint Action, as intended by Social Solidarity (SOS), it was not. There is no nationwide protest.

15 February

The democrats (Yabloko and the Union of Right Forces) have again tried to reach agreement. So far their battlefield is still offices in Moscow rather than the streets of Russia. Everybody is fed up with the democratic functionaries, even their supporters.

Today they almost managed to unite at a meeting of Committee 2008, but once more everything fell through at the last moment. They resolved to continue discussions. The big problem remains the same: who is to be first among equals? How can Yavlinsky make sure that Kasparov and Ryzhkov do not leapfrog him into the front rank? Kasparov and Ryzhkov, meanwhile, have decided to form a new democratic party headed by themselves, as democratic politicians who do not carry the odium of defeat in the parliamentary elections.

I met Kasparov this morning at a session of the Steering Committee of the ailing National Citizens' Congress. He was in a very determined mood and commented that the regions are far ahead of Moscow politically. 'Would you believe it, at one of the meetings they called me – me! Kasparov! – a compromise-monger. What a change of mood in just two weeks!' he kept saying, referring to the wave of protests. Kasparov is urging Committee 2008 to hold a congress of the new party in one of Russia's provincial towns.

16 February

Garry Kasparov went to St Petersburg today to a meeting against monetarisation organised by Petersburg Citizens' Resistance, which unites several of the democratic parties and groups.

First Kasparov said he wanted to found a new political organisation in St Petersburg. He said, 'The capital city of protest is now St Petersburg, and this is where we need to establish a political movement which can throw down a challenge to the powers that be. That is why I am here.' A number of those at the meeting then blocked Antonenko Street next to the Legislative Assembly, demanding the right to broadcast live on St Petersburg television. Nothing came of it. The one thing the authorities will not give them is live air time.

The Moscow Procurator's Office has dropped the charge of violent seizure of power against the National Bolshevik Party members who occupied a reception room in the offices of the Presidential Administration. They have been charged instead with a new offence of 'organising mass disorder' (Article 212). Thirty-nine of Limonov's supporters are in prison in Moscow.

21 February

The Deputy Minister of the Interior, Sergey Shchadrin, has visited Blagoveshchensk where there was a brutal 'cleansing' in December in which about 1,000 people were hurt. The Interior Ministry continues to refer to this outrage as 'the so-called "cleansing"'. In Ufa, Shchadrin called the victims 'seekers after truth', only to claim at a press conference the next day that 'The actions of the militia were justified, although many considered them excessively rigorous.' This was his assessment of the deployment of filtration points, the use of tear gas and the physical violence of December. The operation itself Shchadrin called an 'excess', adding that 'Every society gets the militia it deserves.'

He is right. For as long as people in Blagoveshchensk stand up only for their own rights, people in St Petersburg for theirs and everyone else exclusively for theirs, episodes like this will occur.

23 February

Maskhadov surfaces on the Internet and proposes an extension of the unilateral ceasefire he declared. No official response, as usual.

Nor will there be. The Administration seems to have come up with a way to explain to the West what is going on in Russia. Putin, in an interview given to the Slovak press before his meeting with Bush in Bratislava, says, 'The fundamental principles of democracy, the institutions of democracy, must be adapted to the reality on the ground in Russia today, to our traditions and history. And we shall do that for ourselves.'

Thus is born the theory of 'traditional democracy' (that is, democracy that accords with national traditions). We also hear tell of 'sovereign democracy' and 'adapted democracy', which, being interpreted, means: 'Our democracy will be the way we want it, and we don't need anyone to lecture us on the subject. So the rest of you can just push off!'

Putin was asked about his attitude to the revolutions in the countries of the former Commonwealth of Independent States: 'We are not bothered one way or the other. It is for the peoples of those countries to decide how they build their lives, through revolutions or in accordance with the law.' He plainly is bothered.

24 February

Putin meets Bush in Bratislava. In Russia people were eager to hear what Bush would have to say to Putin. Everybody knew that yesterday, at a meeting in Brussels with the leaders of Nato and the European Community, under obvious pressure from the Baltic States and the states of Eastern Europe, Bush promised that he would raise the matter of Putin's move away from democracy.

We thought that was a breakthrough, but Bush failed to challenge him. Oil, and friendship for the sake of oil, won out. Those in Russia who hope for help from the West need finally to recognise that winning back our democratic freedoms is down to us. It depends on the quality of our people and cannot come about through outside pressure. Only a few individuals in our democratic movement understand this. Most meetings of democrats end with the incantation, 'Let's complain to Europe.' Europe, unfortunately, is tired of hearing how wicked Putin is. It would prefer to be fooled and to hear how good he is.

According even to official results from Romir Monitoring, one-third of the public consider meetings between Putin and Bush to be a waste of time.

26 February

The ultimatum to Murtaza Rakhimov, President of Bashkiria, to restore benefits or resign, has expired. He has done neither, but the leaders of the opposition are nowhere to be seen. People are certain that Rakhimov simply bought them off by giving them a small stake in Bashkiria's petrochemical industry. That would seem to be the end of the revolution in Bashkiria for now. Long years of poverty mean that everything has its price, and until everybody has enough to eat, people will not be too bothered about democracy. What they don't understand is that without a social system based on democratic principles, you are unlikely to get enough to eat.

27 February

Throughout February the official Russian media have very persuasively been assuring us of the impossibility of a revolution in Kirghizia: President Akaev was sincerely striving to introduce democracy for the good of his people; he was inviting his people to set up businesses, although rather few apparently want to. The overall suggestion seemed to be that the Kirghiz were not up to much and that if a revolution did start, it would be at the instigation of criminals wanting to displace Akaev, rather than through any fault of his. Alexey Simonov, Director of the Foundation for the Defence of Glasnost, commented that 'The press is betraying society and society is betraying the press. There is a shortage of professionalism and honesty all round.'

Today, however, parliamentary elections were held in Kirghizia, and it was curtains for Akaev.

*

Akaev came to live in one of the Presidential Administration's dachas in Moscow. After parliamentary and presidential elections, the Kirghiz were to receive worldwide support for their efforts to build a new society. Russia excoriated the new rulers for a while, but then decided to live with them.

8 March

Aslan Maskhadov, democratically elected President of the Chechen Republic of Ichkeria in 1997 and latterly leader of the Chechen Resistance, has been killed in the village of Tolstoy-Yurt.

His stripped dead body was shown all day in close-up on television. In Chechnya even those who did not support Maskhadov said this was the vilest thing Moscow could have done. The Maskhadov era has ended, but whose era has begun?

The new Maskhadov will be Basaev, which means an end to the cease-fire and negotiations. Chechnya has had four presidents, and to date three of them have died a violent death. The legitimacy of the fourth, the still-living Alu Alkhanov, is highly debatable. There is no other territory in present-day Europe with such a chaotic military and political situation and such continual bloodshed.

Maskhadov is reputed to have died, like thousands of other Chechen men and women, as the result of information from one Chechen implicating another. Torture has been the most common method of interrogation and investigating criminal cases during both the First and Second Chechen Wars. To that extent Maskhadov has shared the fate of his people. He will most likely be remembered in Chechnya as a great martyr, whatever his previous actions.

Maskhadov was killed while his unilateral ceasefire was in force, which, if it has not been fully observed, was nevertheless the first such move in the Second Chechen War. It was a gesture of goodwill, a hand held out to the Kremlin indicating willingness to begin negotiations, to stop the shooting, to bring about demilitarisation and a mutual extradition of war criminals.

Maskhadov, almost alone and to the utmost of his ability, restrained extremists on his side who believe Russia must be opposed by all available means, including those demonstrated at Beslan. Now there is nobody to hold them back. The leadership of the Chechen Resistance, regardless of whom the clandestine State Defence Committee of Ichkeria appoints, will devolve to the main opponent of Maskhadov's moderate methods: Shamil Basaev. The end result of the operation to assassinate Maskhadov, which, it is now officially claimed, was organised by the Special Operations unit of the Russian FSB, will be to hand the reins of government to Basaev, who is not the least interested in political legitimacy.

We are left with two figures in Chechnya equally bloodthirsty, loathsome and barbaric: Basaev and Kadyrov Junior. Everybody else, including everybody in the whole of Russia, will find themselves caught in the middle.

In this way, the era of Maskhadov, a former Communist and Soviet colonel who turned to Islam only in his last years, and the unremittingly idiotic campaign fought against him personally, has brought into existence a younger generation that is no longer interested in moderate Islam. They prefer to be extreme towards authorities that destroy moderates.

The hero of this underground is Basaev. For a long time Maskhadov stood in their way, but now the road has been cleared. Basaev has obtained what he has dreamed of for the best part of a decade. It no longer matters that he does not have Maskhadov's political legitimacy. He is interested only in the technical aspects of preparing terrorist acts against Russia and causing as much pain as possible. The killing of Maskhadov proves irrefutably to Basaev the correctness of his well-publicised view that there can be no negotiations, and that all methods are justified in the war against Russia.

This evening the state channels put on our screens the lunatic Kadyrov Junior, who informed us that the killing of Maskhadov was a present to women on 8 March, International Women's Day.

15 March

The FSB claims to have paid someone $10 million for the information on the whereabouts of Aslan Maskhadov.

His body has not been returned to his relatives. Through all this medieval barbarity Putin remains silent, which means it is taking place on his personal orders. I wouldn't be surprised if he had demanded the head of Maskhadov on a charger, as was the wont of the Tsars of medieval Muscovy. For some reason Maskhadov's body was brought secretly to Moscow, though nobody believes it was for a supplementary post-mortem examination. They think it was for Putin to reassure himself. Such is the morality of those at the pinnacle of power in Russia.

Soldiers have again deserted from a frontier post, this time the Sretensky FSB Border Unit in Chita Province. At two o'clock in the morning four of them shot their commanding officer, his deputy and one other officer. When they fled the soldiers took with them four Kalashnikov rifles with 500 rounds of ammunition. Desertion by border troops occurs at least once a month.

In Hasavyurt, Dagestan, the nearest major town to Chechnya and a place where many Chechens live, there have again been attempts to capture fighters. A house in which they were believed to be was surrounded and reduced to rubble, but the fighters apparently escaped through a triple cordon of militia with all their weapons.

The Ministry of Defence has announced that in 2005 it will not be increasing officers' pay in line with inflation. They also failed to index it in 2004. Price increases in 2005 are predicted to be around 25 per cent.

16 March

In Shali in Chechnya, relatives of those abducted recently are picketing the town administration for the third day in a row. The protesters are demanding their release, or at least information about them.

Among them are the family of Timur Rashidov, 28, a Category 1 invalid from the village of Serzhen-Yurt, who was abducted from his home by Russian soldiers. His mother, Khalipat Rashidova, relates that the soldiers arrived in an armoured personnel carrier, burst into the house, turned everything upside down without explanation, and stripped her 18-year-old daughter Polina in order to check 'whether she had any marks left from bearing arms' on her body. They then took Timur and drove off towards the outskirts of Shali, where the Interior Ministry's Special Operations No. 2 Division is deployed.

The family of Ruslan Usaev from Novye Atagi are also outside the administration building. He is 21 and a third-year student at Grozny University. On 13 March he too was abducted by Russian soldiers and taken off in the direction of Shali, since when no more has been heard of him.

The protest secured the release of one villager from Serzhen-Yurt and four men from the village of Avtury. They had all been tortured and brutally beaten. All this passed without comment from the democrats in Moscow.

Now, in early 2005, the Chechen War has finally burst beyond the bounds of Chechnya into neighbouring regions like Ingushetia, Dagestan, North Ossetia and Kabardino-Balkaria. In each republic people protest in their own way. Associations of families whose members have been abducted do not exist there. Chechnya continues to live like a separate state; nobody travels there from the other republics, not even from Ingushetia, and after Beslan nobody sympathises with the Chechens.

19 March

Early this morning, Adam Karnakaev was abducted in Grozny by unidentified armed men. He was on his way to the mosque.

*

On 5 April the Procurator-General's Office asked the family to collect Adam's body from the mortuary in the North Ossetian city of Mozdok. It is a familiar story.

23 March

At about five o'clock this morning, masked soldiers broke down the front door of a home in Nekrasov Street, Achkhoy-Martan. They took Ismail Viskhanov, 31, and his nephew Rustam Viskhanov, 23. The abductors arrived in vehicles without number plates and were a mixture of Chechens and Russians. None of the security agencies of Chechnya admit to being involved. Neither of the men had ever been fighters.

At 5.23 a.m. the same group of 25–30 persons burst into another house in Achkhoy-Martan on Naberezhnaya Street where the Masaevs live. They roused Said-Mahomed Masaev, 31, from his bed. He is the driver of a regular bus between Grozny and Achkhoy-Martan. They took him, without allowing him to get dressed. Nobody has seen him since.

In Moscow everything continues in the old way. The discussion club of the National Citizens' Congress debates the topic: 'Referendums: should they be held, and on which issues?' It is all remarkably dull and flat, with no spark of initiative. A handful of democratic nonentities are there who are clearly not going to play a role in anything. The journalists in attendance titter. Democrats in the capital no longer take an interest even in their own affairs, let alone in Chechnya where purges and abductions are in full swing.

25 March

A big protest meeting on the issue of benefits is held at the farthest reaches of our land in Yuzhno-Sakhalinsk, although the wave of protests is almost over. Here, nevertheless, is part of the resolution adopted by the protesters in Yuzhno-Sakhalinsk:

We, veterans of war and of labour, workers of various organisations, disabled people, pensioners and young people, have come in order to express our indignation at the continuing undermining by government agencies of the social and political rights of all Russian citizens, especially those in the North and Far East. We protest against the curtailing of the basic democratic freedoms guaranteed by the Constitution, against the usurping by the state authorities of the freedom of the mass media, against attacks on social welfare, on the independence of the courts, on local self-government, and on the rights of the people to elect the institutions of state power. We oppose monetarisation, which does not cover the real expenses either of those receiving benefits or of those who provide services for them. We oppose the division of people into blacks and whites, obstacles placed in the way of honest private enterprise, the abolition of conscription deferral for students and militarisation of the country, political exploitation of anti-terrorism, the vulgarisation of the sacred ideals of the Motherland and of democracy. We demand respect for our interests, our wishes, our petitions to the authorities, our right to engage in a dialogue with the leaders of the state so that they should take account of the opinions of those in opposition to them when making important decisions.

A very detailed, comprehensive and rational set of proposals passed by the meeting was published in the local newspaper, *Sovetsky Sakhalin,* but there was no follow-up, despite the fact that the resolution is an elegant and realistic plan of action proposed to the state authorities. Our people can live in the remotest regions and yet can think in a statesman-like way that one only wishes those in the Kremlin could emulate. Yet again the authorities stonewalled.

We know what we need, but lack the tenacity to fight for it. We give up almost immediately. Life passes by while we wait for our aspirations to be bestowed on us from above, as in 1991 when a coup within the elite was latterly supported by the people. But the elite has learned from the experience of 1991, and has no wish to get involved in any more coups. They prefer to come to agreement quietly in offices, and their agreements are not in the interests of the people.

26 March

In the Chechen village of Samashki, at 5.00 in the morning, masked soldiers speaking Russian abducted Ibrahim Shishkhanov, 21. He was taken away in his socks, not even allowed to put his shoes on. They told him, 'Where you are going you won't be needing shoes.' The abduction was carried out by about 20 people, who drove up in four cars without number plates.

*

Twenty-four hours later the family discovered what was going on at Achkhoy-Martan militia station. Ibrahim had been kidnapped under the scheme to take 'counter-hostages', which the Procurator-General of Russia had deemed an acceptable measure in the aftermath of Beslan. The Shishkhanovs were ordered to surrender their relative, Said-Khasan Musostov, a member of the Resistance and cousin of Ibrahim.

He did not surrender, and nothing more is known about the fate of Ibrahim.

*

Today, Saturday, is a day of protest meetings. There is a picket in Khabarovsk demanding 'independence of the courts in the Khabarovsk region'. The protesters had suffered from 'dependent' courts, and decided to send an open letter to Putin:

> Our experience over many years shows that judges in the Khabarovsk region do not protect the rights of citizens in their judgements, as required by the Constitution, but rather the interests of bureaucrats. Many court decisions accord neither with the law, common sense, nor elementary logic.
>
> Judges are grossly and cynically violating citizens' fundamental rights to a hearing, without which there can be no talk of observing and protecting other rights. Journalists are excluded from open court sessions, records of hearings are falsified, as is evidence: court verdicts 'to order' have become the norm in the Khabarovsk region. No written judgement is provided, unfavourable evidence is ignored. Argumentation which refutes a court's verdicts and rulings disappears from the files of the case;
>
> Appeals to the Collegium of Qualification of Judges regarding violation of legal rights are sent back for consideration to the same

courts and are reviewed by the individuals responsible for the original violations;

Complaints about illegal behaviour by judges of the Collegium of Qualification of Judges are not accepted for examination by the courts.

Establishing the public accountability of judges as required by the law 'On the Institutions of the Legal Profession' has become a farce in Khabarovsk. Six of the seven representatives of the public in the Collegium of Qualification of Judges are appointed by the authorities or judicial institutions.

There was no reaction to this. President Putin did not demand the resignation (as only he has the right to) of either the Chairman of the Khabarovsk Regional Court, Mr Vdovenkov, or of his deputy, Mr Voloshin, as the main culprits of the extraordinary state of justice.

In Ufa, the capital of Bashkiria, between 5,000 and 10,000 people attend a protest meeting in Lenin Square. They have come from 14 cities in the republic to demand the resignation of President Rakhimov. The slogans are: 'Sack Murtaza Rakhimov!', 'No to nepotism in the Government'. The enterprises of Bashkiria's Fuel and Energy Complex are controlled by Murtaza's son, Ural Rakhimov.

They demand that the shares in Bashkiria's oil companies should be returned to state ownership, and compensation for moral and material loss of the inhabitants of Blagoveshchensk who suffered the brutal 'cleansing of the city' by the militia and its Special Operations units in December. The organisers are a co-ordinating committee of the United Opposition, which includes the local branches of the Communist Party, Yabloko, People's Will, the Russian Pensioners' Party, the Foundation for the Development of Local Government, the Union of Tatar Associations and the Rus Society.

The meeting passed a resolution demanding repeal of the law on monetarisation of benefits; and the resignation of President Rakhimov, of the Chief Federal Inspector of Bashkiria, of the Minister of the Interior of the Republic, Rafail Divaev, who stated that the militia's 'cleansing' operation in Blagoveshchensk had been justified, and of other top officials.

Having stood in Lenin Square for an hour, the huge crowd marched nine kilometres to the offices of Rakhimov's Administration, but were prevented from approaching the building by a barricade of buses and a cordon of many thousands comprising, apparently, the entire militia of Bashkiria. Rakhimov did not come out. Instead they were met by the Director of his Administration, Radii Khabirov, and the Secretary of the

Security Council of Bashkiria, Alexander Shabrin, who were presented with the resolution, and the people dispersed.

In Moscow, Committee 2008 once more attempts to create a united democratic party and fails. Kasparov proposes inviting to Moscow regional representatives of the opposition and letting them decide who should head the list of democratic candidates. The Moscow leaders are afraid of bringing the provincial opposition together, because they will then quite certainly not head the list. Stalemate.

In Pskov, 300 people gather in Lenin Square to protest about the new Residential Accommodation Code. The meeting was called by the Pskov Communists together with the local branch of Yabloko and the trade unions. None of the local television stations would agree to cover the meeting, which declared criminal the idea behind the new Residential Code, effective from 1 March: 'In recent decades the state has failed in its obligation to repair and modernise residential properties, but has instead very effectively directed national resources into creating a class of property owners from among the ranks of those in power.'

They demand that:

the Residential Accommodation Code should be suspended until the level of pensions and wages in the region is sufficient to meet the market cost of what is provided by the Communal Residential Services Office, and also the cost of health, education, culture, transport, communications, food and other essentials; there should be full transparency in the fixing of prices and tariffs for services provided by the Communal Residential Services Office; those who devised the deplorable Residential Accommodation Code, namely the Government of Russia, should be sacked; the State Duma should be dissolved for failing to represent the interests of the people, packed as it is with functionaries of the United Russia party and Liberal Democratic Party of Russia who voted for adoption of the Residential Accommodation Code; full responsibility for the increase in social tensions within society should be laid on President Putin.

27 March

Today, Sunday, is a day of regional referendums.

In Saratov there is a referendum about how the mayor should be elected. Just over 7 per cent of the people of Saratov turn out to vote.

They don't appear to care whether they elect him directly or have him nominated by the Kremlin-appointed governor. The Popular Front of Saratov Province, a regional association of all the opposition parties, refused to take part.

In Bashkiria a referendum has been called by the Society for Local Government Reform, on the grounds that the new system of appointing civic and regional leaders in the Republic contravenes the European Charter on Local Government, ratified by Russia in 1998.

Here too the turnout was very low, although the issue affects every citizen. The root of all this apathy is a firm belief that elections are rigged and will continue to be rigged, so why bother to vote? In any event, 90 per cent of those who did turn out voted in favour of direct election of mayors.

Moscow is becoming the least politically active of cities. If there is to be a revolution it will come from the provinces.

Yabloko's demonstration in Moscow next to Government House, protesting against the reform of the Communal Residential Services Office, managed to assemble only 200 demonstrators. The Government is insisting that all regions make these services fully self-financing by the end of 2005, and in a country with as many poor people as ours, this will be beyond the means of most. Yabloko's view is that the Government has no right to encourage a further raising of prices; it should be cracking down on the monopolistic mentality of these offices, encouraging those who own accommodation to set up co-operatives, and should encourage small businesses to offer competing services. By putting up prices, the Government is proposing to raise one trillion roubles [£20 billion] and to invest the money raised in the current rotten system of residential services provision.

Yabloko's proposals are very sensible, but the low turnout tells you how seriously people take the party. The leaders are not seeking the support of the people, but rather seats in the Duma by negotiating with the Presidential Administration.

28 March

In Ingushetia attempts to demand the resignation of President Murat Zyazikov have been thwarted. Bearing in mind the way events developed in Kirghizia, the organisers evidently thought that where there is thieving, you can expect a revolution. Everyone is wondering whether Russia can follow Kirghizia.

The authorities suppressed the meeting before it began. The Memorial to the Victims of Political Repression on the outskirts of Nazran was cordoned off at a great distance by armoured vehicles, soldiers and militia. Boris Arsamakov, the leader of Akhki-Yurt, which organised the demonstration, was detained until the day was over. On the eve of the protest President Zyazikov left Ingushetia just in case – he is never around when he smells trouble brewing – and returned only when everything had calmed down.

Although the meeting was not allowed to assemble, the crowd did not resort to violence. When Arsamakov was arrested, protesters wanted to storm the militia headquarters, but were restrained by Musa Ozdoev, a Deputy of the People's Assembly and prominent representative of the Ingushetian opposition. He went into the building to negotiate Arsamakov's release, then called on those outside to adopt a resolution demanding President Zyazikov's immediate resignation and added, 'Since the authorities have shown their cowardice by bringing such numbers of troops into the Republic, we should disperse for today and wait to see whether they implement our resolution.'

This calmed the mood. Murat Oziev, the highly respected Editor-in-Chief of *Angusht*, the only opposition newspaper in the Republic (banned by Zyazikov), also asked the crowd not to take direct action. Two pro-Zyazikov Deputies said they had come to negotiate with the opposition and to consult Zyazikov about the issue of his resignation. They asked the crowd to disperse.

What was behind this behaviour by the authorities? In a nutshell, panic that the Kirghiz scenario was being repeated. Ingushetia is poor, while its officials are rich and getting richer by the day by plundering the state budget. The following is taken from an official audit looking into misappropriation of budgetary funds and carried out by the Central Directorate of the Interior Ministry of the Southern Federal District:

Total losses from misappropriation of federal budget resources amounted to 3.9 million roubles [£76,000], of which 2.8 million roubles was misappropriated in 2003, and 1.1 million roubles in the first half of 2004. During 2003 and the first half of 2004 financial irregularities have been discovered totalling 181.4 million roubles [£3.5 million]. Of this total, those involving resources of the federal budget amount to 72.5 million roubles [£1.42 million], or 40 per cent.

Tiny Ingushetia is even smaller than its neighbour Chechnya, yet in the year and a half of Zyazikov's rule, millions have been filched. Where did these millions come from?

Ingushetia has a number of major problems. The first is refugees: the Federal Government provides aid for them, and for building new houses for those who lost their homes in floods in 2002. The second problem is the Malgobek oilfield, the principal source of wealth in the Republic: all the big local officials are constantly jockeying for control of this, and endless corruption surrounds it. Finally, there is agriculture, since the Republic is primarily agricultural.

The audit continues:

> Without making the necessary budgetary provision, the Government of the Republic illegally granted a budgetary credit to the company Ingushneftegazprom of 30 million roubles [£590,000]. Without making the necessary legislative changes, the amount allocated for subsidising residential accommodation was decreased by the same amount.

The Ingushneftegazprom oil and gas company is the Republic's most important enterprise and financially underpins the authorities. Unfortunately, under Zyazikov, having an oil company is proving expensive for the people living in Ingushetia. There is an acute accommodation crisis, partly due to the thousands of refugees, so cutting residential subsidies and handing the money over to the oil company is the most outrageous act one can imagine, but that is what happened.

> In 2003 Ingushneftegazprom was allocated a loan of 27 million roubles [£530,000] in order to implement a programme of stabilisation and development of the oil complex. Only 10.5 million roubles was repaid on time. On the balance the period of repayment was extended. According to the statistics provided, the extraction of oil is declining year by year. It has been discovered, however, that since 2002 Ingushneftegazprom has been extracting oil without a licence and concealing from audit the true quantity obtained . . .
>
> On 15 August 2003 Ingushneftegazprom signed a contract, guaranteed by the Government of Ingushetia, with a Norwegian firm (name provided) to supply technologies to increase oil production. For the work carried out Ingushneftegazprom was to transfer funds provided by the Republic amounting to US $775,000 to the

company's current account. The money was transferred by two payment orders on 19 December 2003 and 10 March 2004 respectively, but the conditions of the contract were not fulfilled.

Overall:

As a result of impropriety on the part of the management of Ingushneftegazprom, the enterprise and the state have suffered material losses amounting to more than 25 million roubles [£490,000]. In the course of the present audit, the Procurator-General of the Republic has on 5 October 2004 instigated criminal proceedings under Part 2, B, Article 171; Part 2, B, Article 199; and Part 1, Article 201 of the Criminal Code of the Russian Federation . . .

Inspection of the use of resources allocated to deal with the consequences of natural disasters in Nazran, Sunzha and Malgobek districts revealed that in 2003 payments totalling 9.5 million roubles [£186,000] were improperly received by citizens not registered at fixed addresses at the time of the flood. Four criminal cases have been opened for financial irregularities totalling 3.1 million roubles [£61,000] . . . In the Ministry of Construction, because of an overstatement of cost of sewage treatment plants in Malgobek district [to replace those destroyed by the floods], misappropriation of funds was discovered amounting to 546,600 roubles [£10,700] . . . In 2003 and the first half of 2004, the auditing of 253.9 million roubles [£4.98 million] received from the federal budget to implement the federal South Russia aid programme [which is primarily for accommodation] revealed financial irregularities amounting to 48.9 million roubles [£959,000], or 20 per cent of the total allocation. For the period 2003–2004, 185 criminal prosecutions have been instigated in respect of the theft of budgetary funds. These include 38 cases of serious or very serious misappropriation of resources. The majority relate to misappropriation of resources allocated to overcome the consequences of the flood of June 2002. Thirty-three cases relate to losses which total 17.7 million roubles [£347,000].

The criminal cases for embezzlement were indeed opened, but have since been frozen. This is the main technique for ensuring the loyalty of officials in Russia. First, get compromising materials on them, then sit back and watch as they rush to join the United Russia party.

When I published this information and these figures – and there was a ban on publishing them in Ingushetia – Zyazikov threatened to sue me. Not for having defamed or libelled him, but for having supposedly stolen official documents. I was hauled off to the Procurator-General's Office for questioning. Then I was left in peace. These are not secret documents, so why would anyone need to steal them? In order to prove theft they would need my fingerprints on somebody's safe. What a lot of nonsense.

Needless to say, General Napalkov, the Interior Ministry official in charge of this audit and by whom it was signed, has been sacked. The Interior Ministry came under such heavy pressure from the Presidential Administration to sack the whistle-blowing general that they decided it was simplest to sacrifice him.

11 April

Mikhail Khodorkovsky's last words before sentencing: 'I am not guilty of the crimes with which I am charged, and accordingly I do not intend to ask for clemency. It is a disgrace to me and my country that it is considered perfectly legal for the Procurator to directly and openly deceive the court. I was shocked when the court and lawyers explained this to me. It is a very unfortunate state of affairs if the whole country is convinced that the court is acting under the influence of officials in the Kremlin or the Procurator-General's Office.

'The court is in effect being asked to rule that the very creation, management or possession of a successful business is proof of a crime. Today I have no great amount of property left. I have ceased to be a businessman. I am no longer one of the super-rich. All that I have left is the knowledge of my own rightness and my determination to be a free man.'

Most had predicted that Khodorkovsky would plead for clemency. Nobody could believe that an oligarch would remain a decent human being, whatever the cost. The oligarchs are not trusted. Their thieving was too public, and the basis of their wealth is our national impoverishment. People will not forgive that, but they might just feel sorry for Khodorkovsky if he is totally crushed.

15 April

A second sentence has been passed on Mikhail Trepashkin, who was framed for defecting from the KGB and taking part in an independent inquiry into the blowing up of apartment blocks in Russia immediately before the Second Chechen War was started. Five years' imprisonment in a penal colony. The court found him guilty of an even graver charge than the Procurator had proposed. Throughout the trial, Trepashkin was kept in unreasonably severe conditions of detention. His case is being reviewed by the European Court of Human Rights, but meanwhile he is in prison.

17 April

At one of his appearances in Moscow, Garry Kasparov has been struck on the head with a chessboard. Somebody approached him, supposedly wanting him to autograph the board. Recovering from the blow, Kasparov quipped, 'I'm glad Russians prefer chess to baseball.'

23 April

Today Putin received Mikhail Fridman of Alfa Group in the Kremlin. The Moscow business elite have been viewing him as a likely candidate for the Khodorkovsky treatment. The reception in the Kremlin was a typical PR act by Putin, this time for the benefit of the TNK-BP oil company. In the language of the Kremlin, they were 'giving moral support' to Fridman.

Fridman is accordingly in favour for the moment. He has been given the opportunity of sharing his wealth and will certainly avail himself of it. You are in a bad way if the authorities don't even give you the chance of buttering them up. Lord Browne, Group Chief Executive of BP, was also received in the Kremlin. Viktor Vekselberg was there too, the man who lays Fabergé eggs in the Kremlin's basket. Throughout the meeting Fridman and Vekselberg radiated happiness.

Sergey Glaziev, a Deputy of the Duma from the Rodina party who was Minister of Foreign Economic Affairs in the early 1990s and is now in the opposition, commented, 'They prefer Fridman to Khodorkovsky because he does not finance opposition projects.'

23–4 April

Vladimir Ryzhkov has joined the political council of the Russian Republican Party. He has financial backing from Lukoil and this is now his party. Ryzhkov warned that the democrats must unite no later than this summer, if they are to stand a chance in the Duma elections in 2007.

Garry Kasparov was an ally of Ryzhkov in the winter, but has not joined the RRP. They have in common the view that the present political system needs to be done away with, not compromised with. If Kasparov had stayed with Ryzhkov, he could have been the one with charisma, with Ryzhkov as the smarter political fighter. Ryzhkov is saying that the door is still open, and that the RRP is still hoping to welcome Kasparov.

25 April

Putin's annual Address to the Federal Assembly was both sensational and comical. It was a veritable manifesto of liberalism, but by their fruits shall ye know them!

His theme was 'A free country of free people', but how can you be free without an independent judiciary? Or genuine, democratic electoral rights? With a politically directed Procurator-General's Office, and a stifled civil society?

28 April

The Government has decided that recipients of the title of Hero of Russia, of the USSR, or of Socialist Labour will be paid an extra [2,000 roubles, £39] a month in place of their privileges.

*

Thus began the main political scandal of the summer of 2005: a three-week hunger strike by the Heroes, which Putin's Administration called blackmail.

1 May

In Russia, 1 May is traditionally a day of meetings and parades. This year the opposition were at sixes and sevens.

They assembled at Turgenev Square, marched along Myasnitskaya Street past the great gloomy buildings of the FSB, and held a meeting on Lubyanka Square at the Solovki Stone, which commemorates victims of the Communist era. Their placards read, 'For freedom, justice and democracy! Against the violation of civil, political, social, economic and cultural rights in Russia!'

There were about 1,000 people. Not too bad, not a disaster. The day before, in Minsk, 14 of our fellow citizens had been released from custody. They had travelled to Belarus to take part in a procession organised by the local opposition. Ilya Yashin, leader of the youth wing of Yabloko, got back to Moscow this morning. From a rostrum beside the Solovki Stone, he gave us an insider's view of a Lukashenko* prison, and told us that in Minsk Ukrainian supporters got beaten up much more violently than Russian protesters.

As the democrats were finishing, the Union of Right Forces started their meeting right there in Lubyanka Square. The authorities must have been delighted to see that liberals and democrats don't even stop quarrelling on public holidays.

The main protest was organised by the left wing, who assembled almost 9,000 people. Most of the young people were there. The Communist Party, the National Bolsheviks, Rodina, Labour in the Capital, the Union of Soviet Officers and others had agreed to hold a joint meeting. For the first time in four years Eduard Limonov was able to lead the column of the National Bolsheviks, now that his suspended sentence has expired.

Yevgeny Baranovsky, Lev Dmitriev, Alexander Chepalyga have begun a hunger strike at the headquarters of the National Bolshevik Party in Moscow. They are demanding the release of their fellow party members who are in prison.

Overall, throughout Russia, the left brought out one and a half million May Day demonstrators.

In Ingushetia, the May celebrations were marked by arrests. Musa Ozdoev, the leading campaigner for the removal of President Zyazikov, was arrested during the night. The previous day he was in a square where an anti-Zyazikov meeting was to be held and was arrested by the militia. At midnight Judge Ramazan Tutaev was brought to the militia headquarters in Nazran; he dispensed justice in the holding cell, thereby giving symbolic expression to the further melding of the judiciary and institutions of law enforcement into a single repressive state mechanism.

Tutaev sentenced Ozdoev to 72 hours' imprisonment, officially for 'petty vandalism'. It was falsely alleged that he had broken a stool. As a Deputy of the Republican Parliament, Musa cannot legally be arrested without the sanction of the People's Assembly, but, as that is difficult at night, they dispensed with the formality.

In prison, Musa promptly went on hunger strike in protest. He discovered his cellmates were in for a collective suicide attempt.

2 May

Ozdoev has been unexpectedly released, a day early. The decision was taken by Judge Alikhan Yaryzhev of the Nazran District Court. Ozdoev considered this insulting. 'I told Judge Yaryzhev,' Musa told me, 'that I wouldn't leave. I needed no concessions from them.' The militiamen, however, took the oppositionist out into the street and shut the door firmly behind him.

The real reason was evidently that he had entered a world the authorities want kept secret. In the cell he met people who had been tortured into 'voluntarily' confessing that they were 'organisers of and participants in a terrorist act against Murat Zyazikov'. Ozdoev learned that the torture employed by agents of the Interior Ministry against these prisoners was so extreme that the North Ossetian Directorate of the FSB refused to accept some of them for further questioning because of the severity of their injuries. Ozdoev also met Bekkhan Gireyev, whom the Interior Ministry claims was 'the mastermind behind the terrorist plot'. His kneecaps had been shattered and he had no fingernails left on his hands. They had been torn out during interrogation.

'I learned things that I would never previously have believed,' Musa told me, 'if I had not seen them with my own eyes. Of course, after this sort of thing these people and their relatives will rush to join the Resistance.' The Deputy considers his own misadventure entirely trivial.

3 May

From Israel, Leonid Nevzlin has made an offer to the Presidential Administration to sell off Menatep Group's shares in Yukos in return for the freedom of Khodorkovsky and Lebedev.

Through his lawyers, Khodorkovsky from Matrosskaya Tishina prison rejected his friend and erstwhile business partner's offer. Khodorkovsky stated that he did not consider himself guilty and had no intention of allowing himself to be ransomed. He would fight for his freedom by legal means.

Nevzlin became the owner of a controlling share in Menatep after Khodorkovsky transferred 59.5 per cent of the company to him in order to 'concentrate on creating a civil society in Russia'. This focusing of his efforts was the beginning of all his troubles, as the Kremlin decided he was its most dangerous enemy. If he had dutifully paid the Kremlin its cut, no harm would have come to him.

The Yukos shareholders have announced that they see no point in continuing their attempts to save the company.

The authorities are insinuating ever more busily, on television and in speeches by their most prominent figures, that Stalin was really not as bad as he was subsequently made out to be. The unveiling of new monuments to Stalin in recognition of his great contribution to victory in the Second World War features prominently on the news. The Human Rights Association has urged opposition to these attempts to impose official veneration of The Leader. In a statement it commented:

> After all that our people has learned about the superhuman brutality and vileness of Stalin, his moral and political rehabilitation could only mean that in our country any political immorality is permissible and any crime committed by the state can be justified if its enormity is sufficiently mind-numbing. We must never forget that the main victim of Stalinism was the Russian people.

The democrats have missed the boat again. Re-Stalinisation is a reality.

4 May

In the Zamoskvorechie District Court in Moscow, Judge Irina Vasina rejects an appeal by Svetlana Gubaryova. Svetlana was a *Nord-Ost* hostage and lost her 13-year-old daughter and her fiancé, Sandy Booker, a US citizen, in the tragedy.

Svetlana was demanding that the Procurator's refusal to respond to her questions as to where and when her family died should be ruled unlawful; that the directives of the Procurator's Office refusing to review the provision of medical assistance during the *Nord-Ost* siege should be ruled unlawful; and likewise that the decision of the head of the investigating team, Vladimir Kalchuk, not to press criminal charges against the agents of the Special Operations units that carried out the assault should be ruled unlawful.

In a wavering voice, Svetlana read her complaints against the Procurator. She noted that those who killed the hostages, including her family, received awards, and that every attempt is now being made to absolve them of blame for turning the Dubrovka auditorium into a gas chamber. The lack of accountability of the guilty has led to the even greater tragedy of Beslan.

After five minutes of this, the judge abruptly terminated the hearing. Svetlana had been hoping to create a precedent by getting the court to pronounce on the legal basis of the way the inquiry was being conducted.

9 May

The leaders of every imaginable country have come to Moscow to pay homage to Putin, not to Russia's victory in the Second World War. That is how it is being seen by the right, the left and the apolitical.

Putin has hijacked this major patriotic celebration for his own purposes, in order to consolidate his position as one of the world's major leaders. The whole business world has been coerced into contributing to the Victory Fund. All officials have been charged a levy. Even the humblest government employees have had no option but to pay up to celebrate 'Putin's Victory'.

One old man, Pavel Petrovich Smolyaninov, has written to me from the village of Pushkarnoye where his wife is the postwoman. She is paid a mere 2,000 roubles [£40] a month, but even she was forced to contribute. In his words, she was unable to resist the extortion because she has only three months to go before she retires, and didn't want to jeopardise her pension.

11 May

They are going to set up a Social Chamber from 'the best elements of civil society'. These will be selected by Putin so that they can criticise decisions of the state authorities, including Putin himself.

The Steering Committee of the Citizens' Congress has described this as 'an attempt to manipulate civil society in the vested interests of those in power'. On the other hand, they added, they continue to consider it sensible to exploit any opportunity of influencing the authorities, 'and we believe that individual participation of members of the National

Citizens' Congress in the Social Chamber should be regarded as a further practical opportunity to exert such influence'.

Are they really going to allow themselves to be bought in this manner? They sure are.

12 May

In Novosibirsk, FSB agents have arrested two National Bolsheviks, Nikolai Baluev and Vyacheslav Rusakov. Baluev's flat was searched, and the agents removed leaflets, issues of the National Bolshevik newspaper *Generalnaya liniya*, 20 video-cassettes and a jar of saltpetre that Nikolai's mother, Yevdokia, uses at their dacha as fertiliser. Both party members are being charged under Articles 222, Part 2, 'Possession of weapons', and 205, Part 2, 'Terrorism'.

14 May

The 'Anti-Terror Festival'. The *Nord-Ost* siege victims staged a four-hour *tour de force* called 'No to Terror!' They continue the fight under their own steam, but with little support. The large concert hall of the Cosmos Hotel in Moscow is only half full.

In the stalls and the circle are mainly the families of those who died at *Nord-Ost* and survivors. Somewhat to one side is a delegation from Beslan. The event is opened by Tatiana Karpova, the mother of Alexander Karpov who died at *Nord-Ost*, and who is now the driving force behind the association, defending the interests of those involved. The main theme of the evening is: where is the state's concern for the victims of terror? Where are the independent inquiries into terrorist acts? Where is the independent judiciary and the honest procurator's office? Are you listening, Mr President?

An open letter to Putin is distributed. It has been written by Oleg Zhirov, a Dutch citizen whose wife died trying to save their son in the siege:

My main reason for writing this letter is the growing number of victims of terrorist acts in Russia, and the total disregard for their problems and their right to moral and material compensation on the part of the bureaucracy and judicial institutions, including the Supreme and Constitutional Courts. To judge by their verdicts, everything that has gone on in Russia over the past five years of the struggle against terrorism has been in accordance with the Constitution, and the demands and lawsuits of the victims have been without legal justification. It seems at times that there are only two parties to this war: the heroic Special Operations troops; and, on the other side, terrorists and separatists.

In the wings I read Oleg Zhirov's letter together with Svetlana Gubaryova, who lost her daughter, Sasha, and her American fiancé during the siege. Her eyes are full of tears as she tries to hold back her inconsolable grief. She does not believe that writing open letters to Putin will change anything about the way the Russian authorities currently 'fight terrorism', when it is Putin who is the main instigator of policies where those who come off worst are always the hostages.

The stage is taken by familiar faces, diehard supporters of the victims of terrorism: Irina Khakamada, who now heads the Our Choice party; Garry Kasparov, a world champion who this spring retired from playing chess the better to work for political change; and Lyudmila Aivar, a lawyer who for more than two years now has been representing the interests of the *Nord-Ost* victims in the courts.

Many 'new faces' had been invited, but have not appeared. Alexander Torshin, for example, who is leading the parliamentary commission set up to investigate Beslan. It was him that the people from Beslan had been hoping to hear. They believe that Torshin knows every last detail about the assault on the school, can't reveal it for the time being, but will tell the whole truth once he has plucked up enough courage. His absence from this festival evidently means he hasn't plucked up enough courage yet.

Putin is incapable of seeing the Russian people as an ally in the fight against terrorism. He doesn't like that kind of popular involvement, and the lackeys who carry out his orders merely ape the President's behaviour.

The 2005 Festival is already the second. It is becoming a tradition. We, hostages to an uncaring state, can only guess how many more terrorist acts there will be in 2006, and hope they may be few.

16 May

The churlish behaviour of the OMON Special Operations militia outside the Meshchansky Court where the trial of Khodorkovsky and Lebedev is drawing to an end is a clear indicator of the authorities' attitude towards democracy. They broke up a group of those supporting the accused, but ignored the demonstrators opposed to Yukos, who had also materialised from somewhere. In total 28 people were arrested, the militiamen just plucking people out of the crowd and shoving them into a bus when the demonstration was over, as if someone in charge had just woken up. The protesters were taken to militia stations and held there for seven hours. They included Kasparov.

21 May

Every year since 1990, the Andrey Sakharov Foundation and the Moscow State Philharmonia have celebrated Sakharov's birthday by holding a musical evening in the Grand Hall of the Moscow Conservatory. Over the last 14 years the programme has become traditional: a classical concert with brief speeches, by leading public figures and human-rights defenders who were close to Sakharov, about the main problems currently facing us.

It was probably the speeches they were afraid of, because when it was time to arrange the fifteenth celebration this year, for the first time the Philharmonia suddenly told the Foundation it wouldn't be possible. No reason, no explanations.

In order to continue the tradition unbroken, Sakharov's admirers, regrouping after their surprise at such an unexpected manifestation of managed democracy, held an open-air concert in the little square next to the Sakharov Museum and Social Centre. The theme of the evening was 'While Hearts Still Beat for Honest Life'.

There was a good attendance and the evening went well in a familiar, Moscow sort of way. Bards sang, poets recited, the Chechen singer Liza Umarova performed breathtakingly, a letter was read out from Vladimir Voinovich who was unable to attend. Sergey Kovalyov gave a speech, as did Grigorii Yavlinsky and Vladimir Lukin, Russia's Ombudsman for Human Rights. The concert was compèred by Natella Boltyanskaya, an excellent songwriter, singer and presenter on Echo of Moscow, almost the last free radio station broadcasting.

The sense of being embattled, left over from the cancellation of the evening at the Conservatory, dissipated with the first words spoken and sung, to be replaced by a great sense of solidarity, and of being at one with the legacy of Sakharov.

The tricks were not over yet, though. Realising they had failed to humiliate the human-rights movement, the authorities did an about-turn and the Philharmonia started advertising a 'Sakharov Concert' in the Grand Hall of the Conservatory. They set up a doppelgänger, a parallel concert to which, naturally, neither Sakharov's friends nor those who had been prisoners of the Gulag, nor members of the human-rights movement, nor Sakharov's relatives were invited.

'They' seem to have decided to try to privatise even the memory of Sakharov. Most likely the aim was to throw dust in the eyes of the West.

22 May

Sunday, and marches were called across the nation 'for free speech, against censorship, violence, and lies on television'.

I supposed that most of the demonstrators would be members of the press corps, and that they would lead the parade. In fact, apart from journalists covering the event, there were only two representatives of the press marching: Yevgenia Albats, who has left journalism for teaching, and me.

The demonstration had been jointly organised by Yabloko, the Communist Party, the Union of Right Forces, the Russian Union of Journalists, the Moscow Helsinki Group, the Citizens' Congress, Committee 2008, the Committee for the Defence of Muscovites, the Committee for the Defence of Civil Rights, the Human Rights Association, the Solidarity Movement and the National Bolsheviks (in strength). Limonov made a speech.

Everybody assembled at the memorial to Academician Korolyov on Cosmonauts' Avenue and processed to the broadcasting centre at Ostankino, blocking the road.

23 May

The National Bolsheviks held in the Pechatniki women's prison for the 14 December occupation of a room at the Presidential Administration's building have gone on hunger strike.

24 May

Yukos is no more. The company in its former incarnation has been done away with. Its main asset, Yugonskneftegaz, has been prised away with the assistance of German capital. The holding company, Yukos-Moscow, has been liquidated.

28 May

The party conference of the Union of Right Forces. Nikita Belykh was elected chairman of the political committee and head of the party. He is a government man, the Deputy Governor of Perm Province, so the Administration has taken over the Union of Right Forces, too. It has promptly ceased protesting about the abolition of elections for governors, for example.

At the behest of the Presidential Administration, the Duma's main preoccupation throughout its spring session has been to expunge the last vestiges of democracy in the electoral legislation. Laws have been amended to ensure that those out of favour stand no chance of getting into power, no matter what the electorate might think. The main innovations are:

1. The electoral deposit required of political parties has been increased to $2 million.
2. The quorum for a valid election is being sharply reduced in order for them to continue taking place at all. Where previously the minimum turnout was 20 per cent, there will now be no minimum requirement in local elections. It is a complete travesty: if even 2 per cent of the electorate turn out to vote for a mayor, he will get in.
3. There is no longer to be a restriction on the number of remote or portable ballot boxes at polling centres. Machinations involving remote voting were the main tactic for falsifying the last elections, both parliamentary and presidential. They stuffed them with as many votes as were needed, away from the polling stations and hence outside the purview of observers. Indeed, in the municipal elections in St Petersburg this system has proved its worth marvellously, the number of voting slips in remote ballot boxes exceeding those from electors who voted in person at polling stations.
4. The box for voting for 'None of the above' is to be removed from ballot papers. Up to 20 per cent of votes cast have been for 'None of the above' recently, and this has greatly vexed the Presidential Administration. There will now be no way to register a formal protest vote in elections.
5. Observers may no longer be provided by public associations. No independent observers will be allowed, only those nominated by

political parties. International observers will only be allowed if invited by the state authorities. The Presidential Administration will decide which observers to invite, and which to keep out.

Is the Administration desperately afraid of elections, even when they are as 'managed' as the recent ones? Or is it just tired of worrying whether it can get away with its deceptions and wants to impose conditions even more favourable to itself?

All these presidential amendments adopted by the Duma are still not enough for Dmitry Medvedev, Director of the Presidential Administration, who told representatives of the regional electoral commissions that elections were a 'threat to stability' in Russia. Putin did not rebuke the Director of his Administration.

In Moscow, the Communist Party, the National Bolshevik Party, Yabloko and Rodina held a joint protest meeting on Revolution Square in support of political prisoners. They are showing solidarity with the women on hunger strike, and demanding that they should not be held in prison while the 14 December case is pending. They want a stop to further persecution of the opposition on political grounds, and demand a wider amnesty for prisoners in custody who are charged with trivial infringements of the law.

Much the authorities care.

30 May

At 10 a.m. three of Limonov's supporters who have been on hunger strike at NBP headquarters came out and blocked the entrance to Red Square. They locked themselves between the gates of the archway next to the History Museum. The protesters wore T-shirts bearing the legend '29-day hunger strike' and held portraits of the National Bolshevik political prisoners. They demanded their release, and a response from the state to the hunger strikers in the Pechatniki women's prison.

They also scattered leaflets with the statement:

Freedom or Death! The fourth week of our hunger strike has come to an end at the headquarters of the National Bolshevik Party. We have seen once again that the Russian state authorities are indifferent to the life and security of their citizens. There has been no reaction to the hunger strike on the part of the authorities. What more could be expected of people who, without hesitation, poisoned their country's citizens with gas in *Nord-Ost*, fired from tanks at child hostages in Beslan, deprive the aged of their benefits, imprison the innocent, express admiration for the bloody dictator Karimov [of Uzbekistan], and declare an insulting amnesty of a mere 200 prisoners to mark the sixtieth anniversary of victory in the Second World War. We hunger strikers are obliged to come out on to the street in order to voice our protest at such a murderous attitude towards the citizens of Russia. We say no to the power of pitiless officials and police state butchers! Long Live Free Russia!

The protest lasted just over half an hour. At 10.35 the National Bolsheviks were arrested by agents of the Federal Security Service and fined 500 roubles [£10] for 'an unsanctioned picket in the vicinity of the residence of the President'.

7 June

In North Ossetia there has been a sudden transfer of power. President Alexander Dzasokhov, whom nobody could stand any longer, has been demoted to the position of senator and member of the Soviet of the Federation, representing North Ossetia. He bears full responsibility for the deaths of hundreds of children and adults in Beslan, and should have been put on trial. Putin, however, does not put his allies on trial. He has replaced Dzasokhov with Teimuraz Mamsurov, an 'anti-terrorist appointment'. Mamsurov was previously Leader of the North Ossetian Parliament. Two of his children were held hostage in Beslan, but survived. Subsequently, however, all he did was whitewash the actions of the authorities.

In his speech from the throne to the Deputies of the Parliament, Mamsurov declared, 'I shall try to be worthy of the high trust of the President.' Appointees no longer need to aspire to winning the trust of the people.

16 June

Representatives of the opposition on the left and right have signed a charter of alliance, prompting one of Yavlinsky's now rare public appearances, in Yaroslavl. He looked weary and depressed.

He told the local journalists, 'I get invited onto television periodically just to show the public that I'm still alive. They are pleased to know that, but that is as far as their interest goes. What can you do in such circumstances? No more than ask the authorities to grant you a certain percentage of the vote in the elections. It's like a rigged sports match where the result doesn't reflect the game.' Nowadays Yavlinsky lectures at the Higher School of Economics in Moscow. He has postgraduate students, writes books and gives talks abroad.

The new leader of the Union of Right Forces, Nikita Belykh, appears to be urging the Kremlin not to persecute them, but to see them as being useful. 'We are an opposition, a constructive opposition. We have never said we were loyal to the authorities, but at the same time we do not believe in opposition for its own sake.'

His words are completely lifeless. Is there any point in making the effort to resuscitate these old democrats merely because they are familiar faces? Are they capable of doing anything at all for the country as demo-cratic leaders, or should we simply accept the way politics is developing? If we are realistic, none of the movements or parties in the democratic spectrum deserve the support of an honest person unwilling to compro-mise his conscience.

In the absence of grown-up politics, an increasing role is played by youth politics, which does not keep wondering what its role should be or whom it should support. It does not care what Yavlinsky thinks, and most likely has never heard of Nikita Belykh.

20 June

It is six months since the mass outrages committed by the militia in Blagoveshchensk, Bashkiria and the surrounding villages on 10–14 December 2004. It is almost two months since the publication of uncon-stitutional, secret instructions issued by the Interior Ministry of Russia on the permissibility of taking violent measures against Russian citi-zens, instructions highly germane to the Blagoveshchensk violence. Now, finally, a commission has been put together in Moscow under the auspices of the Ombudsman for Human Rights to discuss where we go from here.

A meeting of this commission is the sole official reaction by the state authorities to a whole series of 'cleansings' similar to those in Blagoveshchensk, which have occurred, and are still occurring, in many places including Bezhetsk, Nefteyugansk, the village of Rozhdestveno in Tver Province and the village of Ivanovskoye in Stavropol Region.

The extraordinary brutality of the security services within Russia over the past six months has produced no wider public protest, no social repercussions. The President has continued to consider himself above defending the Constitution, not once apologising to the hundreds of people 'purged', injured and beaten up, for his failure to protect them. Parliament is in the President's pocket and has devoted not a single session to the extraordinary events in Blagoveshchensk and their aftermath. The Procurator-General has failed to demand publicly the immediate annulment of the unconstitutional Interior Ministry instructions.

Now, on 20 June, the Ombudsman, Vladimir Lukin, opened the Commission's first session. The Procurator-General was represented by Sergey Gerasimov, Deputy Procurator-General of the Privolzhiye Federal District. Representatives of the Interior Ministry included the Deputy Head of the Department of Organisational Monitoring, Gennadii Blinov (who did most of the speaking for the lot of them), and Vladimir Vladimirov from the local department of the Federal Drug Control Service. He had nothing to say, like most of the other militiamen present.

Things got off to a brisk start. Lev Ponomaryov of the Human Rights Association, a member of the unofficial Public Commission for Investigating the Events in Blagoveshchensk, asked, 'What is the current situation with criminal prosecutions in connection with the Blagoveshchensk events?'

Sergey Gerasimov: The inquiry has been completed. All the accused have been acquainted with its findings. Ramazanov, the Head of the Blagoveshchensk Internal Affairs Office, has so far read 22 of the 50 volumes. Our prediction is that if he continues to read at his present rate, he will need about another month. The case will then be forwarded to the court.

(The longer he spends reading the evidence, the less it will be in the public eye. The Procurator's Office will not be pressuring Ramazanov.)

Ponomaryov: Certain officers of the Interior Ministry of Bashkiria were initially suspended, but now they have been reinstated. Why is that?

Gerasimov: They appealed, saying they had been unfairly suspended, and the court refused to confirm their suspensions. In my opinion the Interior Ministry of Bashkiria acted incorrectly. If employees of the Procurator's Office were involved in something of this kind, their employment would have been terminated.

Veronika Shakhova (ex-Editor of the Blagoveshchensk newspaper *Zerkalo*, sacked for giving a truthful account of the December events): But our Procurator Izmagilov simply refused to accept statements from the victims! Now he has not been punished, but merely disappeared from view.

Gerasimov: A few days after the events he wrote a statement and was relieved of his post.

Shakhova: Is that the extent of his punishment?

Gerasimov: Yes.

Shakhova: Well, now he has applied to become a judge. Has the Procurator's Office given a reference on him to the Collegium of Qualification of Judges?

Gerasimov (discomfited and unsure how to reply): I don't know. Possibly something has been sent.

Sergey Kovalyov (the first Russian Ombudsman, former Deputy of the Duma, a convinced democrat, a dissident in the Soviet period, comrade-in-arms of Andrey Sakharov): But tell me, is nobody even raising the matter of his breaking the law in the course of performing his duties?

Gerasimov: Dismissal is the severest sanction. No evidence of criminal activity was discovered.

Vladimir Lukin, Ombudsman: Nevertheless, this case has had repercussions, and problems are continuing. Irregularities of the same kind have occurred since Blagoveshchensk in Tver Province, and there are suspicions that on the night of 11–12 June something similar occurred in Stavropol District. How can we ensure that this kind of thing is stopped? Perhaps the fact that the guilty get off with total impunity is causing it?

Gerasimov: The Interior Ministry cannot impose order in its own department. The Minister of the Interior should be the master of his house – he should bang his fist on the table. Any number of procurators are not going to be able to force the militia to put their house in order.

Lyudmila Alexeyeva (Chairwoman of the Moscow Helsinki Group and a member of the Presidential Commission for the Development of Civil Society and Human Rights): At first, when we took on this case, we thought it was simply mismanagement on the part of the local Interior Ministry, but now we know about Order No. 870 DSP. The militia were carrying out this order. We are campaigning to have Order 870 repealed, but are there other departmental orders regarding 'filtration points'?

(Orders No. 174 DSP and No. 870 DSP of 10 September 2002, signed by Boris Gryzlov, who at that time was Minister of the Interior, and Appendix No. 12 to Order No. 870 DSP ('Instructions on the Planning and Preparation of Forces and Resources in Emergency Circumstances') laid down how officers of the Interior Ministry are to react in 'Emergency Circumstances', 'Emergency Situations' and a 'State of Emergency'. They introduce the concept of 'filtration points' and a 'filtration group'. According to these documents, not only can we be punched in the face whenever a militiaman or OMON agent sees fit, but we can also be subjected to arbitrary detention, sent to a filtration point, and, if we resist, they are also allowed to 'exterminate criminals'.

These documents appear to grant a militiaman the right to consider anybody a criminal. Today these orders, which amount to a *de facto* abolition of the presumption of innocence, are to be found in every militia station.)

Gennadii Blinov: As regards the creation of the so-called 'filtration point' in Blagoveshchensk, that was just elementary incompetence on the part of the individual in charge locally. Order No. 870 was approved only to protect the population and our territory in the event of a state of emergency. It applies only in those circumstances.

Oleg Orlov (Co-Chairman of the Memorial Human Rights Centre): But in Order No. 870 reference is made not only to a state of emergency, but also to emergency circumstances and emergency situations. How is the creation of filtration points in a state of emergency regulated? And what are 'emergency circumstances'? These concepts are not to be found anywhere in our legislation.

Blinov: The Interior Ministry has one more week in which to reply. Let us not be over-hasty. An impressive team of lawyers is working on it. Let us wait.

(What are we talking about here? In the corridor, Sergey Gerasimov, who was in charge of the Blagoveshchensk criminal investigation, openly admitted that Order No. 870 had not been sent to him because it was secret. This order, in accordance with which citizens were herded into a filtration point, beaten up, tortured and gassed, can in fact be read on any number of human-rights websites – Memorial, The People's Verdict, the Human Rights Association. It has been translated into English and is available to international human-rights organisations. How else does it have to be brought to the notice of the Deputy Procurator-General?)

Mara Polyakova (Chairwoman of the Independent Legal Commission, which has examined the legality of Order No. 870): Is the

Procurator-General's Office intending to object to such subordinate legislation as Order No. 870 and the Instructions to it as being unlawful?

Blinov: Order No. 870 has been examined and approved by the Ministry of Justice. It is legal.

Sergey Shimovolos (human-rights campaigner from Nizhny Novgorod): The wearing of masks by OMON agents during the 'cleansing' makes it impossible to bring them to justice. Only those who were not wearing masks have been accused in the Blagoveshchensk case. How do we proceed?

Gerasimov: It is impossible to do without masks completely; they are essential when guarding particularly dangerous criminals and when catching armed bandits where a guerrilla war is being waged. Certainly the use of masks should be regulated, which is not the case at present. For the time being, the OMON agents in Bashkiria have escaped punishment. The position of the Procurator-General's Office is that, where masks are used, agents must wear numbered badges; after Blagoveshchensk, it transpired that the Bashkiria militia did not have a single badge, and the same is true of many other regions.

Irina Vershinina (Human Rights Ombudsman for Kaliningrad Province): Are you going to review the legal situation concerning the wearing of masks? There are constant scandals, but nothing is done about it.

There was no reply to this at all.

Sergey Kovalyov: We are not just talking about the 10 officers accused in connection with Blagoveshchensk, nor even only about the Interior Ministry of Bashkiria. That is not the point – the situation is much worse. Where did these filtration points come from? From Chechnya. This sort of thing has been going on there for more than 10 years. They have been suffering from filtration points and a harsh regime under a state of emergency, even though no state of emergency was ever formally declared. This simply creates conditions for brutality. We are speaking about individuals of very high rank. Indeed, we have to ask whether this is not state policy. I fear it is.

*

At subsequent meetings of the Commission those whom Lukin referred to as 'outsiders' were banned. These included victims of the Blagoveshchensk 'cleansing', and an apparently unwelcome number of human-rights campaigners and journalists. At the next meeting an act of collective suicide by prisoners in the penal colony in Lgov was under discussion, where, simultaneously, around 1,000 prisoners slit their veins in protest at the tortures to which the guards were subjecting them, but the discussion was restricted to 'insiders'. Insiders, to Russia's official champion of human rights, are senior officials of the Ministry of Justice, which runs the prisons and penal colonies of Russia.

29 June

In Dagestan, Geidar Jemal has been arrested. He is the Chairman of the Islamic Committee of Russia, one of the most authoritative Islamic philosophers of the present day. He lives in Moscow. Jemal went to Makhachkala at the invitation of the Religious Board of Muslims of Dagestan, an entirely official institution. He was arrested by agents of the Makhachkala Directorate of the FSB, along with another 12 people who had come to discuss how to maintain peace in the Republic, where a war is brewing.

This arrest of unarmed individuals was carried out in a highly aggressive manner by armed agents. Jemal was insulted and beaten up, then taken to the Dagestan Centre for the Struggle Against Terrorism. Subsequently, all except Abbas Kebedov were released, but this is unbelievable behaviour. Jemal is too serious a figure in the Islamic world to be treated like this.

The officially stated reason was suspicion of sympathy for Wahhabism, with which Jemal is totally unconnected. What nowadays we call Wahhabism is in fact the cult of Basaev.

30 June

In the Nikulin District Court, Moscow, the trial of the National Bolsheviks who occupied an office in the Presidential Administration building on 14 December 2004 has begun. They were led into the courtroom fettered to each other like slaves, looking like something from a textbook about the ancient world.

The trial is without precedent. In the first place, there are 39 accused, and trying to find a sufficiently large courtroom with cages to hold them all is well nigh impossible. Cages are an invariable feature of trials in Russia now. In the second place, the state authorities are going out of their way to emphasise that the trial is political.

At first they were accused of 'violent seizure of power in the Russian Federation' (Article 278 of the Criminal Code). The charge was subsequently reduced to 'organising mass disorder' (Article 212, Part 2), which carries a term of three to eight years' imprisonment. The case is being handled specially by the Procurator-General of Russia, Vladimir Ustinov, and the investigation was conducted by a team from the Moscow Procurator's Office (whose leader, Yevgeny Alimov, was to be dismissed in July in connection with a different, corrupt investigation). For more than six months 39 of the 40 National Bolsheviks (15-year-old Ivan Petrov from Tver was released) have been held in detention cells awaiting trial.

By midday, when the hearing was due to begin, the court building on Michurin Prospekt was surrounded by concentric security cordons. There were OMON agents everywhere, militia arriving, dogs, people in camouflage fatigues and plain-clothes agents at every turn. They were openly recording on video those who had gathered, and even looking over the shoulders of journalists to read what they were noting down. There were no liberties here, as there had been at Khodorkovsky's trial. The National Bolsheviks were not brought to court in elegant off-roaders with tinted glass, and parents had no opportunity of seeing how their children were looking.

The accused were transported in windowless prison vans, which were immediately driven into a basement. They were brought up internal staircases to the second floor, which today was completely closed to anybody not actively involved in the trial. To round off these extraordinary measures, militiamen were posted every 10 metres in the outer cordons, as if Putin was expected to show. The only person who did turn up was Eduard Limonov, the National Bolshevik leader, although neither he nor the parents were allowed into, or even anywhere near, the building.

'We sympathise, but this is what the judge has decided,' the colonel in charge of the cordon explains amicably. The judge is Alexey Shikhanov, who has been brought over from the Tver District Court. The hearings should have taken place there, where the alleged offence occurred, but the courtroom isn't big enough.

It has to be said that putting as-yet-unconvicted people in chains and cages seems something of an overreaction; not even terrorists and serial rapists are brought to court in chains. As we can see, those whom the state authorities really fear today are dissidents.

This first day, with the public excluded, the defence tries to have the young defendants released on bail, if only the three boys who are minors and the nine girls. This hardly seems radical, given that the damage they are said to have caused (a torn sofa, a broken safe and a door) is minuscule. Even if they add holding an unsanctioned meeting, that is an administrative offence, not a crime.

Judge Shikhanov, however, emphasises how very serious this all is and what grave concern it gives rise to. He will announce his decision on whether to continue to hold them in jail at 7.00 p.m., after everybody attending other cases has left the court, in case those National Bolsheviks still at liberty cause a disturbance. That is a pretty clear hint that the ruling will be negative.

The judge need not have been so anxious about causing a riot. By evening, with the rain sheeting down, only the most dogged supporters remain; the quiet, sad mothers and fathers huddled under their umbrellas whose only weapons are their tears. The party comrades have gone for tea and Limonov too is absent. It is unbecoming for leaders to stand about in the rain. The decision is announced: keep them in jail.

All the trappings of this trial show us how scared the authorities are of committed political opponents who believe in standing up to Putin.

They need another show trial. First there was Yukos, now they are trying to crush the dissidents, which is the role ascribed to the National Bolsheviks today. Their slogans are 'Stop the war in Chechnya!', 'Down with this antisocial government!', 'Putin out!' What is worse, they don't set about other people in gateways: they read books and think thoughts. What makes their offence all the more heinous is that the authorities haven't been able to break them, even though they have subjected them to all the disgusting methods that our security agencies excel at in places of detention. The authorities have got nowhere: none have appealed for clemency, none have pleaded guilty.

Garry Kasparov is now the leader of a United Democratic Front which, so far, unfortunately, hasn't managed to unite many democrats other than the few like-minded souls who used to work for or support the Union of Right Forces. He continues his travels through the south of Russia. Everywhere Kasparov and his team are refused accommodation in hotels, cannot get meals in restaurants and are denied rooms in which to hold their meetings. The owners refer to a ban – naturally only verbal – by the authorities of the Southern Federal District. 'You will go back to Moscow, but we have to stay here. They are likely just to shut our hotel and restaurant down if we agree to accept you.'

Why is Kasparov so alarming? He has only talked to people, sown seeds of doubt about the 'good Putin' in the minds of some. That is all he has done. His persecution is the doing of the 'good' Dmitry Kozak, Putin's political representative in the south of Russia, a supposed democrat. Many, even in the democratic ranks, see Kozak as the best hope for democracy after Putin, though he looks good only because of a total lack of alternatives. Most in the Government are sluggish and cowardly. People felt sorry for him when he was appointed the Presidential Representative in the South, which was seen as a dead-end job, but Kozak showed that he was no coward. He was prepared to come out and talk to people about their discontents. He helped them let off steam.

Gradually, as he moved from one act of civil disobedience to another through the towns of the South, Kozak started gaining popularity in other parts of Russia. His real political complexion, however, is to be seen in this petty persecution of Kasparov. He is completely on Putin's side.

1 July

In Makhachkala, Dagestan, 10 people were killed on the spot and two more died in hospital when almost 60 conscripts from 102 Brigade of the Interior Ministry's Special Operations unit were blown up outside a bathhouse they attended on Fridays. The home-made mine had an explosive power equivalent to seven kilograms of TNT. This is the sixth terrorist act in Dagestan in the past month.

6 July

In Moscow, Russia's Heroes have gone on hunger strike. This is unheard of for a group traditionally considered the mainstay of whichever regime currently occupies the Kremlin. They should be heroes for the leaders of the state, but something has gone wrong.

Five Heroes, representing 204 Heroes of Russia, of the Soviet Union and of Socialist Labour, have decided they have no other way of helping to improve relations between the Russian populace and the state authorities than to subject themselves to public self-mortification. They are conducting the hunger strike in a former research institute on Smolny Street on the outskirts of Moscow.

Each hunger striker represents a group of Heroes: one, those twice awarded the title of Hero of the Soviet Union; another, the cosmonauts of Star City; a third, the Heroes of Socialist Labour and full Cavaliers of the Order of Glorious Labour; a fourth, those who are both Heroes of the Soviet Union and of the Russian Federation; and so on.

The Heroes have lost patience. On 13 June the Duma adopted at the first reading new anti-benefit amendments, this time relating to the Heroes. The amendments propose a reduction not of income, but of tokens of respect from the state towards those who have served it exceptionally; for example, Heroes will not henceforth be buried with honours: no guard of honour from the Military Commissariat, no farewell volley, unless their estate pays for it.

This is bureaucratic insanity of the highest order. The Heroes are incensed, having always supposed that the state had an interest in honouring them. In April, while these amendments were meandering through the machinery of government, the Heroes wrote to Putin, Fradkov and Gryzlov. Two hundred and four of them asked the authorities to meet their representatives, to hear them out and understand that they felt these amendments were humiliating and unacceptable.

There was no reaction whatsoever. No glimmer of understanding. The bureaucrats of the Presidential Administration, Duma and Government spat in their face. The Heroes were then struck by the thought that if this was the response they themselves got, how would anybody else in the country far'? They decided to go on hunger strike in order 'to draw attention to the problem of dialogue between the state authorities and society'.

'We consider it time to start a protest moment, and to be the "sparks that light a flame",' Valerii Burkov says. 'So that civil society should follow our lead and a law be passed ensuring that the voice of citizens is heard when the state institutions are drafting laws. Our hunger strike is intended to provoke a broad public debate about how political decisions are taken, about a citizen's right to his own point of view and about how the state should be governed. Otherwise the Russian Constitution is just another idealistic Declaration of Human Rights. Where is the intelligentsia? Where are the writers? The members of the Presidential Council? Let us hear what they have to say on the issues that have prompted our action.'

7 July

Terrorist acts in London, as the G8 meet at Gleneagles, near Glasgow. Putin is there. Casualties and blood are shown on our television screens, but it is better not to listen to the commentary: there is very little sympathy and a lot of malicious satisfaction. It is as if we are pleased that the British are suffering the same as we do. They are particularly careful to insinuate that Great Britain is now prepared to extradite Akhmed Zakaev to Russia, although the British Government has said nothing of the sort.

What is it with us? We are always ready to exult at the suffering of others, and never prepared to be kind. Throughout the world we are held to be good, fair people. I have no sense of that at present.

In Moscow, the Heroes continue their hunger strike, but not one television channel reports the fact.

Marina Khodorkovskaya, the mother of Mikhail Khodorkovsky, has delivered to our *Novaya gazeta* an open letter to the cosmonaut Georgii Grechko, who has signed a notorious open letter of 50 actors, writers, producers and cosmonauts – people well known throughout Russia. They write to the effect that they condemn Khodorkovsky and are glad he has been given a severe [nine-year] sentence. The letter is wholly in the spirit of the Stalin epoque, when the populace would write ecstatic exhortations to The Leader to continue destroying his opponents, real or imagined.

'I am hurt and ashamed for you,' Khodorkovsky's mother writes. 'I find it hard to believe that you, a well-informed and not unfeeling person, knew nothing about the vast amounts my son and his company invested in educational projects for young people and teachers in various regions of the Russian Federation. If you did know that, where is your conscience? If you did not know it and are kicking someone who has been condemned on instructions from above, then where are your honour and manliness? I am not asking you to defend Khodorkovsky and to criticise our so-called justice system – every person has a right to their own opinion – but before publicly vilifying someone, you need to be in full possession of the facts, and without that there can be no question of elementary justice.'

We published the letter, but no response was forthcoming from Cosmonaut Grechko, who, incidentally, also opposes his colleagues' hunger strike. That is his choice.

8 July

Hearings continue in the case of the 39 National Bolsheviks. They have been in various Moscow prisons for seven months now. New cages reaching to the court ceiling have been installed, two for the young men, one for the young women. All three are packed tight. Ivan Melnikov, a prominent Communist Deputy of the Duma, and also a member of the Parliamentary Assembly of the Council of Europe, cannot believe what he is seeing: the ridiculous appurtenances of a trial of political prisoners. Working in the Duma, you would never expect such a thing. There the state authorities appear to work by consensus, by deals and accords; here, however, there is no mistaking the pitiless attitude towards 'enemies of the Reich'. Deputy Melnikov also teaches at Moscow University; most of the National Bolsheviks are students, some of them from Moscow University, and he has come to act as a character witness for them, but the judge rules this out.

The defendants are accused of having caused damage amounting to 472,700 roubles [£9,450]. If you divide that between the 39 accused, it transpires that the Procurator-General is demanding that each should be imprisoned for up to eight years for causing just over 12,000 roubles [£242] of damage. Why such severity? Because they shouted, 'Putin – *you* get out!' and other similar suggestions in Putin's public reception area.

They made their view of the President known and here they are, caged like puppies on a dog farm. They look at us so seriously that it breaks your heart. One has grown a bushy, black beard in prison and shaved his head. In photographs before he was locked up he looks quite different. Another is still too young to grow a beard, but he has been eaten alive by bedbugs; he is covered in sores. A third keeps scratching – he is suffering from prison itch, erysipelas. They are a danger to society because of their viewpoint on life in this country.

The judge evidently feels that everything is going to plan, in accordance with the instructions he has received. He knows whose side he is on.

Almost all the liberals and democrats, current and ex-, turned up at the trial of Khodorkovsky and Lebedev. Nobody turns up to this trial. There are no pickets, no demonstrations, no protest meetings, no slogans chanted. This is very odd, because it is by now absolutely clear that this is no less a show trial than the Yukos trial. It is, of course, a show trial to intimidate a different age group, people in a different income bracket. Yukos was about putting the super-rich clearly in the dock, while here the accused are low-income young people, mostly students. The message is, however, exactly the same – see what will happen to you if you dare to defy us: prison, bedbugs, erysipelas, prison camp, doing time with thugs.

For many years we had great hopes that trial by jury would force real independence on the courts. The state authorities had to allow it because, if they hadn't, they could have said goodbye to any prospect of being admitted to the Council of Europe. Since 2003, juries have gradually begun to consider criminal cases, and if conventional courts acquitted fewer than 1 per cent of defendants, jury trials were at least finding 15 per cent not guilty.

Those acquitted, however, were more often than not gangland bosses and 'heroes' of the war in Chechnya, federal soldiers who had committed atrocities there, murders with aggravating circumstances in the main. After the acquittal of Yaponchik, a well-known criminal boss, respect for trial by jury gradually fell to zero. They were just another false dawn.

12 July

Bad news from Blagoveshchensk. The last militiaman held on charges has been released from jail. While human-rights campaigners were making waves in Moscow, in Bashkiria they were quietly releasing Officer Gilvanov, one of the most brutal characters in the whole episode, who had beaten up young men from the village of Duvanei. Now all the beasts are free again. The District Court in Ufa decided that Gilvanov was not a danger to society, although he personally attacked a boy whose leg was in a frame, knowing that he was completely helpless with a complex fracture of his leg. Even more disgusting is the fact that the Interior Ministry of Bashkiria has allowed Gilvanov to return to work as a militiaman.

The authorities are now planning to get their own back for all the fuss that was raised after the outrages.

The materials of the criminal case were lodged, supposedly in complete security, at the Department for the Investigation of Serious Crimes in the Republican Procurator-General's Office. Now, however, it transpires that the lawyers' applications to have major charges brought for illegal detention at the so-called filtration points have disappeared. The current charges are merely for 'exceeding their authority'.

At the same time, the victims of the 'cleansings' are subjected to unprecedented administrative harassment, dismissed from their jobs for refusing to withdraw their statements. This is happening to the victims most brutally mistreated and to their parents, who complained to Moscow-based journalists and human-rights campaigners about the extreme violence of the local militia and OMON. Nor have the lawyers who agreed to represent the victims' interests been having an easy time. When Stanislav Markelov from Moscow and Vasilii Syzganov from Vladimir arrived in Blagoveshchensk at the request of Moscow human-rights associations and met their clients, a drunken hooligan with a knife rushed into the house. It was only because the owner of the apartment, Vitalii Kozakov, took the blows on himself that the lawyers were saved. Kozakov's blood was all over the flat and staircase, but when the militia were called they turned and drove away, refusing even to arrest the knifeman. At this point the attacker spilled the beans; he admitted it was the militia themselves who had instructed him to provoke a drunken brawl. They wanted a pretext to arrest the lawyers defending the victims of their own earlier violence.

The victims of Blagoveshchensk have formed a Society of Victims of Filtration, Cleansing and Militia Violence, appealing to all citizens who have had similar experiences:

We have no rights, just like you. In those dark December days we knew what the civilian population of Chechnya has been through, because we experienced it all ourselves. Militia violence in our city marked the beginning of heavy-handed actions in many regions of Russia. They are starting off in small towns, but in no time at all filtration will also be seen in the great cities. We no longer have any confidence in the state authorities or the courts. We can rely only on ourselves and on mutual help from others in our situation. We ask you, no matter who you are, no matter where you live, no matter what your nationality is, to contact us. We must stop this now, before we are all destroyed.

The hunger strike of the Heroes, which began on 6 July, continues. On 12 July officialdom finally showed itself in the person of Ombudsman Vladimir Lukin, by which time some of those fasting had already had to be replaced. His first act was to ask the journalists to leave. Out we trooped. His visit coincided with the arrival of a delegation of widows of Heroes who had come to show their solidarity.

Larisa Golubeva's husband, Dmitry Golubev, was a Submarine Captain First Class and Hero of the Soviet Union. He was the commander of the second atomic submarine ever built in the USSR. 'When he was dying, he kept saying to me, "What are you crying for? You will have everything. You will be well looked after. You are the wife of a Hero." Of course, that was not what I was crying about, but he could never have imagined how things would turn out.'

Commanding only the second Russian atomic submarine to be built was never going to be good for your health, as the commanders of those vessels were being experimented on. Larisa spent her life in garrisons: Kamchatka, Severomorsk, Sebastopol . . . It was a life of waiting, and hoping that her husband would return alive from his ordeals.

What is Larisa, who shared everything with her heroic husband, entitled to now? Well, nothing. Under the new law, a Hero's widow is entitled to no supplement to her pension. A state that has sunk into unbelievable corruption, bringing equally unbelievable wealth to its top functionaries, is cutting back the budget. The benefit payable to the Hero's widow is so low that she is better off renouncing it and settling for the standard old-age pension, because you can't have both. That is what Larisa has done. She has her old-age pension, and also receives the President's monthly 500 roubles [£10] as a survivor of the Siege of Leningrad. In total, she gets 3,200 roubles a month [£64]. That is the legacy of a Hero.

The hunger strikers have no regrets about their past, but they do regret the present and fear for the future. Their protest will end, they are certain, with the opening of a genuine dialogue between the citizens of Russia and the state authorities.

Gennadii Kuchkin is a 51-year-old Hero of the Soviet Union from Kinel in Samara Province. As a Senior Lieutenant he found himself fighting in Afghanistan with the Tank Corps. He took part in 147 battles, and in 1983 was awarded the title of Hero of the Soviet Union. Only yesterday he flew in from Samara to join his comrades' strike.

'As I understand it, the aim is to force our state authorities to be honourable.' For all his 147 battles, he is still an innocent. He is a romantic, and he needs to be, in order still to feel a hero when his country spits on his heroism. Gennadii had to wait 10 years after the award of his title to get a flat, living in other people's accommodation with his family and his wounds. It took 12 years before he got a telephone.

'The lying begets cynicism,' he says. 'I sometimes give talks in schools. What are the children interested in nowadays? Money, mainly. They want to know if I am a rebel fighter. They generally ask me two questions: how many people have I killed, and how much money do I get for that? When they find out how much I get, they no longer regard me as a hero. They lose interest. It is a very fundamental question, of course, who makes up the elite in Russia nowadays. The elite are anybody with money or power, from the boss of a small district like ours up to our First Citizen.'

I personally asked Boris Nemtsov of the Union of Right Forces to go and visit the hunger strikers: 'Go out there and give them some moral support!' He was not very taken by the idea and said, rather oddly, 'They will expect me to bring them something. I can't go there empty-handed.' Nemtsov assumed they would be expecting him to bring good news of some kind from the regime, but they would have been happy if he had just brought himself, because he wanted to be there.

Our society isn't a society any more. It is a collection of windowless, isolated concrete cells. In one are the Heroes; in another are the politicians of Yabloko; in a third there is Zyuganov, the leader of the Communists; and so on. There are thousands who together might add up to be the Russian people, but the walls of our cells are impermeable. If somebody is suffering, he is upset that nobody else seems concerned. If, in other cells at the same time, anybody is in fact thinking about him, it leads to no action, and they only really remember he had a problem when their own situation becomes completely intolerable.

The authorities do everything they can to make the cells even more impermeable, sowing dissent, inciting some against others, dividing and ruling. And the people fall for it. That is the real problem. That is why revolution in Russia, when it comes, is always so extreme. The barrier between the cells collapses only when the negative emotions within them are ungovernable.

13 July

The Heroes have suddenly been invited to the session of the Soviet of the Federation where the legislation relating to them is to be discussed. They were as pleased as children who had been bought a long-anticipated bicycle. Burkov kept saying, 'The ice is breaking up. I told you, the authorities are beginning to communicate with us. Excellent!'

Their delegation sat for several hours in the Soviet of the Federation, gradually beginning to feel that something was wrong. The law was put to the vote. Burkov jumped up and shouted to the whole chamber, 'And what about us? Is nobody going to listen to what we have to say?'

They were reluctantly allowed to speak. Clearly nobody had been expecting actually to have to listen to them. They had been invited merely to get them to call off their hunger strike.

Burkov began speaking, but was rudely interrupted. The Chairman of the Soviet of the Federation, Sergey Mironov, irritably put the legislation to the vote and the senators passed it. Mironov invited the Heroes to his office and assured them that the Soviet understood their concerns, but that those upstairs had a different view. He repeatedly asked them to abandon the hunger strike, after which 'it will be possible to begin a dialogue with the Administration'. They left feeling they had been humiliated, and returned to their little cell.

14 July

The trial of the National Bolsheviks continues as the Procurator reads out the indictment. The state has decided to use the case to establish the fundamental concept of collective guilt, something not heard of since Stalin's show trials. In later years, Soviet and Russian procurators and judges have always been at pains to personalise guilt as far as possible, distancing themselves from totalitarian practices, but in 2005 they are with us again. Procurator Smirnov gabbled out the names of the National Bolsheviks, claiming that they had all 'participated in mass disturbances involving violent behaviour . . . a criminal plan had been devised to infiltrate . . . obstructed agents of the Federal Security Service . . . leaflets containing anti-presidential sentiments . . . demonstrating manifest disrespect for society . . . chanted unlawful slogans about the removal from office . . .'

During a break in proceedings, defence lawyer Dmitry Agranovsky commented, 'I have participated in a great many trials, and invariably the guilt has related to specific individuals. Here, however, they clearly intend to give a precedent-setting verdict based on collective guilt for dissidence. This is a political fiat from above.'

We are sometimes called a society of millions of slaves and a handful of masters, and told that is how it will be for centuries to come, a continuation of the serf-owning system. We often speak about ourselves in that way too, but I never do.

The courage of the Soviet dissidents brought forward the collapse of the Soviet system, and even today, when the mobs chant, 'We love Putin!', there are individuals who continue to think for themselves and use what opportunities exist to express their view of what is happening in Russia, even when their attempts seem futile.

A rare example of an intelligent, detailed, articulate protest has come from a campaigner of the Human Rights Association in Tyumen. Vladimir Grishkevich has sent the Constitutional Court a supplementary deposition to his complaint about the unconstitutional nature of the law on appointing regional leaders. He agrees to its being considered together with complaints from Committee 2008, Yabloko and a group of independent Deputies of the Duma. His statement is a very important fact in the history of our country, and will show that by no means everybody remained silent in 2005, even though no revolution has come about. Moreover, those who raised their voices were not only to be found in Moscow. After a long and detailed analysis of the illegality of Putin's move to nominate governors, he concludes:

On the basis of the above, I request the Constitutional Court of the Russian Federation to give an official assessment of the circumstances described above in which the federal law was adopted and signed. I refer to the law 'On the Introduction of Changes and Additions to the Federal Law "On the General Principles of Organisation of Legislative (Representative) and Executive Organs of State Power of Constituent Territories of the Russian Federation" and in the federal law "On the Basic Guarantees of Electoral Rights and the Right to Participate in Referenda of Citizens of the Russian Federation"'.

The court failed to respond. Society failed to protest.

15 July

Our people seem to wake up only when it hits them where it hurts, in the pocket. Revolutionary passions run high only when money is involved.

In Ryazan, the trade union of the Khimvolokno factory mounted a picket outside the Provincial Government offices. The trade unionists do not want their enterprise to be closed. They are certain that the synthetic-fibre plant is being deliberately bankrupted to enable someone to buy it on the cheap. A directive was first issued to cease production for three months, then to cease production completely on the grounds that it was making a loss.

This was when the workers woke up. There are very few jobs in the town and the factory's management informed 25 workers, who included members of the trade-union committee, that they were being put on the minimum wage of 800 roubles [£16] a month. The workers from Khimvolokno found no support, however, not even in Ryazan, because they had never supported anyone in the past. They just stood there picketing the government offices, with nobody paying any attention.

Ulianovsk is a more militant town. A sticker protest has begun there: 'No more bureaucracy, no more Putin!' It is being organised by a national youth movement called Defence, together with the local ecological and youth organisations. The activists covered the town in little labels reading, 'No more lies!', 'Say no now and fight back!' They call for non-violent civil protests against a bureaucracy that is leading their region and the country to ruin. They are not trying to defend their pay packet. Theirs is a prologue to revolution.

Why Ulianovsk? The province is one of the poorest, turned into a mere source of raw materials for big companies based elsewhere and, worse, into a rubbish tip for waste materials. This is thanks to the efforts of the Governor, effectively imposed on the voters by the Presidential Administration, that great hero of Chechnya, General Vladimir Shamanov. Under him the crime bosses of Ulianovsk came out of the underground. Shamanov openly depended on them and was surrounded by ex-soldiers who had retrained as gangsters, a minor sideways movement in Russia. Shamanov himself was thoroughly stupid and incapable of managing civilians.

Wrapping themselves in democratic slogans and brandishing the support of Putin, these supposed helpmates of the state openly robbed, and continue to rob, the province, even though Shamanov has now been transferred to the Presidential Administration.

The Defence movement in Ulianovsk is like a local fragment of the Ukrainian protest movement. Members of Defence believe that, within the framework of the law, they can hold non-violent demonstrations, protest meetings, pickets, and distribute leaflets and now stickers. Defence in Ulianovsk has rallied the local youth wing of Yabloko and of the Union of Right Forces, and the ecological organisation Green Yabloko.

In Moscow a demonstration took place outside the Interior Ministry to protest against brutality on the part of the law-enforcement agencies. About 20 people turned out. Their banners read, 'No more secret orders! Press charges against those guilty of violence in Blagoveshchensk and other towns and villages.' The demonstrators demanded the resignation of Rashid Nurgaliev, Minister of the Interior of Russia, the bringing of a criminal prosecution against Rafail Divaev, Minister of the Interior of Bashkiria, and against all the officers and officials of the law-enforcement agencies guilty of acts of violence.

The protest was against attempts by the militia to intimidate the Russian people, but the Russian people didn't show up. It lasted two hours. Nobody came out from the Interior Ministry to speak to the protesters, because they only worry about mass demonstrations. If the numbers are not there, they laugh at us and go about their business.

16 July

The eleventh day of the hunger strike. The participants are very weak. What lies ahead? The regime is silent. Do they need some of these people to die? Most of the hunger strikers are old, disabled or ill. Still not a single politician has come to speak to them.

18 July

The hunger-striking Heroes face a stalemate. The authorities contemptuously ignore all their suggestions.

'What's the point?' I ask Svetlana Gannushkina in bewilderment. We are talking shortly before a meeting, attended by Putin, of the improbably named Presidential Commission for the Development of Civil Society and Human Rights, of which Svetlana is a member. 'Why can't they just listen? Why do they always insist on doing everything in the worst possible manner? Why do they force one stalemate after another?'

'Why? Because they want to create a country it is impossible to live in,' Svetlana replies sadly. She is the only member of the human-rights commission brave enough to agree to hand Putin the Heroes' appeal. Perhaps the *barin* is a good man after all.

This afternoon a jury at the Moscow City Court acquits Vyacheslav Ivankov, also known as Yaponchik, of shooting dead two Turkish citizens in a Moscow restaurant in 1992. All the television stations lead with this, with live link-ups to the court. They also report that Mr Ivankov is intending to write a book. The hunger strike doesn't get a mention, and the trial of the National Bolsheviks gets just a couple of words here and there. We hear nothing of what they might be planning to do if they were to get out of prison.

How can we go on living such a lie? We pretend that justice has been done in the case of Yaponchik, we rejoice that justice was not done in the case of Khodorkovsky. We applaud both these just outcomes. This is not your enigmatic Russian soul; this is the long-standing tradition of living a lie about which Solzhenitsyn wrote long ago, mixed with a lazy refusal to take your backside off your chair in a warm kitchen until they take the warm kitchen away from you. At that point you might join a revolution, but not before.

19 July

The fourteenth day of the hunger strike. Surkov, Putin's chief ideologist, calls them blackmailers: 'We will not allow anyone to twist our arms.'

Actually, what has Surkov to do with anything? Why should it depend on this political manipulator, who has to his credit only the virtual achievements of United Russia and the bloody Chechenisation of Chechnya – that same Surkov who dares to think this makes him a political heavyweight – why should it depend on him whether 204 Heroes of the country get a hearing or not?

*

In the course of the hunger strike, they have written many letters, sending them by fax, email and even by hand to the offices of important persons. They have given many interviews mentioning these letters, although few were ever broadcast.

What this episode has demonstrated is that many of our most prominent figures, leaders and deputy leaders of parties inside the Duma and out, of movements and alliances, and even the leader of the Soviet of the Federation, Sergey Mironov himself, who, according to the Constitution, is the third most powerful man in the country, seem to sympathise with the hunger strikers, their demands, their feelings, their desire to serve the country. They do so, however, only in private. Publicly, for the television cameras and information agencies, for the President, they stand united in opposition to it. They voted in favour of the humiliating amendments that sparked this whole confrontation, one that shows no signs of concluding in dialogue.

Why are the independently minded of our political establishment so two-faced? That is the question. Is it not a matter of straightforward blackmail by the Administration: if you do not say what we require you to, we will take away your perks?

Nobody wants to go without their perks nowadays. Our political 'elite' is profoundly infected with cowardice and scared stiff of losing its power. Not of losing the respect of the people, just its seat. They have no more to them than that.

*

A terrorist act in the Chechen village of Znamenskoye. A vehicle was seen at the central crossroads, in the front passenger seat of which was a dead body. The militia were called, but, when they approached the vehicle, it was blown up, killing 14 of them. A child was also killed, and many, including young boys, were injured.

It turned out that in the early evening of 13 July Alexey Semenenko, 23, was abducted from the hill village of Novoshchedrinskaya. The kidnapping took place in front of his younger sisters. In recent months, Alexey and his young wife had been saving up to get out of Chechnya. His relatives had lived in Novoshchedrinskaya for a hundred years and it was a large, united, hard-working family, but what could they do? The more firmly Kadyrov becomes ensconced, the greater the lawlessness and the more remote the hope that life will come right. That was what Alexey had decided.

He decided to take seasonal employment reaping the harvest, which can bring in good money in a short time. Alexey returned home from the fields on 13 July to find four armed men in combat fatigues waiting for him. They were Chechens and had arrived in two silver UAZ off-road vehicles. Nearly everyone in Novoshchedrinskaya is certain these were Kadyrov's troops. Anyone living in Chechnya can distinguish Kadyrov's from Yamadaev's troops, the OMON from Baisarov's or Kokiev's troops (all of them paramilitaries of the 'Chechen Federal Security Units', as they are called) by the vehicles they drive and the weapons they favour. The paramilitaries talked to Alexey, then bundled him into one of the vehicles and drove off. The neighbours memorised the number plates, but they turned out to be false.

The following morning, the family notified the authorities of the abduction, and Chechen local militiamen who had known Alexey from childhood spent two days looking for him in all the security subdivisions. They didn't find him. At this point the local Procurator's Office scented danger and reverted to its usual cataleptic state.

On 19 July, the first person to approach the vehicle was a nearby militiaman. He opened the door and saw a corpse in the passenger seat, which, judging by the smell and state of decomposition, had been dead for a considerable time. He also noticed that the body had bullet wounds to the face.

He went to call reinforcements, and thereby saved his own life. When a crowd of his colleagues arrived to inspect the vehicle, it was blown up. The button was pressed by someone who could see it and intended to kill as many militiamen as possible. After the explosion, Sergey Abramov, the Moscow-appointed Chechen Prime Minister, made some dark remarks about Basaev and Umarov, but did not himself go near the scene. A state of mourning was declared.

The Semenenko family, meanwhile, had been continuing to scour Chechnya for Alexey. Two days later they were visited at home and asked to go to Mozdok in neighbouring North Ossetia to identify a body. All murder victims are taken to the forensic medical centre there, as Chechnya does not have one of its own.

Tatyana Semenenko, Alexey's mother, still not suspecting any link with the bomb in Znamenskoye, found the victims of the explosion laid out in the mortuary refrigerators, except for one bag of remains that had been dumped on the floor in a puddle of water.

In this bag, which was being treated as if it contained the body of a terrorist, she found the remains of her son. She was able to identify him only from a tattooed letter L on his arm. There was no face to speak of. The family subsequently buried this arm and the head. The militiaman who had first approached the vehicle, and seen Alexey's body while it was still in one piece, said it had been dressed in combat fatigues. His kidnappers had evidently dressed him this way before shoving him in the mined vehicle.

That is the end of the story. The Semenenkos have nowhere to turn. There was no public reaction. Nobody – not Kadyrov, Alkhanov or Kozak – bothered to offer their condolences to the family. Nobody offered to compensate them for the death of their son. Nobody tried to pay them just to keep quiet. A criminal case in respect of the abduction of Alexey Semenenko was opened and closed, but they didn't even bother to open a criminal case in respect of his murder. Because he killed militiamen, Semenenko is officially classified as a terrorist. Admittedly, he was dead at the time of committing this crime.

There are really only two possibilities as to what happened. If those who kidnapped Alexey were indeed Kadyrov's troops, as everybody in the village believes, then the Kadyrov gunmen may themselves have staged this terrorist act, knowing that for as long as there is terrorism, paramilitaries are in work. If peace were to return, they would all be thrown straight in prison.

The second possibility is that the paramilitaries sold Alexey's body to the fighters, Basaev's or others. This is also plausible, because it has long been known that the dividing line between Kadyrov's troops and Basaev's is increasingly permeable, despite Kadyrov Junior's endless idiotic talk of how he dreams of shooting Basaev. Those preferred by Putin's regime are the most sly, cynical and criminal elements in the land.

Who now in Chechnya is protesting about the saga of Alexey Semenenko? Nobody. His family are terrified of Kadyrov's paramilitaries because his two younger sisters saw the faces of the abductors. It is more prudent to forget their son than to risk making waves. These are the effects of Putin's war, on the way people think in Chechnya, and it is a way of thinking that is rapidly spreading to the rest of Russia. You find a similar blind panic gripping the families of those abducted throughout the North Caucasus, in all those towns and villages where Chechnya-style mass 'cleansings' have been taking place.

The more violent the rampaging of the security agencies, the higher Putin's approval rating, for the simple reason that very few people want to risk life and limb by opposing him.

Such is daily life in Russia today. Crimes, a lack of honest investigation, and even a lack of any attempt at it. The result is the endless replication of tragedies and terrorism.

For the first time in recent years, my newspaper refused to print the story about Alexey Semenenko. *Novaya gazeta* wants to stay out of trouble, so it is best not to give Ramzan Kadyrov too much grief, since he is in favour with the President.

20 July

Today Putin received human-rights campaigners and members of his Presidential Commission on Human Rights in the Kremlin. Svetlana Gannushkina was not allowed to speak, but handed Putin the letter from the hunger-striking Heroes. The matter was also raised directly by Alexander Auzan, another activist present. Putin was not pleased. He stated, 'Everything has settled down there now. I have had a report.' Auzan was insistent, however, and repeated what he thought the President ought to be told on the subject. Ella Pamfilova, the chairwoman, became impatient and demanded that no further time should be spent on the topic. The argument came to an end and Putin continued to regard the Heroes as part of the enemy opposition.

The discussion then moved on to ecological matters. The human-rights campaigners missed their one opportunity to speak openly to him. Many of them are too afraid they might not be invited back.

According to Svyatoslav Zabelin, Co-Chairman of the Socio-Ecological Alliance,

Putin raised three issues: firstly, how best to inform citizens about reforms being implemented; secondly, how the Social Chamber could be used as a channel to make public opinion more influential; thirdly, how the voluntary sector in Russia could be developed with less reliance on Western resources.

On the second question, about the Social Chamber, the campaigners maintained a collective silence. On the third, Putin unexpectedly announced that he was prepared personally to oblige the Government to find ways of empowering voluntary associations by channelling state and private-sector resources. He seemed to me to be genuinely concerned that this support should not be seen as an attempt to bribe civil society and public associations. He was being very practical.

On the subject of ecology, I told Putin: 'We need public ecological accountability, and public ecological audits. We have neither of these things at present. As a result, there are quite extraordinary things going on in the state sector. In 2002 the public sector had four ecological inspectors per district, but in 2005 there are four districts per inspector. How can we hope to avoid violation of ecological guidelines without public participation?

'We also find extraordinary liberties being taken with ecological audit. Here the problem is that businesses are required by law to take reasonable steps to ensure that industrial projects are discussed with the public, so that the interests of society and the overall interests of the state are properly considered. This is simply not happening. Most worryingly, the worst offenders are those companies in which the state has the largest financial stake.

'One well-known company involved with the pipeline from East Siberia to the Pacific is said to be behaving in a thoroughly devious manner. In order to comply with the requirement for a public ecological audit, it has set up a "public" association of its own and registered it in Moscow. This body has taken decisions on what should be done for people living on the coast, what should be done for people in Irkutsk, what should be done for the Buryats, and where it would be in their best interests for the pipeline to pass. When a project of this kind is being built in Russia, there are international repercussions. Their behaviour is now common knowledge, there is a lot of fuss, and that can only be to our disadvantage. These companies, in which the state has a substantial presence, need to be told politely that this kind of conduct is just not acceptable.

'We have a system for assessing ecological costs. Eighty-five per cent of the private companies we approached were prepared to give us, the public, access to their own ecological accounts: not a single state enterprise would do so.'

Putin replied, 'I would like you to understand the logic of the situation in which state organisations find themselves in respect of ecological audit. You have just mentioned one of our most vital projects, comparable in importance with the Baikal–Amur Highway, which took decades to build. I hope this will not be such a megaproject, but its value to the state might eventually be much greater than the BAH itself, which is already struggling to cope with the demands on it. This pipeline gives us an outlet for our energy resources to the markets of the rapidly developing countries of the Asia-Pacific region, to the Chinese market where we are both buyer and seller, to South Asia, Japan, and so forth.

'Let me draw your attention to the fact that our country lost five major seaports in the West after the collapse of the Soviet Union. In effect, we became dependent on the countries through which our energy resources have to pass, and they abuse their geopolitical situation. We come up against this all the time. It is extremely important for Russia to have a direct outlet to other markets. When we were talking about a pipeline from East Siberia directly to Datsin, in China, along the southern end of Lake Baikal, we decided to diverge from that route after taking account of the opinions of ecological associations, ecologists and inspectors. The cost went up by hundreds of millions of dollars. It was decided to skirt the northern shore of Lake Baikal and go further to the east.

'These ecological audits should not be allowed to hold back the development of the country and the economy. I do not for a moment question what you have just said. No doubt we need to look very closely at the situation, but one of the ways of attacking us is invariably by raising ecological issues. When we started building a port adjacent to Finland, our partners in the neighbouring countries (and I have this from reliable sources) put money into ecological associations purely in order to torpedo the project, because it would create competition for them in the Baltic. Our partners, including those from Finland, came and inspected ten times, but in the end were unable to find anything to object to. Now the "ecological problems" have moved to the Danish Straits, and there is some objection to the vessels we are using. These are not even Russian vessels, they are leased from international companies. In the Turkish Straits, the Bosphorus, there are "ecological problems" too.

'Why do I mention this? I mention it because, of course, we need more contact and trust if we are to interact properly with national ecological associations working in the interests of our country, and not as agents whom our competitors can use to obstruct the development of our economy. This is precisely why I said that when this kind of ecological work is financed from abroad, it raises suspicions and ends up compromising all sorts of voluntary associations. That is what I am talking about. We need associations that help to resolve our own problems, so that major decisions can be taken optimally. For that, of course, we need them to have more contact with state organisations too.'

Zabelin: 'Certainly, the most important thing is establishing contact, and our national interests. As far as that great pipeline is concerned, the main thing is that it should be built. No reputable ecological association is saying it is not needed. We are talking about specific issues of routing and where the terminal should be located. The current choice, purely from the viewpoint of minimising ecological damage, is the very worst option. There are plenty of alternatives, and I am prepared simply to hand over to you the analysis of those scientists in the Far East who say there are other options that are more beneficial economically, socially and ecologically. We are partners in this, just as in respect of public ecological monitoring. As regards ecological audits, people just need to obey the law. We have an excellent law on ecological auditing, dating from 1995. It needs to be observed.'

Putin: 'I would like to return to this in the future. I think it would be right to establish a more sensitive mechanism for interacting with our national ecological associations, because we cannot afford to make mistakes, and at the same time we cannot allow this issue to be used, as I have said, as a lever by our competitors. Just look at what is happening in the Caspian: Lukoil had only to erect an oil rig there to be told the ecology meant they couldn't. None of the other companies there have technologies as clean as ours. It is more expensive, but we have taken that on board. The same thing is going on now in the Baltic Sea.'

21 July

In Astrakhan, as throughout the country, the authorities are waging a war on the people for money and property. There the main weapon is arson. It is a war in which people die, looters sift the ruins, and ordinary people become homeless refugees.

The Ostroumovs are the last people not to have been burned out of their part of Maksakova Street, where an opulent house is being built in the prestigious old town. Of course, building sites are to be found now in all our cities; there are wealthy people around. The rules for how things should be regulated in such cases are that the local authorities allocate land to the developers and, if anybody is living on it, they are rehoused. After that the site is fenced off and building commences.

That is not quite how things are done in Astrakhan. A company called Astsyrprom obtained the rights to a development site on Maksakova Street. Unfortunately, it was covered with buildings where people were living in their recently privatised flats. Astsyrprom brought in a sub-contractor, a certain Nurstroy, both to build the new house and to move the current owners out. At first Nurstroy negotiated terms with some and bought their houses, but then the approach suddenly changed. Nurstroy began offering people in exchange flats that were manifestly unacceptable. The Ostroumovs were offered a one-room flat for the five of them.

When the residents began to dig their heels in and make demands, the response was an ultimatum, followed by military-style action. The Director of Nurstroy, Mr Timofeyev, told Alexander Merzhuev straight to his face, 'I'll burn you out.' Shortly afterwards his house was indeed consumed by fire. The conclusion of the Fire Department's inspection team was arson using an accelerant but the evidence was deemed insufficient for a prosecution. The problem of the encumbrance of the left-hand side of Nurstroy's building plot had been resolved. The Ostroumovs occupy the right-hand part of the site.

The Kosa district, close to the Astrakhan Kremlin, is lined with historic houses from which you can see the Volga, that same Volga in which, in the seventeenth century, the local brigand Stenka Razin drowned his ill-starred bride. No. 53 Maxim Gorky Street is a fine merchant's villa, which even today, after the fire in March, is still magnificent.

Last winter investors, as they called themselves, began visiting the people here. They said, 'We will move you to a new house.' People said, 'Thanks, only we want to stay in this area. We are used to living here.'

On 20 March, 78-year-old Lyudmila Rozina was visited by 'investors' for the last time. 'The old lady condemned us,' Alexey Glazunov, a pensioner who used to live in the no longer existent Flat 7, tells me. 'She said she would move, but only into this new upmarket apartment block they are building next door.'

That night the villa was set alight from all four sides. In two or three minutes the place was roaring like a furnace. Some old ladies jumped from the windows, breaking limbs, but others didn't manage even that. Lyudmila was burned in her bed, because the walls of her flat had been doused with accelerant, as the subsequent investigation revealed.

Lyudmila's son, 55-year-old Alexander Rozin, survived and was taken to hospital with severe burns. Three days later an unidentified criminal arrived at the hospital, supposedly bearing humanitarian aid from the mayor's office. The food brought was poisoned, as the later inquiry showed, and on 12 April Rozin died. Anna Kurianova, 86, who had been carried alive from the burning building, succumbed to the stress and died shortly afterwards.

The appalling truth in Astrakhan is that, in recent months, six people have died in fires, and 17 houses have been destroyed in confirmed arson attacks. There have been a total of 43 fires, but it is not easy to obtain the rigorous investigation that might lead to a criminal prosecution. Most cases relating to them are immediately closed, or there is a complete, mysterious lack of evidence, which means they are never opened. Meanwhile, the construction of prestigious houses, casinos, restaurants and commercial offices on sites cleared by fires continues apace.

Viktor Shmedkov is the head of the Kirov District Interior Ministry Office, and it is on his territory that most of the instances of what is known in Astrakhan as 'commercial arson' occur.

'I would not say that the problem is too serious,' he opines, looking straight into the eyes of old ladies who had been left in the street in their nightdresses. 'The Kirov District Office is pursuing five cases relating to five instances of arson,' he continues. 'I would not say that the militia are not doing all they can. The causes are being investigated, and all possibilities considered . . .' The eyes of the militiaman suddenly widen and he says, lowering his voice, 'Even the most audacious . . .'

The 'audacious' hypothesis is that the entourage of Mayor Bozhenov are party to the arson. They have a commercial interest in clearing the city, sharing out real estate between the mayor's deputies and the commercial organisations which support them, and thus repaying 'election debts'. Somebody, after all, paid for the mayor's election campaign. It was an investment. Now it is time for them to realise their profit.

The militia bosses admit there is nothing they can do about the wealthy brigands of Astrakhan, who enjoy an incestuous relationship with the city administration. They are powerless in the face of the total criminalisation of the top level of government. The laws do not operate. There was a time when the militia used to catch brigands, and knew it was doing its job. Now the person appointed to guarantee the effective functioning of the law is himself a brigand. The arson has been going on for half a year, and yet no inquiry has been set up to look into those far from random fires. Nobody wants to piece together the overall picture of serial commercial arson.

'What happened after our fire?' Alexey Glazunov asks. He is a member of the Society of Astrakhan Fire Victims. 'The chronology is this: the fire at fifty-three Maxim Gorky Street began at half-past three in the morning,' Glazunov points out. 'At around nine a.m. workmen arrived with sledgehammers and started knocking everything down, wrecking what the fire had not destroyed, right in front of the militia. During the day, those victims who were not hospitalised went to see the mighty Madame Svetlana Kudryavtseva, accommodation tsaritsa of Astrakhan, the mayor's deputy for building and architecture, and she made it clear that she was glad the house was being demolished. She said the city needs to get rid of these ancient buildings, and that the victims would be rehoused in a hotel.'

What is the moral of this story? The elite are interested only in getting their hands on money and property, which they can do only if they first get their hands on political power. They see an opportunity, and the citizen ceases even to be noticed. You can burn citizens if they get in the way. You can dump them in a slum 'hotel' if they fail to die, and they can die there. There is a moral vacuum at the heart of the present political system in Russia, and in Astrakhan it has reached crisis point.

27 July

Another hearing for the National Bolsheviks, and cross-questioning of the witnesses begins. The judge invites Natalia Kuznetsova to say how the National Bolsheviks behaved on 14 December. She works at the Kitai-Gorod Internal Affairs Office, close to the Presidential Administration's building, from where she observed what was going on. Natalia proves to be a guileless woman and admits that actually she had only seen the 'disorder' on television. She does, however, have first-hand evidence relating to the metal detector, which, according to the charge against them, they wrecked and which is the main item in the claim for damages from the President's residential services office. Well, anyway, this metal detector, Natalia testifies, had been mended by the morning of 15 December, and has been working fine ever since. Has Judge Shikhanov taken that in? Has the main charge just self-destructed? Can the accused all be released? No. You cannot deprive Russian young people who have dared to question the fairness of the authorities of their right to go to prison, and they must be fully re-assured on that score. Especially if they are starting to get ideas about politics.

28 July

Everybody has justified complaints about the militia, but they did actually manage, after searching for more than a year, to catch Sergey Melnikov, extortionist and right-hand man of the head of the Togliatti mafia. The jubilant militiamen went to seek powers to detain him from the Office of the Procurator-General of Moscow, and Vladimir Yudin, Deputy Procurator of Moscow, told them to get lost. He refused to issue a warrant because, in his view, the extortionist Melnikov was not a danger to society. The grounds written by Yudin on the rejected application are, 'There is no incontrovertible proof of guilt.'

The gangster was duly set free. This is the same Yudin who concocted the charges against the National Bolsheviks and insisted that they should be kept in prison for month after month, and fettered in court, because of the immense danger they pose to society. That is the reality of selective justice. Criminals are freed while political prisoners get put in chains, thrown in prison, kept in cages. The authorities rely on criminal elements to prop up the system of state power.

That this really is their doctrine recently received further confirmation when the Presidential Administration created a clone to oppose the National Bolsheviks. It is called Nashi (Our People), and was cobbled together in February at a meeting between Vasilii Yakemenko, leader of that earlier clone, Marching Together, and Vladislav Surkov. Yakemenko is the 'federal commissar' of Nashi, which is the Presidential Administration's very own street movement to insure against revolution. The stormtroopers of the Nashi youth movement are football hooligans armed with knuckle-dusters and chains. So far they have confined themselves to assaulting the National Bolsheviks, and the authorities prevent the investigative agencies from bringing criminal charges against them. They have two units, one consisting of thugs who support the Central Sports Club of the Army football team, and the other of thugs who support the Spartak team. They all have an impeccable record in street fighting. Under the leadership of Vasya the Hitman and Roma the Stickler, thugs who support Spartak, Nashi has also set up a private security agency called White Shield. Vasya the Hitman is one of our most violent football hooligans, and it is his followers who organise attacks on the National Bolsheviks. They have twice occupied the National Bolsheviks' bunker, from where Vasya once gave a press conference. Vasya (known on his passport as Vasilii Stepanov) and Roma had a number of criminal cases pending against them, which were first put on hold, and then kicked into the long grass.

Roma was even seen at the famous shish-kebab meeting between Putin and the 'Nashists', when our President was lecturing them about how young people are already Russia's civil society. When this obnoxious event, dreamed up by Surkov, was shown on television, one National Bolshevik who had been beaten up by 'unidentified persons' recognised his assailant as Roma the Stickler, known in secular life as Roman Verbitsky.

Why did Khodorkovsky come to grief? He was no different from the rest of those who have amassed fabulous fortunes in record time, no different from others who had the opportunity and the inclination. When he was a billionaire, however, he said, 'Stop! Yukos will become the most transparent and non-criminal company in Russia, using Western business methods.' He began creating a new Yukos, but all around him people remained at large who had absolutely no desire for transparency, people whose very nature is to work in the shadows, away from the light. They set about devouring Yukos, because light is unwelcome in the midst of darkness.

Discriminating against bad political prisoners in favour of good crim-inals has deep historical roots in Russian justice and Russian politics. It is not easy to eradicate, but it would be a disgrace to become reconciled to it. The only question is: who is going to protest? There are no meet-ings outside the Nikulin Court. There are plenty of militia, vast numbers of police dogs, but almost nobody to show solidarity with these illegally detained political prisoners: only a small handful of National Bolsheviks, and occasionally Limonov. It is a bacchanalia of indifference.

Khodorkovsky had the best lawyers in the country, and they managed to attract supporters for the persecuted oligarch, but the poor have almost nobody. The National Bolsheviks are from lower-income groups, the children of research workers, engineers, the impoverished Russian intel-ligentsia in general. They are students and school students. Occasionally a lone human-rights campaigner turns up, but that is the extent of their support.

3 August

At 4.00 a.m. today in Syktyvkar, capital of the northern Republic of Komi, the editorial offices of a democratic opposition newspaper, *Courier Plus*, were burned down. The building also accommodated two opposi-tional television programmes, *Tele-Courier* and *The Golden Mean*, produced by Nikolai Moiseyev, a local Yabloko party member and Deputy of the City Council.

Moiseyev was highly critical of the Mayor of Syktyvkar, Sergey Katunin, and on 14 July he and a group of other Deputies tried to strip the mayor of his powers, but he fought them off. In the Procurator's Office they have no doubt that it was arson; Moiseyev recently had the door of his flat and his car set on fire. The previous Syktyvkar opposition news-paper, *Stefanov Boulevard*, ceased to exist in August 2002 when it too was burned out.

4 August

Jihad in Russia. Again. The beginning of September will see the sixth anniversary of the 'counter-terrorist operation' in Chechnya. Peaceful life, according to the Kremlin's propaganda, has long since returned to the towns and villages, and almost all the fighters they wanted to get have been put out of action by the pro-federal forces. But what is this? Jihad? Against whom? Nor is this the first Jihad to be declared in Chechnya in the 11 years since the First Chechen War began. They have been declared, they have been called off.

This time it is Jihad against Wahhabis and terrorists, and the official line is that it was declared by the pro-Moscow boss of the Republic's Muslims, Mufti Sultan Mirzaev. He summoned the mullahs of all the districts for a pep talk at which, in the presence of the commanders of all the Chechen security units (Yamadaev, Kadyrov, Alkhanov, Ruslan, et al.) he read out the directive. It means that now the troops of Yamadaev, Kadyrov, Kokiev and the rest, and Chechen militiamen, can with a clear conscience murder other Chechens and, needless to say, non-Chechens, if they suspect them of terrorism or Wahhabism. There will be no need for court proceedings or investigations. They can also be sure that, as Muslims, they are doing the right thing. Mirzaev went so far as to declare that he was prepared to take up arms himself.

Given that all these Chechen paramilitaries and their commanders are technically federal soldiers subject to the law of Russia, which does not recognise Jihad, this would seem to mark a further stage in 'Chechenising' the war.

So why has Jihad been declared today? After the events at the hill village of Borozdinovskaya on the border of Chechnya and Dagestan (a brutal 'cleansing' on 4 June, during which Yamadaev's troops abducted 11 people and carried out mass robbery, murder and arson), hundreds of the inhabitants fled to Dagestan. There was, however, great consternation among all these state cut-throats. In Chechnya the Russian-imposed system of extra-judicial rough justice and executions looked like being under threat.

For a long time the arrangement has been, 'We kill those you tell us to, and in return you look after us.' 'We' refers to the foot soldiers. 'You' refers primarily to the Yamadaevs and to Ramzan Kadyrov. These are the field commanders of Chechenisation, the protagonists of a civil war pitting Chechen against Chechen, for which success they have been given federal epaulettes, weapons and immunity from prosecution.

After the Borozdinovskaya incident, the rank-and-file soldiers of Chechenisation demanded an additional indulgence for working as hired killers. Ramzan Kadyrov fixed it with the Mufti, who agreed to declare Jihad. For some of the Russian state's Chechen hitmen, this is very important. They feel much better with the backing of a Jihad. Much better means much less inhibited.

Confirmation of this was not long in coming. The very evening Jihad was declared, the hitmen celebrated by committing a murder in the hill village of Shelkovskaya, in the Yamadaevs' territory. It was a murder of exceptional brazenness and brutality.

At about 10 p.m. several silver Niva off-roaders drove up to the house of Vakhambi Satikhanov, a teacher of Arabic and the fundamentals of Islam at the local school and the 40-year-old father of a large family. Armed Chechens wearing camouflage fatigues took him some 100 metres from his house and drew their Nivas up in a circle to form a small arena. His neighbours and fellow villagers tried to intervene, but the paramilitaries threatened to shoot them. Throughout the night people saw cars driving off and others appearing out of the darkness; they heard cries and shooting, but only at dawn did the butchers lift their blockade and drive away. Where the circle had been they found the body of Vakhambi with dozens of knife wounds, his fingers broken, his nails ripped off.

Vakhambi's neighbours are certain that he was murdered by men from the Vostok battalion of the Central Intelligence Directorate of GHQ. Its commander, Sulim Yamadaev, was awarded the title of Hero of Russia by Putin after the atrocities in Borozdinovskaya, thereby giving the highest possible sanction to what Yamadaev's paramilitaries had done there.

The declaration of Jihad in Chechnya is further proof that the Republic is allowed to live by customary law, to take life in defiance of Russian law. How does this differ from the lawless executions of Maskhadov's time?

The silence and failure to take corrective action are also the surest sign that the Jihad has the tacit blessing of Putin himself. It is simply one more step along the dead-end road of Chechenisation that Putin is travelling. Now the entire muftiate of Chechnya is implicated, just as at one time the Russian Orthodox Church was complicit in sanctifying the crimes of the Stalin and Khrushchev eras.

Life is savage now, even more savage than in the Soviet period, but the Russian people appear not to mind. Nobody has called upon the Procurator-General to declare the Jihad null and void.

9 August

The mysterious deaths of people very close to the state authorities continue. In Sochi, Pyotr Semenenko has fallen from a window on the fifteenth floor of the White Nights Hotel. For the past 18 years he had been the CEO of Russia's largest machine-tools factory, the Kirov, which produces everything from sanitaryware to the turbines for nuclear submarines.

Semenenko was a major industrial player, and from St Petersburg to boot. Most people suppose the main reason he was murdered is because of disagreements over the sharing out of major industrial assets under the Putin system of state capitalism. That he was helped to fall from the fifteenth floor nobody has any doubt.

In the Matrosskaya Tishina prison, meanwhile, Mikhail Khodorkovsky has been moved from investigative detention cell No. 4, which holds four prisoners, to investigative detention cell No. 1, which holds 11. He is no longer allowed to receive newspapers or watch television. The reason is undoubtedly his article 'Left Turn', written in prison and published in the newspaper *Vedomosti*. These are its main ideas:

> In spite of all the state's deviousness, those on the left will win in the end. What is more, they will win democratically, in complete accord with the expressed will of a majority of the electorate. There will be a turn to the left, and those who continue to pursue the policies of today's authorities will lose their legitimacy . . .
>
> We should not overlook the fact that our compatriots have become much cannier than they were ten years ago. People who have been fooled on more than one occasion will not fall for another bluff, no matter how ingenious or eloquently presented. Pulling off the Successor-2008 project is not going to be that easy. The resources of the post-Soviet authoritarian project in Russia have been exhausted.

Not completely, I fear.

Novaya gazeta invited our readers to submit questions to Khodorkovsky by email and published replies that he sent from prison.

> Sergey Panteleyev, a student from Moscow: The bureaucrats have decided to own the state, not to be its hired servants. Am I right in believing that this was the real reason for the seizure of Yukos?
>
> Khodorkovsky: Dear Sergey, they do not want to own the state, but to own tangible assets, and in particular the most successful company in the country, Yukos. More precisely, they want to get their hands on its income. You are right that the seizure and plundering of Yukos is being carried out behind a smokescreen of talk

about the interests of the state. Of course that is not the reality. Destroying Yukos will cause colossal damage to the interests of Russia. These bureaucrats are simply trying to deceive society by presenting their personal interests as those of the state.

A question from Goblin (presumably a pseudonym): Are you not hurt that your friends fled abroad, instead of ignoring all the risks and coming back to join you and Platon Lebedev?

Khodorkovsky: Dear Goblin, being thrown into prison is not something I would wish on my worst enemy, let alone my friends. Accordingly, I am very happy for all my friends who have managed to avoid arrest. What I most regret is that some of my comrades and colleagues have been arrested in connection with the Yukos affair, notably Svetlana Bakhmina, who is the mother of two small children.

A question from Vera, Tomsk: You are being forced to start life all over again. Will you find the strength in yourself, or is your life's main work already in the past?

Khodorkovsky: Dear Vera, in prison I have understood one simple but difficult truth: the main thing is not to have, but to be. What matters is the human being, not the circumstances in which he finds himself. For me business is a thing of the past, but I am not starting my new life from scratch, because I carry forward an enormous amount of experience. I even thank fate for the unique opportunity of living two lives, despite having paid so heavily for the privilege.

On the same day, 9 August, Khodorkovsky's and Lebedev's lawyers received an order setting a deadline for completing their study of the records of the court hearings. They had been allowed to see them at the Meshchansky District Court from 27 July, but all kinds of difficulties now began to arise. On 28 July, lawyer Krasnov was not given the records to read 'for technical reasons'. Lawyer Liptser was also turned down the same day, because part of the record was 'currently being studied by the state prosecutor'.

Between 29 July and 8 August the lawyers were able to read only the records for 2004, because those for 2005 were said to be with the state prosecutor. On 5 August the lawyers received through the post a 'second' notice (although there had been no first) instructing them to come to the court on 5 August (i.e., that same day), to receive 'copies of the records of the court hearing'. When they read these, they discovered that they differed from the original and from the audio recording of the court hearings. Moreover, the supposed copies had not been officially certified, nor was there any numbering of the volumes, internal pagination or a list of contents. The lawyers were indignant and lodged complaints and an official refusal to accept 'copies' that did not correspond to the originals. In reply the court dumped the unsatisfactory 'copies' on them through their chambers.

On 9 August permission to view the original records was refused point-blank. In order to prevent the lawyers from being able to complain to Strasbourg, Acting Chairman of the Court, Kurdyukov, refused to confirm in writing that they would not be given access to the official records of the court hearings and must work solely from the 'copies'. They were given until 25 August to comment on them.

Why is Svetlana Bakhmina, whom Khodorkovsky mentioned in one of his replies, being held in prison?

The employees of Yukos saw their colleague's arrest as a warning. It was obvious to practically everybody in the company that, as part of the campaign against Yukos, the Procurator-General was targeting rank-and-file employees. In fact, if Khodorkovsky was being accused of things that could apply to the vast majority of leading Russian businessmen, then the accusations against Bakhmina could be applied to nearly all ordinary citizens.

Svetlana Bakhmina was paid a salary by Yukos throughout the almost seven years she worked there. According to the accusation concocted by the Procurator-General, for the greater part of this time she was guilty of a crime under Part 2 of Article 198 ('Non-payment of exceptionally large amounts of tax by private individuals'). Under this Article, Bakhmina faces three years in jail, even though she has not in fact broken any law, any more than Yukos has when paying her through a so-called 'insurance scheme'.

These schemes became widespread in Russia during the period when income tax was set at the punitive level of 35 per cent, with even more punitive social-welfare contributions. The essence of the scheme was that the employee insured his or her life using the company's money, and then received contractual insurance payouts, which were effectively the wages due. Since insurance payments were not subject to income tax and were permissible under the tax legislation then in force, the system was used by many private companies, state institutions and ministries, including, let it be noted, the Ministry of Taxation and Excise Revenue.

Now it transpires that you can be imprisoned for this. You could imprison the vast majority of the adult working population for exactly the same offence. If the court finds Bakhmina guilty, the country's workers will be in serious jeopardy. The authorities would be able to bring criminal charges against huge numbers of people at will. No matter how law-abiding you might be, you could still be imprisoned for the tax policies of your employer, even if you knew nothing about them.

Putin was supposed to have nominated by today the 42 citizens he wanted as the leading lights of his Social Chamber. He has been unable to, because those he would like to get, especially those with a reputation for independent-mindedness, have no wish to be involved, while those who do want to get in are too minor to attest to the democratic credentials of Putin, or so servile that the Chamber would be a laughing stock.

11 August

In Urus-Martan six unidentified paramilitaries have abducted Natasha Khumadova, 45, the sister of the Chechen field commander Doku Umarov. Umarov is the second most senior field commander after Basaev. Nothing is known of her fate. In Urus-Martan this is thought to have been the work of Kadyrov troops.

The seizure of counter-hostages is becoming increasingly common, and this was clearly one such manoeuvre, intended to coerce Umarov into surrendering to federal forces. Some Chechens think this is fair enough, and that primitive methods work better than legal methods. Others are simply waiting for the right moment to wreak revenge on Russia.

12 August

In Krasnoyarsk, Siberia, 45 members of the Union of Communist Youth have held a march for freedom and democracy. They marched through the centre of town bearing anti-Putin slogans. People called after them, 'Well done! To hell with their Putin!', but didn't join in. By no means everybody cares for the Communist Youth. People are even rather afraid of them, with their portraits of Che Guevara and his ilk. I would not march under those portraits. These young people have no experience of the consequences of revolution and were born at the very end of the 'period of stagnation', or in the Gorbachev–early Yeltsin era; the ideas of Communism appeal to them.

Kasparov's United Citizens' Front is aiming to bring everybody together: the Young Communists, provincial supporters of Rodina, what remains of the democratic right, Yabloko supporters in the regions who have given up on Yavlinsky, the National Bolsheviks and the anarchists. All unite against the regime! After we have won, we can decide what to do next. That's the best programme the democrats can manage.

Today, an appeal was heard in Zamoskvorechiye court, with Judge Yelena Potapova presiding, against Deputy Procurator Yudin's refusal on 22 July to grant the militia a warrant for the arrest of Sergey Melnikov, a 'simple Russian entrepreneur'.

Attempting to challenge the actions of the Procurator's Office is highly unusual, if not impossible. It is also very rare for Russians to agree to be witnesses against mafiosi, as the retaliation can be brutal and the state authorities give no support. Corruption, now more widespread than ever, ensures that those who can't pay get no protection. Accordingly, when Yudin refused to sanction the arrest of Melnikov, those of his victims who had given evidence were in quite a quandary when the Deputy Procurator decided to use his powers in favour of their tormentor rather than them.

Judge Potapova was nervous and irritable, but lawyer Alexey Zavgorodny appealed to her to put herself in the shoes of Melnikov's victims, from whom he had been extorting protection money. Melnikov himself, of course, was not there, but his lawyer and confidante, Natalia Davydova, was.

Ms Davydova is a loud, sarcastic woman who has been representing and advising some 40 members of the Togliatti mafia for several years. The Moscow City Procurator's Office ought to be taking no nonsense from a lawyer with clients like these, but today its representative in court is Yelena Levshina. Levshina repeats to the court exactly what Davydova has already said. We seem to be listening to a monstrous, well-rehearsed duet, as the two ladies insist to the judge that it is impossible to create a precedent where the Procurator might appear not to be in the right: he is always right. It is a reduction to absurdity of the principle that the Procurator must be independent of the courts.

Davydova turns up the pathos, and paints a touching picture of decent, law-abiding gangsters. Melnikov gave himself up to the militia voluntarily, they heard what he had to say, were sympathetic and let him go on his way. Accordingly, Melnikov had *de facto* invalidated the federal search warrant, and his detention on 22 July was illegal; Deputy Procurator Yudin had merely restored the rule of law which had been violated. This, of course, is complete poppycock. There is no suggestion in the Melnikov file that he voluntarily surrendered himself to anybody.

Judge Potapova retired to consider her verdict, and soon returned to declare that the Procurator is always right, and had been right in this case too when he decided not to sanction Melnikov's arrest, even though a nationwide manhunt had been conducted to find him. She rejected the complaint, and found that the Deputy Procurator's actions did not infringe the constitutional rights of Melnikov's victims. Other, of course, than the very important right to life.

'Russia's social and political arrangements are profoundly unjust,' Vladimir Ryzhkov tells everyone. He is one of the hopes for a democratic revival, young and from the provinces, which goes down well with the public.

It is, however, precisely these 'unjust arrangements' that reinforce social apathy and keep people extremely reluctant to stick their necks out. The habit of considering yourself a 'small person' is like the red button in the President's nuclear suitcase – he has only to press it and the country is in his hands. I am quite sure that Putin and his entourage fight corruption solely for PR purposes. In reality, corruption is very much to their advantage; it plays an important role in conditioning people to keep quiet. While the courts are pulled this way and that by the criminals and the politicians, he has nothing to fear.

Today is the third time Poles have been beaten up in Moscow, and this cannot be coincidental. Polish Embassy staff and a Polish journalist have been attacked in the course of just a few days.

This is the response of Nashi to the fact that on 31 July the children of Russian diplomats in Warsaw were beaten up after a disco: an outbreak of brotherly Slavonic xenophobia with a political subtext, which is very much in the style of Putin's Russia. The Poles have been getting above themselves recently, people are beginning to say, including some who are perfectly decent and educated. What Lenin called 'vulgar great-power chauvinism', which Putin suffers from, is back in fashion. So, if you beat up three of ours, we beat up three of yours. The fact that the official government response has been very sluggish and formal only shows that they approve.

Yabloko demanded that Putin should intervene personally and afford the Polish Embassy special protection. The problem is that all the liberals and democrats can do nowadays is appeal to Putin, and appealing to Putin while simultaneously demanding his resignation is just not sensible.

Nikita Belykh, the leader of the Union of Right Forces, has declared that 'In the heart of most Russians is an urge to be better people. Our task is to make this clear to them.'

Unfortunately, in the heart of most Russians is an urge to not stand out, and it is particularly in evidence today. We do not want to attract the evil eye of repressive institutions. We want to stay in the shadows. What you get up to in the shadows depends on your personality. Many would not want to emerge under any circumstances; there is a striving for self-improvement, of course, but keeping to the shadows lies much deeper in the heart of every Russian. After all that has happened here in the twentieth century alone, it is perhaps hardly surprising.

An official survey has put Russia seventieth in the world in terms of the use it makes of its human potential.

13 August

The latest grass-roots initiative to give Putin a third term has come from Adam Ima-'aev, a Deputy of the Legislative Assembly of the Primorsky Region and well-known political boot-licker. He announces that he has found a loophole in the legislation which would allow Putin to be elected for a third time. The Legal Committee of the Primorsky Parliament instantly resolved to examine the matter in September.

16 August

The Supreme Court has caused a sensation by rescinding the Moscow Provincial Court's ban on the National Bolshevik Party. Old man Limonov was so touched that he said outside the court building he had almost had his faith in Russia restored. The Procurator-General is very upset and has vowed to appeal against the decision to the Presidium of the Supreme Court.

The National Bolsheviks celebrated by infiltrating the inaugural day of Putin's pride and joy, the prestigious Moscow Aerospace Show 2005. All sorts of Arab sheikhs had flown in, as had representatives of the Indian military-industrial complex, and King Abdullah II of Jordan, a descendant of the Prophet. Despite incredible security measures, as soon as Putin began his speech opening the show, the National Bolsheviks (God only knows how they had got in) started yelling only 30 metres away from him, 'Down with Putin!' and something about his being responsible for Beslan. They were immediately pinioned and bundled off to the militia station in the nearby town of Zhukovskoye.

Three hours later they were released without so much as a fine. They were totally amazed, having expected to end up in jail. It is possible that the militiamen at Zhukovskoye have no time for Putin. Strange things do happen.

Putin got into a bomber at an airfield near the Aerospace Show and flew off with great aplomb to Murmansk Province. The defence people were quietly grinding their teeth; it might be good PR for Putin, but it was a security headache for them. Our generals are well trained, however, and know when not to answer back. They gave orders for Putin to be put in the cockpit, even though it is categorically against regulations. He briefly piloted the aricraft while it was cruising. The state-run mass media wept with delight: Putin was personally inspecting our military aviation! But why? Perhaps to boost his popularity rating?

That evening the Nashists again beat up the National Bolsheviks. There is no point in even trying to talk to the Nashi, none of whom can explain coherently why they have joined the organisation. The National Bolsheviks and other left-wing young people are a complete contrast, and highly motivated. Poor people on the left are potentially the most dynamic revolutionary force in Russia. The middle class is very plodding and aspires to no more than a bourgeois way of life, regretting only that, so far, they haven't quite got the means to support that level of consumption.

Active left-wing organisations include the youth wing of Yabloko, which has become the backbone of Defence, the Russian equivalent of the Pora movement which was so important to the success of the Ukrainian Orange Revolution. Defence also includes the youth wings of the Union of Right Forces, Marching without Putin, Collective Action and Our Choice. The co-ordinator is Ilia Yashin, leader of the youth wing of Yabloko, which has about 2,000 members. Defence is drifting increasingly towards the left and their protests resemble those of the National Bolsheviks more and more. For their part, the National Bolsheviks are moving towards mainstream democratic policies.

The most high-profile groups are the National Bolsheviks, although their core has been depleted by the arrests; the Avant-Garde of Red Youth; and the Union of Communist Youth. They handcuffed themselves to the railings of the Procurator-General's Office, demanding a meeting. They did not get it.

The ideology of Nashi was worked out by official spin doctors like Sergey Markov. He declared, 'Youth organisations with the ideology of Russian sovereignty, like Nashi, are a panacea against the Orange Plague.' It is interesting that no anti-Orange movement appeared spontaneously. Many are afraid of Nashi, but I think they will just fall apart after a while.

18 August

It is still a moot point what will bring about the demise of this regime. How will it collapse? The present opposition is too weak and lacking in purpose to bring it down. Spontaneous protest from the Russian people appears even less likely.

One possibility is that, if Putin does construct a neo-Soviet system, it may collapse, as before, through economic inefficiency. The trademark of Putin's Administration is building state capitalism, creating a loyal bureaucratic oligarchy by taking control of all the main national revenues (which are mostly delegated to Deputy Heads or others in the Presidential Administration). For this, they need to renationalise successfully functioning enterprises, turning them into financial industrial conglomerates or holding companies.

That is proceeding apace. Conglomerates such as Vneshekonombank, Vneshtorgbank and Mezhprombank (so-called 'Russian' major financial holdings to counterbalance the more Western-looking Alfa Group and others) swallow ever greater chunks of collateral, successful enterprises raised from their knees after the Soviet collapse.

This is facilitated by the Administration, naturally. Swallow it they may, but they can't really digest it, as they don't have sufficient highly qualified managers. The conglomerates can't cope effectively with what they already have their hands on and the enterprises begin to fail after being taken over. As a result, economic growth in the last half-year has slowed to 5.3 per cent, the export of capital was more than 900 billion roubles [£18 billion] and the rate of growth of incomes halved. These statistics were provided by the People's Government, formed as an alternative to the one we've got, by an independent Duma Deputy, Gennadii Semigin.

Oleg Shulyakovsky is resigning. He has managed the Baltic Factory, the most important surface shipyard in the north-west of Russia, since 1991. Shulyakovsky was such a major figure that he was retained by all its various owners after it was privatised in the early 1990s. He is finally leaving now because of the de-privatisation model imposed on the factory in 2005, after it was bought by United Industrial Corporation, which belongs to Mezhprombank. It is being merged with three design bureaux and some other enterprises, with an obvious loss of efficiency. What the Presidential Administration does now without Shulyakovsky at the helm (and Mezhprombank was only able to swallow the 150-year-old company because of its contacts with the Administration) remains to be seen.

Shulyakovsky was a pillar of the ship-building establishment, but even he has given up because Mezhprombank is creating a state capitalist holding of naval ship-building. The defence companies Almaz-Antei and Milya Helicopters were both de-privatised in a similar way recently. Mezhprombank is controlled by Sergey Pugachev who, although a senator and hence disqualified from running a bank, continues *de facto* to do so. He is one of the so-called Orthodox oligarchs, a comrade-in-arms of Putin in creating a state oligarchy.

The only problem with Putin's system is that it will take decades to collapse through creeping stagnation. Nobody doubts that this fate awaits the Baltic Factory, even if Putin manages to prevent foreigners and those of other tribes from advancing another inch on to Russian territory. In order to preserve their system, they will start passing down the presidency from one useless successor to the next. Their principal characteristic will be their facelessness, and they will get in after elections rigged in the Soviet fashion.

The main problem is that while collapse is inevitable, we will not see it in our lifetime. That's a pity, because we would like to.

19 August

Today's court hearing of the National Bolsheviks' trial descends into farce.

'On 14 December I look and see a commotion. I was standing beside Room 14. I saw everything that happened. I was there the whole time. So then I see the frame of the metal detector lying in a horizontal, prone position . . .' With the single-mindedness of a provincial sleuth, Yevgeny

Posadnev delivers this damning evidence from the witness stand. He used to be the director of some Soviet corrective labour institution, and now works for the Presidential Administration as a 'Reception Adviser', which means that he mediates between Putin and his suffering people. Posadnev's countenance is extremely grave. He is denouncing enemies.

'What condition was the metal detector in after these young people knocked it over?' the state prosecutor asks.

'It was lying down like a letter L,' Posadnev explains, 'but it should have been standing up like a letter 'Haitch'.

Even Judge Shikhanov is laughing.

'The lads from our security unit,' the witness continues, as if telling teacher that Vasya has been stealing apples again, 'blocked their route with this metal detector, so that this group of persons should be prevented from dispersing throughout the entire Administration building. The lads from the unit blocked the corridor with this L and thereby diverted the mob into Room 14!'

The prosecution roll their eyes in horror. What on earth is their witness saying?

'That is, the crowd were directed into Room 14?' the defence immediately interjects. 'They didn't burst in there themselves?'

The indictment, in support of which Posadnev is supposed to be testifying, says in black and white that the gravity of the offence committed by the 39 defendants was that they had seized Room 14. This impertinence is the official reason they have been held in jail for almost nine months.

'No, they didn't go in there by themselves,' the witness insists, trying to show how bravely the Federal Security Service had acted and supposing that he is bringing out the full gravity of the invaders' offence. 'They wanted to run all through the Administration, but were forced into the room with the L-shaped metal detector.'

'And were the doors of the room locked?' the defence asks.

'No, they were open.'

'But then they locked the doors?'

'No, the first of the doors, the outer one, stayed open.'

'Then why was it broken?' Total destruction of that door is the second most serious item of material damage of which they stand accused.

'I saw it, I saw everything, I saw them barricading the second door with a safe. Barricading themselves in.'

'But the outer door was not locked? So why did they break it? And where is it now?'

'It was repaired. It was scratched.'

One might well ask who scratched it. The state prosecutors realise this only too well. They are scowling at 'their' witness, their lips moving. Can they be cursing? The level of all their witnesses has been so abysmal as to be laughable.

'But nevertheless, did you personally witness any of these people creating a riot?' the defence team ask sternly. This is the crux of the accusation.

'No,' the crestfallen witness murmurs. 'There was no riot.'

He hangs his head. After all, how much can they expect you to make up?

This trial is without legal foundation, but there is an ideological imperative to demarcate those who are, from those who are not, 'on our side'. This is part of a wider national process of demarcation. The National Bolsheviks are to have the shit kicked out of them – pardon my use of the President's French – whether there is a legal basis or not.

Of course, the methods on display in the Nikulin Court are ridiculous, but who can see or hear them? Only the handful of people present. The rest of the country gets the message that the authorities are not joking, and that you go to jail for not being on our side. Beat the hell out of people like these. Show them no mercy, and your career will flourish.

Platon Lebedev, Khodorkovsky's friend and co-defendant, has meanwhile been transferred to a punishment cell for refusing to go out for exercise. One week ago, Lebedev, who suffers from cirrhosis of the liver, was transferred from the prison hospital to an ordinary communal cell and his health deteriorated sharply. He refused to go out to exercise because he was not fit enough. They have latched on to this: a punishment cell is an extremely hard place; there is no bed linen, no heating, and the diet is bread and water. The second reason is that the Michurin Court has given him until 25 August to read the records of the Yukos court hearings. Lebedev will be in the punishment cell until 26 August and, as you are not allowed to take any papers or books in there, he will be unable to prepare an appeal against the verdict.

Lebedev, of course, still has Khodorkovsky, and Khodorkovsky is evidently writing up his comments at present. The verdict is effectively shared between the two of them and they have excellent lawyers. Nevertheless, such vindictiveness towards someone whose only crime is to have failed to plead guilty is quite monstrous.

There is good reason to worry about this country. Today's world leaders put their tails between their legs and exchange kisses with Putin rather than pull him up short.

21 August

Another anniversary of the 1991 putsch against Gorbachev and our liberation from it. About 800 people went to a celebration organised by the Free Russia Party. I felt no inclination to stop as I drove past the meeting. There is no freedom, so what is there to celebrate? The years since then have been spent bringing back what we had before, only now in an even more twisted form.

Officially, 58 per cent of those surveyed approve of the slogan 'Russia for the Russians'. Another 58 per cent, when asked what they would do if they earned a decent salary, said they would immediately buy property abroad and emigrate. That is a death sentence for 'Free Russia', and it also explains why we have not had any revolutions of late. We're waiting for someone else to do it for us.

23 August

Some of the mothers of children who died at Beslan have locked themselves in the court building in Vladikavkaz, North Ossetia, where Nurpasha Kulaev is being tried. Officially, he is the only surviving terrorist of all those who seized the school.

After the tragedy, the mothers said they trusted only Putin and had every confidence he would ensure an objective inquiry. Putin promised that he would. A year has passed. The inquiry, however, exonerated all the bureaucrats and security agents who planned and carried out the assault that led to the deaths of so many children and adults. The women are now demanding that they themselves should be arrested. They consider themselves responsible for the deaths of their own children, because they voted for Putin. Their sit-in is an act of desperation.

Khodorkovsky has gone on a total hunger strike in Matrosskaya Tishina prison, refusing even water, as a mark of solidarity with his severely ill friend Platon Lebedev. Through his lawyer Khodorkovsky stated that moving Lebedev into a punishment cell was evidently in retaliation for the articles that he, Khodorkovsky, published in the newspapers after the verdict.

Bravo, Khodorkovsky! I didn't think he had it in him. I am glad I was wrong. Now he is one of *us*. Oligarchs do not go on hunger strike; it is people like us who do that.

In the past six months hunger striking has become the sole means of asserting the right to free speech, a right supposedly guaranteed by the Constitution. There is much you can no longer say, but you can still go on hunger strike to show that you have been silenced. Sounding off at protest meetings has become virtually useless, mere preaching to the converted; those who share your views already know the situation, so why keep telling them about it? Standing in picket lines is pointless, unless it is to salve your conscience. At least you'll be be able to tell your granddaughter that you did more than vent your spleen in your own kitchen. Even writing books that don't get published in Russia because they are off-message doesn't have much impact. They are read only by people living abroad.

So, in 2005, the hunger strike is one of the few ways of getting your protest noticed. Moreover, it is something any of us can do. We all eat. We can all not eat. What is more, you don't need to apply for a permit from the state before you can do it.

Another important plus: in Russia everybody suspects everybody else of hypocritical PR spin, but what kind of PR is a hunger strike? It is clearly evident that it is being done by someone who is in despair.

So, as we enjoy this Indian summer, what has the new tactic achieved? For three weeks in July the Heroes of Russia, the Soviet Union and of Socialist Labour were on hunger strike. Putin in the meantime gave PR support to neo-fascist thugs by eating shashlik with them in a clearing in Tver, ostentatiously insulting the Heroes. Nevertheless, their hunger strike was very effective.

The prisoners in the Lgov penal colony also went on hunger strike to draw attention to the torture they were enduring. Although the consequences were grim, they are being tortured less. In any case, there was a big enough rumpus to disturb the smooth working of the European Court of Human Rights. The Government was obliged to react, and who knows, perhaps the brutes who run other prisons in Russia will be just a bit more circumspect in future.

Victims of beatings by the militia in Rasskazovo in Tambov Province went on hunger strike, warning that, 'We will no longer endure humiliation, insults and physical violence from the law-enforcement agencies.'

The aggressors laid off. One more hunger strike, and the butchers may even be put behind bars.

Finally, the National Bolsheviks in the 14 December case went on hunger strike in their Moscow detention cells, demanding the release of all political prisoners. Who now can fail to see that the National Bolsheviks are themselves political prisoners?

The authorities have quietly taken note of this summer of hunger strikes, even if they refer to it only obliquely, as they did today in Sochi when they remarked that officials should remain at arm's length from the people. The state is, however, plainly wising up to the fact that people are not joking. These are people who will not under any circumstances come to terms with them. A hunger strike is not a dialogue with the authorities, but with your fellow citizens.

I catch myself reflecting that you could never imagine Prime Minister Fradkov, Surkov or Putin himself going on hunger strike. It's not their style. To take a ride in a bomber or a beat-up Volga, supposedly without bodyguards, is fine. Protest, however, of the kind that Khodorkovsky has now shared with the people, is out of the question.

24 August

The mothers have gone back to Beslan.

'We, the mothers of Beslan,' Marina Park says, 'are guilty of having given life to children doomed to live in a country that decided it did not need them. We are guilty of having voted for a president who decided children were expendable. We are guilty of having kept silent for ten years about the war being waged in Chechnya, which has brought forth rebels like Kulaev.'

Ella Kesaeva, another orphaned mother, breaks in: 'The main culprit is Putin. He hides behind his presidency. He has chosen not to meet us and apologise. It is a tragedy that we live under such a president, who refuses to take responsibility for anything.'

Shortly after this it became known that Putin was inviting representatives of the Committee of Mothers of Beslan to meet him in Moscow on 2 September. At first the women were indignant: 2 September was a day of commemoration of the dead. They could not possibly go. The Presidential Administration then bluntly informed them that a meeting between Putin and the people of Beslan would go ahead with or without them; someone would be found to tell Putin in front of the television cameras how much everyone in Beslan loves him. You can always find some of those in Russia.

What should they decide? Immediately after the atrocity Putin promised that the whole truth would be made public. Many believed him, including the 'black mothers' who had lost their children. At the President's personal behest, a Parliamentary Commission was set up to investigate the causes and circumstances of the events in Beslan, chaired by Alexander Torshin, who promised that the Commission's detailed and honest report would appear no later than March 2004.

Nothing happened. To this day there is no report, and the investigation has become a mockery. Large numbers of those held hostage in the school were so incensed that they refused to give evidence in the absurd, face-saving trial of Kulaev.

'Obviously nobody was guilty, or they would not all have been given medals,' as Marina Park puts it caustically. The citizens of Beslan are still alone with their grief. People come to photograph them, like animals in the zoo, and depart. They are asked if they need money, and reply that the only thing they want is the truth.

27 August

The Chairman of the Parliamentary Commission on Beslan, Alexander Torshin, Deputy Speaker of the Soviet of the Federation, admits that the report for which Beslan has been waiting so long simply does not exist. 'There are only a few odd pages.'

Russia shrugs its shoulders.

29 August

In the Nikulin Court, in the entire course of the summer, only 13 of the 26 witnesses for the prosecution have been questioned. None of those for the defence have yet been called.

The authorities are deliberately dragging out the National Bolsheviks' trial while keeping them in prison, because they imagine it will make others think twice. In fact, it only strengthens their convictions. The parents of the 39 have, while their children have been in prison on plainly trumped-up charges, started following their lead. They are organising protest meetings, shouting in picket lines, joining opposition movements.

The Communists now let the National Bolsheviks hold their weekly meeting at their premises, and the alliance of those on the left is becoming very solid. This evening, however, as the National Bolsheviks were arriving, they were attacked and brutally beaten by masked individuals in combat fatigues wielding baseball bats.

After the attack the assailants calmly got into a bus which was waiting for them and drove off. The militia were called and pursued and stopped the bus. They entered it, only to come back out stating that it was full of 'our people'. What was going on? Quite simply, those 'on our side' have a licence to beat those who are 'not on our side'. The Nashists have been attacking the National Bolsheviks with baseball bats since early January. On 29 January and 5 March there were large-scale attacks by Nashi activists on the National Bolsheviks' bunker, which they ransacked. Then as now, politically inspired hooligans arrived and left on a small bus, equipped with baseball bats. They even brought a mobile generator with them in order to saw through the door.

The hooligans were ticked off by the militia and released. On 12 February, on the Moscow Metro Circle Line, thugs waylaid and beat up not only National Bolsheviks, but also the father of one of the 39 in prison. Again, they were taken to a militia station, then released. Each time the militia made a record, subsequently even began to press criminal charges, but then either dropped them or put them on ice. 'You must understand,' the investigators sighed. 'It's politics . . .'

'There is no urgency on the part of the investigators,' Dmitry Agranovsky, the lawyer representing the father who was assaulted, tells me. 'The files have not even been sent to court yet, even though the offences are far clearer than those of the National Bolsheviks who invaded Putin's reception area, and the violence was far greater. So many people were seriously injured. We are trying to prevent them from closing the case completely, but it is clearly going nowhere.'

Now this new attack. The Gladiators of Spartak needed protection from the law. They found it, and now they are using their fists to repay the trust placed in them by the Presidential Administration.

It is all just the way it is in Chechnya. The regime takes people under its wing who have, preferably, several criminal cases pending against them. These are quashed in return for a guarantee that 'While you are with us, nobody can raise a finger against you. You beat up those we point out.' (In Chechnya, 'You kill on our say-so.')

Are we really going to see the day when the President decrees that

Roma the Stickler, following in the footsteps of Ramzan the Nutter, should receive honours from the Russian state?

It is also very obvious that the regime is eager to pit one youth group against another so that, when the chips are down, there will be a balance between the two sides, so that the hatred should not just leach away out of society. Fear and confrontation are far more useful; the pursuit of social harmony is not their agenda. They are hoping that having different social groupings at loggerheads will be the magic carpet on which they fly to their goal of another four years in power and in control of the country's revenues, while the rest of us carry on beating each other up. This is what I see behind the attacks on the National Bolsheviks by well-organised teams wielding baseball bats.

30 August

The Military Collegium of the Supreme Court has been considering an appeal against the acquittal of a Special Operations unit by the North Caucasus Military Court. The unit, subordinate to the Central Intelligence Directorate, shot six people and burned their bodies in the Shatoy District of Chechnya in January 2002. The verdict has been deemed unlawful and the case sent back for reconsideration.

This is extremely unusual. The basic objections to the earlier verdict were gross procedural violations in the selection of jurors, and the conduct of the judge in giving them political instructions before they withdrew to consider their verdict.

Eduard Ulman's unit was acquitted on the grounds that while the soldiers had indeed killed and burned their victims, they could not be held responsible because they were only carrying out the orders of their superiors, which they were not at liberty to dispute. The court entirely ignored the fact that there were no written orders, only veiled hints from a shadowy director of the operation whose voice was heard over a walkie-talkie. The Supreme Court also disregarded this very important detail.

What happens next? This will be the third time the case has been reviewed, but unfortunately it is still going to be tried in Rostov-on-Don. If the Military Collegium was seriously expecting a guilty verdict, Ulman and his unit would be back in detention and the case would not have returned to Rostov, where it is quite impossible to form a jury radically different from the earlier ones. The Rostov jurors took the red-blooded view that Ulman was perfectly within his rights; he was carrying out a mission for the Motherland, and anyway, all Chechens are *a priori* guilty. Strong anti-Chechen sentiment is a fact of life in the south of Russia.

Why has the verdict been set aside on this occasion? The Supreme Court has, after all, a long record of turning a blind eye to inconvenient matters. They are playing up to Putin. When he met the human-rights campaigners at the beginning of the summer, the President said he had been shocked by the acquittal of Ulman and his co-defendants. The Supreme Court has accordingly hastened to help him over his shock by referring the case back, and whatever happens after that is not their concern.

The Central Intelligence Directorate, the GRU, may nevertheless be forced to pull in its horns for a short time. The Special Operations sub-divisions of this murderous organisation continue their 'sanitising' of Chechnya, which is what Ulman and his detachment were involved in, and the fact that we do not know of similar major cases is simply because they do not get reported. The atrocities in the hill village of Borozdinovskaya on 4 June were also committed by a GRU detachment. The assassination on 4 July of Abdul-Azim Yangulbaev, Head of the Administration of the hill village of Zumsoy, is another example.

The background to Yangulbaev's case is that, in January, four people were abducted from Zumsoy by a group of soldiers parachuted from helicopters. Nothing has been heard of the four since. The soldiers then went berserk, beating up villagers and helping themselves, for example, to 250,000 roubles [£5,000] that had just been received by one of the families as compensation for the destruction of their home. Abdul-Azim Yangulbaev, the village Head of Administration, made every effort to find the abducted villagers. He appealed to human-rights organisations and spoke out forcefully about the soldiers' excesses, which is unusual in Chechnya nowadays. And not only in Chechnya.

In the spring, he forwarded to the Memorial Human Rights Centre and the Procurator's Office a draft report by one of the soldiers involved in the January operation, which gave the names of those in command of the abductors, and mentioned the shelling of homes and the murder of one of the villagers.

On 4 July, Yangulbaev's UAZ jeep was stopped on a mountain road by three masked gunmen, who presented GRU credentials and ordered him to get out of the vehicle to show them his ID. When, on their orders, he went to open the boot of his vehicle to allow them to inspect it, he was shot three times at point-blank range with a gun fitted with a silencer.

31 August

In Beslan there is a split. Should the mothers go to Moscow to meet Putin on 2 September or not?

Putin, it seems, is very keen that they should: a special plane will be sent to collect them. This is unprecedented, but then, so was Beslan. Many of the mothers, however, are refusing. Today the delegation of those going to the Kremlin does not consist solely of mothers who lost their only children and who had for so long wanted to tell Putin everything that was on their minds. It includes, of course, Teimuraz Mamsurov, the father of two children who survived in the school, and who, at the time of the terrorist act, was Leader of the republican parliament.

He is now the 'Director' of North Ossetia. The republics no longer have presidents, but if he is its Director he clearly enjoys Putin's trust. Mamsurov is not going to make a fuss in the presence of Putin to discover the truth about the terrorist outrage. He is not going to commit political suicide.

Another member of the Beslan delegation is Maierbek Tuaev, Director of the Public Commission for the Distribution of Humanitarian Aid. Maierbek's daughter, a pupil in one of the senior classes, was killed, but after the atrocity, when humanitarian aid flooded in to the town from around the world, he was appointed to distribute it. There is also Azamat Sabanov, the son of Tatarkan Sabanov, a former headmaster of the First School who, as he did every year, had gone to the 1 September parade and was killed in the attack. Azamat is Maierbek Tuaev's deputy for distributing humanitarian aid, which is like a narcotic in a town that spends most of its time at the cemetery.

I ring Marina Park and she tells me, 'I am at the cemetery.' I can hear many voices around her. She is an extremely active member of the Committee of the Mothers of Beslan. Marina was one of the leading signatories of the Committee's many letters to institutions involved in the inquiry into the tragedy, but she has decided against attending the meeting with Putin on 2 September. 'There is no point in going a thousand kilometres to receive condolences,' Marina is adamant as she stands in the cemetery. 'He is receiving us not to move the inquiry forward, but because he wants to be photographed with us.'

Alexander Gumetsov, whose 12-year-old daughter Aza was killed, also no longer wants to see the President.

I have known Alexander for almost the whole of this year. He was, and still is, deeply depressed. Aza was his only child. There was a time when he very much wanted to tell all about what their family went through before they finally received the remains of their daughter, identified only after DNA testing. Now, however, like most people in the town, Alexander feels he has been deceived so many times in the past year that nothing is likely to restore his faith in the state authorities. Even if Putin were now to spend the whole of 2 September with the people from Beslan; if there were to be no mention of money and only discussion of the need for a genuine inquiry; if Putin were to compel the Procurator-General, the Director of the FSB, the Minister of the Interior and all those bemedalled 'heroes of Beslan' to report the truth to the mothers in his presence; even if he were himself suddenly to repent and kiss the hands of these women, before whom he will forever be guilty, and swear a terrible oath to beat the truth out of his security services – even then they would not believe him.

And so, two or three mothers, out of the 20 who were invited, will be going to the Kremlin. They will serve to leaven the more politically reliable men invited to Putin's meeting with the Committee of the Mothers of Beslan.

Aza's mother, Rimma Torchinova, is one of those going. She wants to look Putin in the eye as she asks him some important, unanswered questions. Rimma has no illusions, but this is how she understands her duty to her daughter's memory. She is going to Moscow, come what may. She will be seeking answers about the headquarters from which the operation was directed, about the assault, the grenade-launchers, the role of the federal helicopters overhead.

We can only try to imagine how difficult this will be for her on 2 September, as also for the other women who are going to see the President. What solidarity can society offer them at this moment? We could at least hold out a hand so that they should feel not only their pain, but also the country's support as they confront the chill of the Kremlin. Perhaps our President would then find it more difficult to cynically 'manage' everything, and be forced to answer their questions honestly.

There is little evidence of social solidarity. We watch the drama of the mothers of Beslan on television. We see them weeping in the court-room in Vladikavkaz, locking themselves in in protest, holding meetings, blocking the highway, demanding to see Deputy Procurator-General Shepel, who is visibly wilting from having to lie to them endlessly. The country is sedated by this soap opera, inclined to murmur only that 'they are out of their minds with grief' and, after all, time will heal them and there is nothing to be done.

We will watch the evening edition of the *Vremya* news programme, and go to bed forgetting the women wearing black headscarves until the next episode of *The Mothers of Beslan*. The men of Beslan will carry on going out of their minds, blaming themselves for everything, while the women continue to live at their town's new cemetery.

Tomorrow is 1 September. A year has passed and not one of the bungling bureaucrats, generals, directors of the intelligence services, officials at the operational headquarters or even the heads of the militia have been called to account. Nobody is really demanding that anyway. Whatever happened to public opinion?

By 1 September 2005 it has become clear that the democratic movement is in a state of collapse. There is not going to be any united front, either in reality, or in the elections to the Chechen Parliament in November, the Moscow Duma elections in December or, indeed, in the Duma elections in 2007. Committee 2008 has given up the ghost. The Citizens' Congress is in a coma. The Russian intelligentsia does not have a single forum in which it could exert itself to real purpose and influence the governance of the state.

Yes, Garry Kasparov has created his United Citizens' Front, although it does not seem to be attracting many members. It formulates its mission as follows:

In the near future, stagnation under Putin will be replaced by a severe political crisis created by the state authorities themselves, and not at all by the democrats. The main task facing us before this crisis occurs is to create an organisation capable of uniting all responsible citizens against the regime when it finally loses its mind. We must learn to organise our opposition.

Those are very true words, but the problem that stifles all good words is that everybody in the United Citizens' Front, apart from Kasparov himself, has a record of electoral failure. Among these people, who were part of the democratic movement in the early pre-Yeltsin years, there are some who behaved disastrously in the late Yeltsin period and made possible the coming of the era of Putin.

To put it bluntly, I do not believe their democratic convictions run that deep. I do not trust any of them, other than Kasparov, and I doubt that he will be able to move mountains on his own. Millions of other Russians do not trust them, either.

Vladimir Ryzhkov is still running the Republican Party of Russia, and people view it with even greater scepticism. It has been around for 15 years. It grew out of an improbable grouping of the Yeltsin period, the 'Democratic Platform of the Communist Party of the Soviet Union', because there was such a monster, and very progressive it seemed at the time. People are not signing up with him, either.

Yavlinsky has publicly quarrelled with the Union of Right Forces, to the extent of refusing to have anything to do with Nikita Belykh, their new leader. That puts paid to any hope of uniting the URF and Yabloko. The only active element in Yabloko is its youth section under Ilia Yashin. Its protests increasingly resemble those of Limonov's National Bolsheviks. Young Yabloko does not think too highly of Yavlinsky himself, perhaps because its members are far purer, more honest and, most importantly, more impassioned than the old democrats, of whom Yavlinsky is typical. The view that the old democrats are past it is very widespread now.

The Union of Right Forces is busy trying to curry favour with the Presidential Administration by emphasising that it 'has nothing against Putin'. Over the summer Belykh stumped through 45 regions of the country trying to mobilise people on the right. He failed.

Anybody trying to do anything worthwhile in Russia at the moment is moving towards the left. Khodorkovsky is correct, although all the democrats condemned his thoughts from prison. Russia's Left March is a fait accompli, which also rules out any Russian Orange Revolution. There will be no splendid revolutionary breakthrough with oranges, tulips or roses in Russia.

Our revolution, if it comes, will be red, because the Communists are almost the most democratic force in the country, and because it will be bloody. The Orange Revolution in Ukraine brought all our democrats and liberals together for a time, but subsequently it divided them all even more. In their place, like a carbuncle, has come the Presidential Administration's 'democratic' Nashi movement.

The threat of a bloody revolution comes today from the state authorities themselves, or possibly from oppositionists who lose their cool when confronted by Nashi. As things stand, the colour of any revolution in Russia will be red, and nobody can be sure that Surkov's street-fighting Nashists will not turn their knuckle-dusters and chains against their present political masters.

Am I Afraid?

People often tell me I am a pessimist; that I do not believe in the strength of the Russian people; that I am obsessive in my opposition to Putin and see nothing beyond that.

I see everything, and that is the whole problem. I see both what is good and what is bad. I see that people would like life to change for the better, but are incapable of making that happen, and that in order to conceal this truth they concentrate on the positive and pretend the negative isn't there.

To my way of thinking, a mushroom growing under a large leaf can't just hope to sit it out. Almost certainly someone is going to spot it, cut it out and devour it. If you were born a human being, you cannot behave like a mushroom.

I cannot reconcile myself to the official demographic forecast from the State Statistical Committee covering the period to 2016. By 2016 many of my generation may no longer be around, but our children will be alive, as will our grandchildren. Do we really not care what kind of life they will have, or even whether they will have a life at all?

Many seem not to care. If we continue with the same political and economic policies, the Russian population will fall by 6.4 million people. That is the optimistic forecast: that by 2016 Russia will have a population of 138.8 million people.

The pessimistic forecast is not so easy to come by, but you can dig it out if you are sufficiently persistent, and it makes you want to do something about changing the situation in Russia right now. The pessimistic forecast is that we will be down to 128.7 million people. Millions of the poor, unable to afford privatised medical services, will die. Young people will continue to be killed in droves in the Army. In wars and also outside of wars, all those who are 'not on our side' will be shot or sent to rot and die in prisons.

That is if everything remains as it is now. If, in a fundamental manner, we do not tackle poverty. If the disgraceful neglect of healthcare provision and our environment persists. If we do not embark on a determined national campaign against alcoholism and drug addiction. If the war in the North Caucasus is not ended. If a humiliating social-welfare system is not changed, which allows a person barely to survive, with no prospect of living a fulfilled and dignified life, eating well, resting properly, enjoying sports.

So far there is no sign of change. The state authorities remain deaf to all warnings from the people. They live their own life, their faces permanently twisted by greed and by irritation that anybody should try to prevent them from getting even richer. In order to head off that possibility, their priority is to cripple civil society. On a daily basis they try to convince the Russian people that civil society and the opposition are funded by the CIA, the British, Israeli and, for all anyone knows, Martian intelligence services, plus of course the worldwide spider's web of al-Qaeda.

Our state authorities today are only interested in making money. That is literally all they are interested in.

If anybody thinks they can take comfort from the 'optimistic' forecast, let them do so. It is certainly the easier way, but it is also a death sentence for our grandchildren.

Glossary

An asterisk in the text indicates the first instance of the following significant individuals and organisations:

People:

Basaev, Shamil: a leading commander of the Chechen guerrillas when Russia invaded Chechnya in 1994. Russian bombing killed 11 members of his family, after which he became a pitiless warrior. Accused of masterminding the hostage-takings at *Nord-Ost* and the First School in Beslan, both of which the Russian Government ended bloodily. Killed in an explosion in 2006.

Berezovsky, Boris: became an oligarch in the Yeltsin era and built a media empire that aided Yeltsin's re-election, only to fall out with Putin over his opposition to the Chechen War and support for liberal and democratic causes in Russia. Now living in London. Accused Putin of responsibility for the murder of Alexander Litvinenko, a close associate, in 2006.

Bonner, Yelena: tireless human-rights campaigner whose father, an Armenian-born secretary of the Communist International, was murdered by the regime in 1937. Widow of the Nobel Prize-winning physicist and human-rights activist Andrey Sakharov.

Chubais, Anatoly: Deputy Prime Minister in 1994–6 associated with the 'shock therapy' programme of free market reforms, with privatisation and the creation of the oligarchs under Yeltsin. Became a co-leader of the Union of Right Forces political party.

Fradkov, Mikhail: former director of the Federal Tax Police and representative to the European Union, appointed Prime Minister of Russia in 2004 by Putin to replace the more turbulent Mikhail Kasianov.

Fridman, Mikhail: co-founded Alfa Group in 1988, which now owns

Russia's largest private bank and has interests in oil, retailing and telecommunications.

Gorbachev, Mikhail: last General Secretary of the Soviet Communist Party (1984–90) and first executive President of the USSR (1990–1). His attempts to democratise the Communist regime led to its collapse.

Kadyrov, Akhmed: pro-Moscow Chechen mufti, later 'President' of Chechnya, assassinated the day after attending Putin's second-term inauguration in the Kremlin.

Kadyrov, Ramzan: fought against Russia in the First Chechen War of 1994–6. Changed to support Russia in the Second War (1999 to the present). Appointed Prime Minister after the assassination of his father, Akhmed Kadyrov. Heads a paramilitary force.

Kasparov, Garry: youngest-ever World Chess Champion in 1985, at the age of 22. Abandoned chess politics for Russian politics in 2005.

Khakamada, Irina: entrepreneur and candidate in the March 2004 presidential election; Chairwoman of the Free Russian Democratic Party.

Khodorkovsky, Mikhail: formerly Russia's wealthiest oligarch and founder of Menatep Bank and Yukos oil company. Supported democratic opposition parties and proposed the introduction of transparent Western business practices. Fell foul of the Putin regime, was arrested in 2003 for alleged tax irregularities and sentenced to nine years' imprisonment.

Kuchma, Leonid: second President of Ukraine (1994–2005). Officially accused in 2005 of involvement in the 2000 murder of journalist Georgii Gongadze.

Limonov, Eduard: Russian writer, founder of the nationalistic but still unregistered National Bolshevik Party. Imprisoned in 2002 for two years for alleged illegal arms purchase.

Lukashenko, Alexander: authoritarian President of Belarus since 1994.

Maskhadov, Aslan: foremost Chechen military leader in the First Chechen War; elected President in 1997 and signed a peace treaty with Yeltsin in the Kremlin, but was unable to prevent a split between secular nationalists and Islamic fundamentalists. Killed by the FSB in 2005, apparently while attempting to negotiate a peaceful settlement of the conflict. His body was not returned to his family for burial.

Mironov, Sergey: since 2001 Speaker of the Soviet of the Federation, the upper house of the Russian Parliament. Since 2003 Chairman of the Russian Party of Life, which merged in 2006 with the Rodina and Russian Pensioners' Parties to form the Russian Justice Party, which he leads. Pro-Putin.

Pamfilova, Ella: Duma Deputy in the 1990s and presidential candidate in 2000. Chairwoman of the Presidential Commission for the Development of Civil Society and Human Rights.

Putin, Vladimir: resigned from the KGB in 1991 with the rank of lieutenant-colonel. Director of the FSB (1998–9) and succeeded Boris Yeltsin as President of the Russian Federation in 2000. Re-elected in 2004. His term as President expires in 2008.

Rakhimov, Murtaza: elected President of Bashkortostan in 1993, and re-elected in 1998 and 2003. The Organisation for Security and Cooperation in Europe described the 2003 election as marred by 'elements of basic fraud'.

Rogozin, Dmitry: leader of the nationalist Rodina (Motherland) Party, which loudly defended the rights of ethnic Russians until early 2006 when, seemingly under Kremlin pressure, he stepped down. His party was apparently posing an increasing challenge to the state authorities' United Russia party.

Ryzhkov, Vladimir: Duma Deputy since 1993 and Co-Chairman of the Russian Republican Party.

Saakashvili, Mikhail: leader of the 2003 bloodless Rose Revolution in Georgia, which obliged Eduard Shevardnadze to step down after elections considered to have been rigged. Became President of Georgia in 2004. Successfully defused separatist confrontations in Adjara and Abkhazia, but still has serious problems with South Ossetia.

Sakharov, Andrey: regarded as the father of the Soviet hydrogen bomb, Sakharov became one of the regime's most courageous critics. Awarded the 1975 Nobel Peace Prize, but was unable to travel to receive it. His stand against the corruption and lack of legitimacy of the Soviet regime was highly influential within the elite itself. Died in 1989.

Surkov, Vladislav: foremost Kremlin ideologist and spin doctor, who held senior positions in Menatep and Alfa Banks during the 1990s. Public-relations director of ORT television company (1998–9). Deputy Head of Putin's Presidential Administration. Himself half-Chechen, Surkov is believed to be the main supporter within the Kremlin of Ramzan Kadyrov and the policy of Chechenisation of the war in Chechnya.

Yavlinsky, Grigorii: author in 1990 of an unsuccessful programme to transform Russia from a communist to a free-market economy in two years. Co-founded the Yabloko political party in 1995, which later attempted to impeach President Yeltsin. Refused to run for the presidency in 2004 on the grounds that Putin had rigged the 2003 parliamentary elections to ensure no Yabloko representation in the Duma.

Yeltsin, Boris: first President of the Russian Federation (1991–9). Succeeded in banning the Communist Party within the Russian Republic and dismantling the USSR in favour of a Commonwealth of Independent States. Believed to have started the First Chechen War in order to retain his personal power with Army backing, and to have handed over power to Vladimir Putin in 1999 to outflank his rivals' bid for the presidency in 2000.

Zakaev, Akhmed: presently Foreign Minister of the separatist Government of the Chechen Republic of Ichkeria, hero of the resistance in the First Chechen War, representative of Chechnya in 1996 at peace talks which led to a Russian withdrawal, then Deputy Prime Minister, later Foreign Minister. Wounded early in the Second Chechen War (1999 to the present), Zakaev left Chechnya in 2000 and became the most prominent representative of the Maskhadov government in Western Europe. Granted political asylum by the UK in 2003 and lives in London.

Zhirinovsky, Vladimir: outspoken populist and ultra-nationalist politician, and leader of the Russian Liberal Democratic Party. Commented on the poisoning of former KGB agent Alexander Litvinenko in London in 2006 that 'a traitor must be eliminated using any methods'.

Zyazikov, Murat: President of Ingushetia, a republic that borders and has close ethnic links with Chechnya. A member of the KGB in the 1980s, he was elected President (with heavy FSB involvement) in 2004.

Organisations:

Commonwealth of Independent States (CIS): established in 1991 and loosely binding all the former republics of the Union of Soviet Socialist Republics except for Georgia and the Baltic states of Estonia, Latvia and Lithuania.

Duma: the Russian Parliament, which, under the Yeltsin Constitution, replaced the Supreme Soviet in 1993. Consists of 450 elected Deputies.

FSB (Federal Security Bureau): the present domestic state-security organisation; successor to the Federal Counter-Espionage Service.

KGB (Committee of State Security): the Soviet secret police, replaced in 1991 by the Federal Counter-Espionage Service after its involvement in the attempted anti-Gorbachev coup.

Liberal Democrats: the first opposition party to be registered, in 1989, after the breaking of the Communist Party's monopoly. A confusingly named, vociferous nationalist party led by Vladimir Zhirinovsky, believed to have been subsidised by Yeltsin to draw support from the Communist Party.

OMON (Special Operations Unit of the Militia): first established in 1979 to protect the 1980 Summer Olympics in Moscow from terrorist attack. Subsequently used as riot police, a unit is to be found in every territory of the Russian Federation.

Rodina: nationalist and generally socialist party founded in 2003, led by Dmitry Rogozin. Some believed it was set up by the Kremlin to take votes from disillusioned Communist Party supporters. In the 2003 elections it won 37 seats in the Duma and now says that it is 'For Putin, but against the Government'.

Russian Federation: successor state, from 1991, to the USSR, but does not include the USSR's autonomous republics.

Union of Right Forces: liberal party formed in 1999 from a number of small parties dedicated to introducing free-market reforms and sharply critical of Putin's curtailment of democratic freedoms. Officially polled 4 per cent in the 2003 parliamentary elections, depriving it of Duma representation, which requires 5 per cent support, prompting widespread suspicion of electoral fraud by the Kremlin.

United Russia: party created in 2001 by the Kremlin to support Vladimir Putin; holds a constitutional majority in the Duma.

Yabloko: liberal party set up in 1995 in reaction to infighting within the democratic camp; speaks out against infringements of freedom of the press and of democratic political practices, supports Russia's ultimate integration into the European Union, opposes the war in Chechnya and has called for the removal of Putin's regime by 'constitutional means'.

Others:

Bashkortostan, or Bashkiria: formed partly by the southern Urals mountains and adjacent plains; population of four million, of which 36 per cent are ethnic Russians, 29 per cent Bashkirs and 24 per cent Tatars.

Chechnya: situated in the eastern part of the North Caucasus and predominantly Sunni Muslim. Most of its economic potential has been destroyed in the two Chechen Wars, together with huge loss of combatant and civilian life. According to the Russian Government, more than US $2 billion have been spent on reconstruction since 2000, though the Russian economic monitoring agency considers that no more than US $350 million were spent as intended.

Dagestan: located in the southernmost part of Russia, in the North Caucasus mountains. Ethnically very diverse.

Georgia: the first republic to declare its independence from Russia, shortly before the collapse of the USSR. Separatist problems with Abkhazia and South Ossetia in particular are fomented by Russia. Rich in natural resources, attractive to tourists and famed for its wine-making, Georgia is combating corruption, which holds back the economy.

Ingushetia: comprises mainly Sunni Muslims of various Sufi orders. It has many refugees from the war in Chechnya. Population of half a million made up of 77 per cent Ingushes, 20 per cent Chechens and 1.2 per cent Russians.

Kyrgyzstan, or Kirghizia: landlocked and mountainous, sometimes referred to as the Switzerland of Central Asia. Had its own Tulip Revolution in 2005 in protest at rigged elections and the suppression of oppositionists, but the new regime is struggling to keep its promises to combat corruption and decentralise authority.

Orange Revolution: triggered in Ukraine in late 2004 to early 2005 by massive rigging of the presidential election by the pro-Moscow authorities. A re-run in December 2004 led to a win for Viktor Yushchenko, who had been poisoned shortly before the first election and who received 52 per cent of the vote to Viktor Yanukovych's 44 per cent.

Rose Revolution: a series of protests in Georgia in late 2003 to early 2004 in response to massive rigging of the parliamentary elections of November 2003. President Eduard Shevardnadze's inability to cope with separatist problems and pervasive corruption caused him to lose the election to Mikhail Saakashvili. Shevardnadze claimed victory, but was forced to concede defeat after the Parliament building was seized by Saakashvili's supporters, bearing roses as a symbol of non-violence; elite military units sided with the protesters. The election was re-run in January 2004 and Saakashvili's party won by a landslide.

Ukraine: declared independence from Moscow in 1991, but was slow to implement free-market reforms; heavily dependent on Russia for energy supplies, which Russia has attempted to exploit for political advantage. Its population of 46 million is 78 per cent Ukrainian and 17 per cent Russian.

Wahhabism: the dominant form of Islam in Saudi Arabia, Qatar and western Iraq, which advocates a puritanical and legalistic stance in matters of faith and religious practice. Russian-speaking Wahhabi Arabs flooded Chechnya at the end of the First Chechen War, allowing the Russian Government subsequently to present Chechnya as a bridgehead of Islamic fundamentalism.

Index